First World War
and Army of Occupation
War Diary
France, Belgium and Germany

GUARDS DIVISION
1 Guards Brigade
Grenadier Guards
2nd Battalion
1 August 1915 - 31 January 1919

WO95/1215/1

The Naval & Military Press Ltd
www.nmarchive.com
Published in association with The National Archives

Published by

The Naval & Military Press Ltd

Unit 10 Ridgewood Industrial Park,

Uckfield, East Sussex,

TN22 5QE England

Tel: +44 (0) 1825 749494

www.naval-military-press.com

www.nmarchive.com

This diary has been reprinted in facsimile from the original. Any imperfections are inevitably reproduced and the quality may fall short of modern type and cartographic standards.

© **Crown Copyright**
Images reproduced by permission of The National Archives, London, England, 2015.

Contents

Document type	Place/Title	Date From	Date To
Miscellaneous	Appear to Have Been Conserved Already		
Heading	1915-19 Guards Division 1st Guards Brigade 2nd Bn Gren Gds Aug 1915-Jan 1919		
Heading	1st Guards Brigade Guards Division War Diary 2nd Battn. Grenadier Guards August 1916		
Miscellaneous	On His Majesty's Service.		
War Diary	In Trenches At Givenchy	01/08/1915	02/08/1915
War Diary	In Billets At Le Preol	03/08/1915	04/08/1915
War Diary	In Trenches At Givenchy	05/08/1915	06/08/1915
War Diary	In Billets At Le Preol	07/08/1915	08/08/1915
War Diary	Relieved Irish Guards At Givenchy	12/08/1915	17/08/1915
War Diary	Brigade Relieved in Givenchy	15/08/1915	15/08/1915
War Diary	In Billets at Bethune	16/08/1915	18/08/1915
War Diary	Ham-En-Artois	19/08/1915	19/08/1915
War Diary	Renescure	20/08/1915	20/08/1915
War Diary	In Billets at Houlle	21/08/1915	21/08/1915
War Diary	In Billets at Houlle	22/08/1915	23/08/1915
War Diary	Lumbres to Campagne-Les-Boulonnais	24/08/1915	24/08/1915
War Diary	In Billets at Campagne-Les-Boulonnais	25/08/1915	25/08/1915
Heading	1st Guards Brigade. Guards Division. War Diary 2nd Battn. Grenadier Guards. September 1915		
Miscellaneous	On His Majesty's Service.		
War Diary	Campagne-Les-Boulonnais	01/09/1915	09/09/1915
War Diary	In Billets at Campagne	10/09/1915	14/09/1915
War Diary	Merck St Lievin	15/09/1915	15/09/1915
War Diary	In Billets at Campagne	16/09/1915	22/09/1915
War Diary	In Billets at Coyecque	23/09/1915	23/09/1915
War Diary	In Billets At Westrehem	24/09/1915	27/09/1915
War Diary	Trenches Near Le Rutoire	28/09/1915	30/09/1918
Heading	1st Guards Brigade Guards Division War Diary 2nd Battn. Grenadier Guards October 1915		
Miscellaneous	On His Majesty's Service.		
War Diary	Mazingarbe	01/10/1915	03/10/1915
War Diary	In Trenches In Front of Vermelles	04/10/1915	05/10/1915
War Diary	In Old German Line	06/10/1915	07/10/1915
War Diary	At Vermelles	08/10/1915	09/10/1915
War Diary	In Old German Line	10/10/1915	12/10/1915
War Diary	In Billets At Verquin	13/10/1915	15/10/1915
War Diary	In Billets At Sailly Labourse	16/10/1915	17/10/1915
War Diary	In Billets At Vermelles	18/10/1915	23/10/1915
War Diary	In Reserve Trenches	24/10/1915	26/10/1915
War Diary	In Billets at Lapugnoy	27/10/1915	31/10/1915
Heading	1st Guards Brigade Guards Division War Diary 2nd Battn. Grenadier Guards November 1915		
Miscellaneous	On His Majesty's Service.		
War Diary	In Billets at Lapugnoy	01/11/1915	10/11/1915
War Diary	In Billets as Above	11/11/1915	13/11/1915
War Diary	Billets at La Gorgue	14/11/1915	19/11/1915
War Diary	Trenches Opposite Pietre	20/11/1915	20/11/1915
War Diary	In Billets At Riez Bailleul	28/11/1915	28/11/1915

War Diary	In Line Opposite Pietre	29/11/1915	30/11/1915
War Diary	In Line Opposite Pietre	21/11/1915	22/11/1915
War Diary	In Reserve At Bout Deville	23/11/1915	23/11/1915
War Diary	In Billets at Bout Deville	24/11/1915	24/11/1915
War Diary	In Line Opposite Pietre	25/11/1915	26/11/1915
War Diary	In Billets At Riez Bailleul	27/11/1915	27/11/1915
Heading	1st Guards Brigade Guards Division War Diary 2nd Battn. Grenadier Guards December 1915		
Miscellaneous	On His Majesty's Service.		
War Diary	In Billets At Riez Bailleul	01/12/1915	02/12/1915
War Diary	In Billets At Merville	03/12/1915	08/12/1915
War Diary	In Billets At Laventie	09/12/1915	20/12/1915
War Diary	In Billets At Merville	21/12/1915	26/12/1915
War Diary	In Billets At Riez Bailleul	27/12/1915	31/12/1915
Heading	1st Guards Brigade. Guards Division. 2nd Battalion Grenadier Guards January 1916		
Heading	War Diary January 1916 2nd Battalion Grenadier Guards		
War Diary	In Billets At Riez Bailleul	01/01/1916	07/01/1916
War Diary	In Billets at Calonne	08/01/1918	12/01/1918
War Diary	In Billets at Arrewage	13/01/1916	25/01/1916
War Diary	In Billets At Riez Bailleul	26/01/1916	31/01/1916
Heading	1st Guards Brigade. Guards Division. 2nd Battalion Grenadier Guards February 1916		
Heading	2nd Battalion Grenadier Guards. War Diary February 1916 Vol XIX		
War Diary	In Billets At Riez Bailleul	01/02/1916	07/02/1916
War Diary	In Billets at La Gorgue	08/02/1916	15/02/1916
War Diary	Camp of Huts And Tents West of Poperinghe	16/02/1916	25/02/1916
War Diary	Calais-Coulogne	25/02/1916	25/02/1916
War Diary	In No. 6 Large Rest Camp Calais	26/02/1916	29/02/1916
Heading	1st Guards Brigade. Guards Division 2nd Battalion Grenadier Guards March 1916		
Heading	War Diary 2nd Battalion Grenadier Guards March 1916 Vol XX		
War Diary	In No. 6 Large Rest Camp, Calais	01/03/1916	05/03/1916
War Diary	In Billets at Herzeele	06/03/1916	14/03/1916
War Diary	Camp "M" Near Poperinghe	15/03/1916	27/03/1916
War Diary	In Line East of Potije Village	28/03/1916	31/03/1916
Heading			
Heading	2nd Battalion Grenadier Guards. War Diary For The Month Ending 30th April 1916		
War Diary	In Camp "C" Near Vlamertinghe	01/04/1916	16/04/1916
War Diary	In Cellars And Dug-Outs In Ypres	17/04/1916	26/04/1916
War Diary	In Billets At Poperinghe	27/04/1916	30/04/1916
Heading	1st Guards Brigade Guards Division 2nd Battalion Grenadier Guards May 1916		
Heading	War Diary For The Month Ending 31st May, 1916. 2nd Battalion Grenadier Guards. Vol 23		
War Diary	In Billets At Poperinghe	01/05/1916	04/05/1916
War Diary	In Billets At Ypres	05/05/1916	19/05/1916
War Diary	In Billets At Tatinghem	20/05/1916	31/05/1916
Heading	1st Guards Brigade. Guards Division 2nd Battalion Grenadier Guards. August 1916		
Heading	War Diary For The Month Ending 30th August. 1916. 2nd Battalion Grenadier Guards.		

War Diary		01/08/1916	01/08/1916
War Diary	In Billets At Sarton	02/08/1916	17/08/1916
War Diary	In Billets at Courcelles	18/08/1916	25/08/1916
War Diary	In Billets At Meaulte	26/08/1916	31/08/1916
Heading	1st Guards Brigade. Guards Division. 2nd Battalion Grenadier Guards. September 1916		
Heading	2nd Battalion Grenadier Guards. War Diary of the Above Battalion For The Month Of September 1916		
War Diary	In Bivouacs South West of Bois Caftet	01/09/1916	03/09/1916
War Diary	In Billets At Meaulte	04/09/1916	10/09/1916
War Diary	In Bivouacs At Carnoy	11/09/1916	12/09/1916
War Diary	In The Line At Ginchy	13/09/1916	20/09/1916
War Diary	In Bernafay Wood	21/09/1916	30/09/1916
Miscellaneous	Narrative of Events From Sept. 13th-17th, 1916	19/09/1916	19/09/1916
Miscellaneous	2nd Battalion Grenadier Guards.	18/09/1916	18/09/1916
Miscellaneous	Narrative of Events From 24th-26th Sept. 1916	28/09/1916	28/09/1916
Miscellaneous	2nd Battalion Grenadier Guards.	28/09/1916	28/09/1916
Heading	1st Guards Brigade. Guards Division. 2nd Battalion Grenadier Guards. October 1916		
War Diary	Morlancourt	01/10/1916	01/10/1916
War Diary	In Billets at Aumont	02/10/1916	31/10/1916
Miscellaneous	Fourth Army No. 373 (G)	06/10/1916	06/10/1916
Heading	1st Guards Brigade. Guards Division. 2nd Battalion Grenadier Guards, November 1916		
War Diary	In Billets at Aumont	01/11/1916	10/11/1916
War Diary	The Camp At The Citadel	11/11/1916	12/11/1916
War Diary	H1 Camp Near Montauban	12/11/1916	15/11/1916
War Diary	In Camps "A" And "B"	16/11/1916	19/11/1916
War Diary	In "H1" Camp Montauban	20/11/1916	21/11/1916
War Diary	In Billets At Meaulte	22/11/1916	30/11/1916
Heading	1st Guards Brigade. Guards Division. 2nd Battalion Grenadier Guards. July 1916		
Heading	2nd Battalion Grenadier Guards. War Diary For The Month Ending 31st July 1916.		
War Diary	In Camps "G" And "P" (A.16.a.8.4 and A.15.d.5.4 Sheet 28 Respectively)	01/07/1916	06/07/1916
War Diary	In Dugouts on the Canal Bank	07/07/1916	27/07/1916
War Diary	In Billets Round Herzeele	28/07/1916	30/07/1916
War Diary	In Billets At Neuvillette	31/07/1916	31/07/1916
Heading	1st Guards Brigade. Guards Division. 2nd Battalion Grenadier Guards. June 1916		
Heading	2nd Battalion Grenadier Guards. War Diary For The Month Ending 30th June 1916.		
War Diary	In Billets At Tatinghem	01/06/1916	07/06/1916
War Diary	Camp "M" Near Poperinghe	08/06/1916	16/06/1916
War Diary	In Billets at Elverdinghe	17/06/1916	30/06/1916
Heading	1st Brigade. Guards Division. 2nd Battalion Grenadier Guards. December 1916		
War Diary	In Billets At Meaulte	01/12/1916	02/12/1916
War Diary	In Trench Camp 108	03/12/1919	03/12/1919
War Diary	In Trench Camp 15	04/12/1916	05/12/1916
War Diary	Maltzhorn Camp Near Trones Wood	06/12/1916	07/12/1916
War Diary	Combles	08/12/1916	11/12/1916
War Diary	In Camp At Maltzhorn	12/12/1916	12/12/1916
War Diary	In No. 1 Camps	13/12/1916	14/12/1916
War Diary	In Combles	15/12/1916	17/12/1916

War Diary	Trones Wood	18/12/1916	18/12/1916
War Diary	In Camp 15	19/12/1916	19/12/1916
War Diary	Plateau Siding	20/12/1916	20/12/1916
War Diary	In Combles	21/12/1916	23/12/1916
War Diary	In Camp 15	24/12/1916	25/12/1916
War Diary	Combles	26/12/1916	29/12/1916
War Diary	In Camp 15 Bronfay	30/12/1916	01/01/1917
War Diary	In Billets At Meaulte	02/01/1917	06/01/1917
War Diary	In Camp 15 Bronfay	01/01/1917	01/01/1917
War Diary	In Billets At Meaulte	02/01/1917	25/01/1917
War Diary	At Priez Farm	26/01/1917	29/01/1917
War Diary	In Billon Camp	30/01/1917	10/02/1917
War Diary	In Camp At Maurepas	11/02/1917	15/02/1917
War Diary	In Camp At Maurepas	16/02/1917	26/02/1917
War Diary	In Billon Camp	27/02/1917	13/03/1917
War Diary	In Camp At Maurepas	15/03/1917	31/03/1917
War Diary	In Camp At Ginchy	01/04/1917	07/04/1917
War Diary	In Camp Near Rocquigny	08/04/1917	17/04/1917
War Diary	In Camp 108 Bronfay	18/04/1917	12/05/1917
War Diary	In Camp Near Les Mesnils	13/05/1917	20/05/1917
War Diary	Bray to Billets at Sailly Le Sec	21/05/1917	21/05/1917
War Diary	In Billets At Sailly Le Sec	22/05/1917	31/05/1917
War Diary	In Billets At Renescure	01/06/1917	29/06/1917
War Diary	In Camp At Cardoem Farm	30/06/1917	07/07/1917
War Diary	In Billets At Roussel Farm	08/07/1917	11/07/1917
War Diary	In The Support Line	12/07/1917	14/07/1917
War Diary	In Billets Near Honflond	15/07/1917	31/07/1917
Miscellaneous	Narrative of Operations by Lieutenant Colonel C.R.C. de Crespigny D.S.O. Commanding 2nd Battalion Grenadier Guards	06/08/1917	06/08/1917
War Diary		01/08/1917	02/08/1917
War Diary	Plumstead Camp	03/08/1917	21/08/1917
War Diary	In Bivouacs At Bluet Farm	22/08/1917	31/08/1917
War Diary	Camp Near Elverdinghe	01/09/1917	08/09/1917
War Diary	In Bivouacs At Rugby Camp	10/09/1917	13/09/1917
War Diary	In Camp At De Wippe	14/09/1917	22/09/1917
War Diary	In Plumstead Camp	23/09/1917	10/10/1917
War Diary	In Camp At Charterhouse Near Elverdinghe	11/10/1917	19/10/1917
War Diary	In Billets At Tournehem	20/10/1917	31/10/1917
Miscellaneous	Narrative of Operations by Lieutenant Colonel G.E.C. Rasch D.S.O. Commanding 2nd Battalion Grenadier Guards	12/10/1917	12/10/1917
Miscellaneous			
Miscellaneous	G.D. No. 1199/3/A.	20/10/1917	20/10/1917
Miscellaneous	Special Order Of The Day	22/10/1917	22/10/1917
War Diary	In Billets At Tournehem	01/11/1917	30/11/1917
Miscellaneous	2nd Battalion Grenadier Guards. Narrative Of Operation For Period	30/11/1917	30/11/1917
War Diary	2nd Battalion Grenadier Guards. Narrative Of Operation For Period	30/11/1917	30/11/1917
War Diary		01/12/1917	30/12/1917
War Diary	Second Battalion Grenadier Guards Narrative Of Raid- March 5th		
Heading	Guards Division 1st Guards Brigade War Diary 2nd Battalion The Grenadier Guards April 1918		
War Diary	Map. Lens 11. 51 B. S. W. 1/10,000	01/04/1918	30/06/1918

War Diary	Saulty	01/07/1918	01/07/1918
War Diary	Ayette Combined Sheet 1/20000	05/07/1918	31/08/1918
Miscellaneous	2nd Battalion Grenadier Guards. Narrative Of Operation by Lieut: Colonel G.E.C. Rasch D.S.O. Commanding 2nd Battalion Grenadier Guards		
Miscellaneous	The Following Letter Has Been Received By The 1st Guards Brigade	31/08/1918	31/08/1918
Miscellaneous	The Total Casualties During This Operation Were As Follows		
War Diary		01/09/1918	30/09/1918
Miscellaneous	2nd Battalion Grenadier Guards Narrative Of Operations	01/10/1918	01/10/1918
Heading	War Diary 2nd Bn. Grenadier Guards October 1918.		
War Diary		01/10/1918	31/10/1918
Miscellaneous	Narrative of Operations by Major C.F.A. Walker M.C. Commanding and Battalion Grenadier Guards	26/10/1918	26/10/1918
War Diary		01/11/1918	30/11/1918
Miscellaneous	Narrative of Operations by Lieut Colonel C.F.A. Walker M.C Commanding 2nd Battalion	04/11/1918	04/11/1918
Miscellaneous		01/12/1918	31/12/1918
War Diary	Ehrenfeld Cologne	01/01/1919	31/01/1919

Appears to have been canvassed already

[signature] 15/3/2012

1915-19
GUARDS DIVISION
1ST GUARDS BRIGADE

2ND BN GREN. GDS. AUG 1915-JAN 1919

From 2 DN 4 GDS

1st Guards Brigade.
Guards Division.

2nd BATTN. GRENADIER GUARDS.

A U G U S T

1 9 1 5

On His Majesty's Service.

2nd Battn. Grenadier Guards.

August 1915.

War Diary. 2nd Bn. Gren. Gds.
August 1915.

1st Aug. 1915.
In Trenches at GIVENCHY. Some shelling during the day. About 10.50 p.m. the enemy exploded a small mine without doing much damage. Much Bombing during the night. Casualties. Nil.

2nd Aug. 1915.
In Trenches at GIVENCHY. The Brigadier and the Prince of Wales came round our lines in the morning. During the night we exploded three mines at 8.30 p.m. near Sunken Road, it is believed we blew in some of the enemy's galleries. Relieved by Irish Guards at 5.0 p.m. who occupied the near edge of the Craters. The Battalion marched to Billets at LE PREOL.
Casualties. 2 men killed, 2 N.C.O's and 2 men wounded, and 5 men slightly wounded.

3rd Aug. 1915.
In Billets at LE PREOL.

2nd Battn. Grenadier Guards.

August 1915.

4th Aug. 1915.
In Billets at LE PREOL.
Relieved Irish Guards at GIVENCHY at 5 p.m. Enemy very active with "minenwerfer" all night and threw many hand grenades, which mostly fell short, over the craters. Consolidating our positions on edge of craters.
Casualties, 1 man slightly wounded.

5th Aug. 1915.
In Trenches at GIVENCHY.
The Brigadier and the Prince of Wales came round our lines. The Prince went up the saps out to the craters and down the Red House mine. The enemy shelled our Trenches with Heavy Howitzers for about an hour doing some damage. Fairly quiet night. Our Howitzers silenced minenwerfers, which only fired a few rounds.
Casualties 1 man killed. Lieut. D. A. Smith and 1 man slightly wounded.

6th Aug. 1915.
At 3.40 a.m. the enemy exploded two mines in the Orchard, blowing in the gallery of our mine and destroying our saps out to the craters and also the trench joining the sap-heads. A number of men were

injured and buried, and two miners were killed in the mine. The enemy opened a sharp rifle fire and commenced shelling the vicinity of the craters, which made the work of digging out buried men difficult. All were, however, successfully dug out and we re-occupied the edges of the craters. 2nd Lieut H. J. C. Brookshank was completely buried in about 4 feet of earth, but when dug out was none the worse. Some men who were buried were suffering severely from shock, contusions, etc. Relieved by Irish Guards at 5.0 p.m. and marched to Billets at LE PREOL.

Casualties. 1 N.C.O. killed, Captain P. A. Clive wounded, 3 N.C.O's and 9 men wounded and 1 N.C.O and 17 men slightly wounded.

7th Aug. 1915.
In Billets at LE PREOL. A draft of Drummers arrived from home last night and played "Retreat" in the village street.

8th Aug. 1915.
Divine Service in the morning. Relieved Irish Guards at GIVENCHY about 5.0 p.m.
Casualties. Nil.

12th Aug. 1915.
Relieved Irish Guards at GIVENCHY at 5 p.m. Heard that Lieut. E. P. Williams had been accidentally killed in the Trench Mortar School, ST. VENANT, where he was undergoing a course. A fight with hand bombs and trench mortar bombs went on all night across the craters near the Sunken Road. He threw bombs into the craters to prevent the enemy working there and eventually succeeded in stopping them working. Our machine guns on the left played at intervals all night on the gaps in the enemy's wire destroyed by their mine.

Casualties. Nil.

13th Aug. 1915.
A quiet day. At night, we bombed the enemy's craters, but they did not attempt to work and did not reply.
Casualties. 3 men wounded. 1 man slightly wounded.

14th Aug. 1915.
Enemy shelled the vicinity of Gent but and village in the morning, but did no damage. The rest of the day quiet.

14th Aug. 15. (Continued)
Relieved by Irish Guards at 5 p.m. and marched to Billets at LE PREOL.
Casualties. Nil.

15th Aug. 1915.
Brigade relieved in GIVENCHY Section by 5th Brigade. The Battalion was relieved in Reserve Billets at LE PREOL by Glasgow Highlanders at 2 p.m. and marched to BETHUNE. The Battalion billetted in Ecole Paul Bert, Ecole Sevigne, and Skating Rink.
The Battalion entered BETHUNE with drums playing.

16th Aug. 1915.
In Billets at BETHUNE.

17th Aug. 1915.
In Billets at BETHUNE.
All Officers of the Brigade photographed together in the morning. The Drums of the 2nd Bn. Grenadier Guards and 3rd Bn. Coldstream Guards played "Retreat" in the Grande Place before a large crowd.

18th Aug. 1915.

Our Officers photographed together in the morning. The Drums again played "Retreat" in the Grande Place. A German areoplane came over the town about 7p.m. and dropped bombs, causing some casualties including 1 Grenadier killed and 1 wounded. Officers entertained General Horne, General Feilding, C O's of Brigade and principal Staff Officers, 2nd Divn to a farewell dinner in the evening. The following order was published by Major General H. S. Horne. C.B. Comdg 2nd Division:-

"The 4th Guards Brigade leaves the 2nd Division tomorrow. The G. O. C. speaks not only for himself but for every officer, non-commissioned officer, and men of the Division, when he expresses sorrow that certain changes in organisation have rendered necessary the severance of ties of comradeship commenced in peace and cemented by war. For the past year, by gallantry, devotion to duty and sacrifice in battle and in the trenches, the Brigade has maintained the high traditions of his His Majesty's Guards, and equally by thorough performance of duties, strict discipline, and the exhibition of many soldier-like qualities, has set an example of smartness, which has tended to raise the standard and elevate the moral of all with whom it has been associated.

Major General Home parts from Brigadier General Feilding, the Officers, non-commissioned officers, and men of the 4th Guards' Brigade with lively regret - he thanks them for their loyal support, and he wishes them good fortune in the future."

"Sgd. S. H. Robinson."
Lieut. Colonel.
"A. A. & Q. M. G. 2nd Division."

19th Aug. 1915.
Marched at 8 a.m. about ten miles to HAM-EN-ARTOIS, on leaving the 2nd Division to join the Guards' Division now forming. Representatives of all units of the 2nd Division lined the road to see the Brigade off and the Divisional Band played the Battalion out of BETHUNE and past General Home.

20th Aug. 1915.
Marched at 8 a.m. about 12½ miles to

RENESCURE. The Battalion marched past Sir Douglas Haig Candg 1st Army, on the road just South of AIRE. They looked and marched very well. No men fell out.

Sgt Major A. Wood joined the Battn from England and a draft of 35 N.C.Os and men joined.

The following order was published today by General Sir Douglas Haig, Candg 1st Army:-

"The 4th Guards Brigade leaves my command today after over a year of active service in the field. During that time the Brigade has taken part in military operations of the most diverse kinds and under very varied conditions of country and weather, and throughout, have displayed the greatest fortitude, tenacity and resolution."

"I desire to place on record my high appreciation of the services rendered by the Brigade and my grateful thanks for the devoted assistance, which one and all have given me during a year of strenuous work."

"Sgd. D. Haig" General"
"Commanding 1st Army."

21st Aug. 1915.
    Marched at 8.55 a.m. about ten miles to HOULLE. The Brigade marched past Sir John French in the big square of ST. OMER and presented a very fine appearance. A great crowd of generals, staff officers and others were present to see the Brigade march through. Bad Billets at HOULLE. We were notified that the Brigade now becomes the 1st Guards Brigade. 2nd Lieut. Hav. H. Parnell joined. The following order published in the 2nd Division and forwarded to the 1st Guards Brigade:-

    "The Commander-in-Chief has intimated that he has read with great interest and satisfaction the report of the mining operations and crater fighting which have taken place in the 2nd Division area during the last two months. He desires that his high appreciation of the good work performed be conveyed to the troops, especially to the 170th and 176th Tunnelling Companies, R.E. the 2nd Bn. Grenadier Guards, the 1st Bn. Irish Guards, the 1st Bn. K.R.R.C. and the 2nd Bn. South Staffordshire Regiment.

    The G.O.C. 2nd Div. has great

pleasure in forwarding this announcement."

"(Sgd) H. V. Horne."
"Major General"
"Commanding 2nd Division."

The following message was also received:-

"The C. in C. wishes to thank all ranks for the splendid services they have rendered. He is much impressed by their soldier-like bearing, and very much regrets that owing to pressure of work he is unable himself to come and visit all units and speak to them himself."

22nd Aug. 1915.
In Billets at HOULLE. Various Officers of the 3rd and 4th Bns. came over to see the Battalion.

23rd Aug. 1915.
In Billets at HOULLE
Orders received to move next day to CAMPAGNE-LES-BOULONNAIS in order to make room at HOULLE for troops arriving from England.

24th Aug. 1915.

Marched at 8 a.m. via LUMBRES to CAMPAGNE-LES-BOULONNAIS, nearly 18 miles. Halted for three hours at mid-way for dinners. A very hot day but the Battalion marched well and only three men fell out. The Brigade now much scattered in different villages. The Headquarters, Guards Divn. at LUMBRES. Poor and very scattered Billets at CAMPAGNE-LES-BOULONNAIS.

2nd Lieut. A. G. H. Sandeman joined.

25th Aug. to 31st Aug. 1915.
In Billets at CAMPAGNE-LES-BOULONNAIS.

H. Seymour
Major
Comdg 2nd Bn. Grenadier Guards

1st Guards Brigade.
Guards Division.

WAR DIARY

2nd BATTN. GRENADIER GUARDS.

SEPTEMBER

1915

On His Majesty's Service.

2nd Battn. Grenadier Guards.

September 1915.

War Diary.
September, 1915.

1st Sept. 1915.
The Battalion paraded and took part in Divisional Field Day under command of Major General, The Earl of Cavan.
Returned to Billets at CAMPAGNE-LES-BOULONNAIS.

2nd Sept. 1915.
In Billets at CAMPAGNE-LES-BOULONNAIS.
The Battalion received sudden orders to proceed to AVROULT to dig trenches forming part of the 17th line of defence. Actual digging took place at DOHEM. Billeted at AVROULT. Very heavy rain during the evening.

3rd Sept. 1915.
Digging at DOHEM. Very heavy rain all day.

4th Sept. 1915.
Digging in the morning at DOHEM. Battalion marched back to billets at

CAMPAGNE-LES-BOULONNAIS at 2 p.m. Very heavy rain.

5th Sept. 1915.
In Billets at CAMPAGNE-LES-BOULONNAIS. Divine Service at 4 p.m.

6th Sept. 1915.
In Billets at CAMPAGNE-LES-BOULONNAIS. Companies doing Coy Drill and Training.

7th Sept. 1915
In Billets at CAMPAGNE-LES-BOULONNAIS. Battalion Field Day in the morning. Practised Battalion in moving across country in Lines of Columns.

8th Sept. 1915.
In Billets at CAMPAGNE-LES-BOULONNAIS. Battalion doing Coy Drill and Training.

9th Sept. 1915.
In Billets at CAMPAGNE-LES-BOULONNAIS. Companies doing Company Training.

10th Sept. 1915.
　　In Billets at CAMPAGNE.
　　Battalion Field Day.
Lines of Columns and Assaults.

11th Sept. 1915.
　　In Billets at CAMPAGNE.
　　Company Training.

12th Sept. 1915.
　　In Billets at CAMPAGNE.
　　Major C. R. C. de Crespigny transferred to 1st Bn. as Second in Command.

13th Sept. 1915.
　　In Billets at CAMPAGNE.
　　Held Battalion Sports in the afternoon. A fine day and plenty of entries. A considerable number of Officers of 1st, 3rd and 4th Bns. came over, also G. O. C. Guards' Divn. and G. O. C. 1st Guards' Brigade.

14th Sept. 1915.
　　In Billets at CAMPAGNE.
　　A wet day.

15th Sept. 1915.
    Brigade Field Day near MERCK.
ST. LIEVIN. Marched off at 7.15 a.m.
about 6½ miles. At the conclusion of
operations. Officers were addressed by
the new Commander of the 11th Corps,
Lieut. General Haking. Battalion had
dinners out and arrived back at CAMPAGNE
about 5.45 p.m.

16th Sept. 1915.
    In Billets at CAMPAGNE.
    Practised Battalion getting into
and out of motor buses, 25 in each
bus.

17th Sept. 1915.
    In Billets at CAMPAGNE.
    Companies doing Drill and
Training.

18th Sept. 1915.
    In Billets at CAMPAGNE.
    Companies doing Drill and
Training. The Commanding Officer
went to reconnoitre new trenches

19th Sept. 1915.
    In Billets at CAMPAGNE.
    Battalion paraded for Service
at 9 a.m.

20th Sept. 1915.
    In Billets at CAMPAGNE.
    Battalion Field Day in
THIEMBRONNE WOOD.

21st Sept. 1915.
    In Billets at CAMPAGNE.
    Battalion practised outpost
across FAUQUEMBERQUES Roads.

22nd Sept. 1915.
    In Billets at CAMPAGNE
    Battalion fired 10 rounds rapid
per man with smoke helmets on.
Lieut. J. C. Craigie slightly wounded
accidentally by bomb.
    Battalion marched at 6 p.m.
and arrived at COYECQUE about
9.45 p.m.

23rd Sept. 1915.
    In Billets at COYECQUE. A very hot
day. Battn. marched at 6 p.m. and
reached WESTREHEM about 10.15 p.m.
    A very wet march.

24th Sept. 1915.
  In Billets at WESTREHEM. Rained all day. Orders to move at midnight cancelled. Later, orders to move at 6 a.m. Informed that a big British Offensive takes place on 25th, in which 11th Corps, consisting of 21st & 24th Divisions and Guards Divn, is in reserve.

25th Sept. 1915.
  Lieut. J. A. Buchanan went sick. Battalion marched at 5.50 a.m. and halted for 3 hours at AUCHEL, where the troops had dinners. Marched at 12.30 p.m. to NOEUX-LES-MINES. A very wet march and continuous checking owing to the tremendous amount of transport, cavalry and guns on the road. Arrived about 10.30 p.m. Men tired after tedious march, but came in well. Heard of complete success of first attack, which captured enemy's trenches and penetrated over a depth of about a mile beyond the German positions on the line from HULLUCH to LOOS.

26th Sept. 1915.
  Orders received in morning that 21st & 24th Divisions continue the attack. News received about noon of complete failure of 21st & 24th Divns' attack and that these Divns were retiring in disorder.

Guards' Divn ordered forward to hold the line. Marched at 1 p.m. via SAILLY LABOURSE and VERMELLES to the old British Trenches near LE RUTOIRE. Enemy shelling locality considerably. Two Coldstream Battalions held the line of the captured German Trenches East of LE RUTOIRE. Casualty. 1 man wounded.

27th Sept. 1915.

Battalion occupying old British line, East of LE RUTOIRE, in support to two Coldstream Battalions in captured German Trenches. Raining heavily all day. Enemy shelled our position intermittently all day and used gas shells, causing everyones eyes to water, otherwise not doing much harm.

Casualties. 2nd Lieut. C. Crosland and 5 N.C.O's & men wounded.

28th Sept. 1915.

Still in Trenches near LE RUTOIRE. The 1st Infantry Brigade came back after dark to the trenches we occupied, causing some confusion and difficulty in fitting in. 2nd & 3rd Guards Brigades made an attack on the right capturing CHALK PIT and HILL 70, East of LOOS, both of which had been lost during the retirement of 21st and 24th Divns on

Sept. 26th. Battalion ordered to move up to the old German first line trenches about 9 p.m. Moved in pouring rain, going very difficult owing to mud and darkness. The Battalion eventually got into position about midnight.
Nos 3 & 4 Coys in old German second line, 1 & 2 Coys and Bn. H.Q. in rear in the old German first line.
Casualties 2 men killed & 5 wounded.

29th Sept. 1915.
Heavy rain and very cold.
Lieut Buchanan rejoined. Battn consolidated the position, buried dead and collected equipment, of which there was a considerable quantity everywhere, left by the 21st and 24th Divns.
A few Shrapnel.
Casualties 2 men wounded and 2 slightly wounded.

30th Sept. 1915.
Very wet and cold. Relieved by 9th Bn. R.S. Fusiliers, who arrived about 10 p.m. Orders received for the Bn. to dig new line in front before leaving. Nos 1 & 2 Coys took the first relief and eventually left the trenches about 1 a.m and marched to Billets at MAZINGARBE under Major

Lord Henry Seymour. No. 3 + 4 Coy took the 2nd relief. Left the trenches about 4 a.m. and arrived at MAZINGARBE about 6.30 a.m. It was a fine performance doing the work in such a short time, as it was raining heavily and the soil was of a chalky nature and difficult to get out.

Casualties 4 N.C.O's + men wounded, and 1 slightly wounded.

W. Grey.
Lieut. Colonel.
Comdg 2nd Bn. Grenadier Guards.

1st Guards Brigade.
Guards Division.

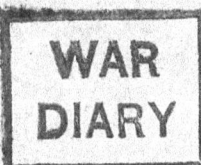

2nd BATTN. GRENADIER GUARDS.

OCTOBER

1915

On His Majesty's Service.

2nd Battn. Grenadier Guards.

October 1915.

War Diary.
October, 1915.

1st October, 1915.
In reserve billets at MAZING-ARBE. Heard of many casualties of 2nd & 3rd Guards Brigades, including many officers of the Regiment.

2nd Oct. 1915.
In reserve billets at MAZINGARBE. Lieut. F. E. B. Witts and 2nd Lieut. J. H. Ingleby transferred to 4 Coys. to replace casualties. Also 2nd Lieuts. G. R. McCreery and A. H. L. Hermon-Hodge to 3rd Bn.

3rd Oct. 1915
Battalion marched at 2 p.m. and took over a section of old British trenches west of VERMELLES as support Battalion. Two Coldstream Battns. in old German trenches south of HOHENZOLLERN REDOUBT. Hq. was scarcely in position when the Germans shelled our line heavily, blowing trenches in in several places

and causing some casualties. At the same time they retook the HOHENZOLLERN REDOUBT held by a Brigade of the 28th Divn on our left.
Casualties 1 man killed, 3 men wounded and 3 slightly wounded.

4th Oct. 1915.
In Trenches in front of VERMELLES. At daybreak, the East Yorks Regt. tried to retake HOHENZOLLERN but failed. The Battalion commenced digging communication trenches forward to the German line, which is now occupied by us.
Casualties. Nil.

5th Oct. 1915.
Completed two communication trenches forward during last night and to-day. Took over line of old German trenches from 3rd Bn. Coldstreams at 4 p.m. A good deal of enfilade and reverse fire coming from Fosse No. 8 and HOHENZOLLERN. Also some hand bombing from the other side of blocks in the trenches.
Casualties. 1 man wounded.

6th Oct. 1915.

In old German Line. Heavily bombed by trench mortars in the morning. Our snipers got the enemy well under cover, killing eight. The Battalion working hard at improving trenches — very hard digging in chalk. Very cold.

Casualties. 2 men killed and 10 N.C.O's & men wounded.

7th Oct. 1915.

In old German Line. Battalion worked very hard all last night and today on line which is now fairly good. Relieved by 3rd Bn. Coldstreams at 4 p.m. and went back to reserve billets at VERMELLES.

Casualties. 2 men wounded and 2 slightly wounded.

8th Oct. 1915.

At VERMELLES. Heavy artillery fire started about 11 a.m. and continued all day. A considerable number of shells falling in and about the village, but doing little damage. The enemy attacked the

line held by 3rd Bn. Grenadiers, just South of HOHENZOLLERN, and got in but were bombed out by 3rd Bn. Coldstreams. They also attacked all along the line to LOOS, but were repulsed everywhere with heavy loss. A deafening din from our own guns all day.
Casualties. 2 men wounded.

9th October, 1915.
   At VERMELLES. A quiet day. Took over the old German line from 3rd Bn. Coldstreams about 4.30 p.m. and were much bothered by aerial torpedoes which did some damage.
   Casualties. Nil.

10th Oct. 1915.
   In old German line. Bombed by aerial torpedoes all day. At 7.30 p.m. our No. 1 Coy. attacked and captured 150 yds of German trench by bombing up it. The trench was successfully consolidated and double block established with bombing post behind it. The Germans made two counter-attacks and a third determined one at daybreak

all of which were driven off. Our
bombers doing excellent work. Our
position bombarded all night by
torpedoes and shells. Lieut. Craigie
and 2nd Lt. A. G. H. Sandeman
led the bombing party.

Casualties. Lieut J. C. Craigie
wounded. 11 N.C.O's & men killed.
1 missing. 39 wounded and 16 slightly
wounded

11th Oct. 1915.
 A quiet day until 5 p.m. when
the trenches were bombarded heavily
for two hours and were badly
knocked about. Battalion worked
hard all night to repair damage.
Major Lord Henry Seymour left
to take command of the 4th Bn.

12th Oct. 1915.
 In old German line. Intermittent
shelling in the morning, and
heavily shelled in the afternoon. A
severe bombing attack made on the
trench which we captured on 10th.
This was beaten off by No. 4 Coy.
The chief anxiety being whether the
supply of bombs would hold out

We threw nearly 2,000 bombs and the enemy a similar number. Two violent explosions occurred in the German line on their side of the block, apparently caused by our bombs exploding in the enemy's bomb stores. During the whole attack, our line was heavily bombed by aerial torpedoes and shelled with heavy shells. About dark, the enemy attack gradually died away but intermittent shelling continued for some hours. No. 4. Coy bombers did very good work, their "Mills" Bombs outranging those of the enemy. Had it not been for the attack, we were to have been relieved about 6.45 p.m. but the relief was greatly delayed and the relieving Battalions did not arrive until nearly midnight. The left Company of the Battn. relieved by 5th Sth Staffs (T) of the 46th Division, the remainder of the Battalion by 7th (K) Bn. Suffolk Regt of the 12th Divn. The relief completed about 3 a.m. and the Battalion marched to billets at VERQUIN, the last Company arriving about 8.a.m. The Battalion very tired.

Casualties for 11th & 12th. 17 N.C.O's & men killed. 40 wounded & 21 slightly wounded.

13th Oct. 1915.
    In Billets at VERQUIN.

14th Oct. 1915.
    In Billets at VERQUIN

15th Oct 1915
    At VERQUIN until 5 p.m. when the Battalion moved to SAILLY LABOURSE and billeted. 2nd and 3rd Guards Bdes now in front line again. 1st Guards Bde in Divisional Reserve.

16th Oct 1915.
    In Billets at SAILLY LABOURSE

17th Oct 1915.
    In Billets at SAILLY LABOURSE The Battalion marched at 2.15 p.m. to Billets at VERMELLES.

18th Oct. 1915.
   In Billets at VERMELLES.

19th Oct. 1915.
   The Battalion took over support trenches from 4th Bn. Grenadiers opposite "Big Willie". Moved about 3 p.m. No 3 Coy was in the front line, No 4 in support. Great difficulty in getting Nos 1 & 2 Coy in owing to no orders having been received as to where they should go. Eventually, they were put into same old trenches for the night, which were in a very dirty condition and needed a great deal of cleaning. Several unlucky shells caught No 1, as they were coming up. Lieut. J. A. M. Browning joined.
   Casualties 9 N.C.O's & men killed and 8 wounded.

20th Oct. 1915.
   Battn Headquarters and Nos 1 & 2 Coy moved back to reserve trenches by VERMELLES. A quiet day.
   Casualties: Nil.

21st Oct. 1915.
The Battn relieved 3rd Bn.
Coldstreams in an old front line
opposite Fosse No 8. No 1 & 2 Coy
being in front and No 4 in support.
No 3 in reserve in the old British
front line. Major A. St. Leger
Glyn joined the Battalion.
Casualties. 1 man (R.A.M.C.
attached to Battn) wounded.
Draft of N.C.O's & men arrived,
a total of 36. Further casualties
2 men killed and 1 wounded

22nd Oct. 1915.
In trenches as above. A quiet day.
No 3 & 4 Coy deepened and widened
new communication trench known as
"King's Head" by night. Very bad
digging owing to hard chalk. No 3
moved up in to the British front
line. An urgent and secret message
received to the effect that a big
attack was to be expected in the
course of the next three days. Our
artillery in a perfect state of chaos —
no communication to their batteries,
none of the observing officers knew
where their guns were firing or what
their night lines were.
Casualties. Nil.

23rd Oct. 1915.

2nd Lt. H. J. C. Crookshank wounded during the night while wiring in front. Our guns shelled German trenches in village of ST. ELIE. The enemy retaliated by heavy shelling of our front line and all down "King's Head" communication trench blowing it in very much. 3rd Bn. Coldstreams relieved us about 8 p.m. and we returned to reserve trenches north of VERMELLES. 2nd Lieut A. J. Irvine joined.

Casualties 1 killed and 10 wounded.

24th Oct. 1915.

In reserve trenches north of VERMELLES. A quiet day. A few shells fell in VERMELLES but no damage was done to the Battalion.

Casualties. Nil.

H.et.

25th Oct. 1915.

In reserve trenches north of VERMELLES. Officers of the relieving brigade came to look round.

26th Oct. 1915.
Relieved by the 35th Bde about 2 p.m. Lt Col G. D. Jeffreys took leave of the Battalion on taking command of 35th Bde. Battalion was formed up in mass near Fosse 8. Lt Col. Jeffreys congratulated them for what they had done and thanked them for the magnificent way in which they had supported him and also his predecessor, the late Lt. Col. H. R. A. Smith, C.M.G., who died of wounds on 19-5-15. The Battalion marched via BEUVRY and BETHUNE, with Major J. St. Leger Glyn in command, to billets at LAPUGNOY arriving about 8.30 p.m.

27th Oct. 1915.
In Billets at LAPUGNOY. Good billets. Companies had arms drill under Captains in the morning. The Batt. paraded under Major Glyn in the afternoon to practise for inspection by H.M. The King. Steady rain all day.

28th Oct. 1915.
In Billets at LAPUGNOY. At 11 a.m. the Battn. marched to CHOCQUES on the way to inspection by H.M. The King. Halted for one hour at CHOCQUES and were informed that His Majesty had met with an accident and that the inspection was cancelled. Returned to LAPUGNOY about 1.15 p.m. A very wet day.

29th Oct. 1915.
In Billets at LAPUGNOY.
Companies doing Drill and Training.

30th Oct. 1915.
In Billets at LAPUGNOY.
No. 3 & 4 Coy. had a route march to HESDEGNEUL to hear the Regimental Band. Nos. 1 & 2 Coy. doing Drill and Training.

31st Oct. 1915.
In Billets at LAPUGNOY.
Divine Service at 11.30 a.m. at which the Band attended.
2nd Lt. A. J. V. B. Ashley and a draft of 60 other ranks arrived.

31st Oct. 1915 (Continued)
Arrangements with the local brewery for the Battalion to have Baths. Wet morning.

AS Lyndhyn
Major
Comdg 2nd Bn. Grenadier Guards

22

1st Guards Brigade.
Guards Division.

WAR DIARY

2nd BATTN. GRENADIER GUARDS.

NOVEMBER

1915

1st Guards Brigade.
Guards Division.

WAR DIARY

2nd BATTN. GRENADIER GUARDS.

NOVEMBER

1915

On His Majesty's Service.

2nd Battn. Grenadier Guards.

November 1915.

November 1915.

1st Nov. 1915.
In billets at LAPUGNOY. A very wet day. Companies did Drill and Training. One Company had hot baths.

2nd Nov. 1915
In billets at LAPUGNOY. A very wet day. Unable to carry out any training.

3rd Nov. 1915.
In billets at LAPUGNOY. A fine day. Nos 1 & 2 Coys fired with smoke-helmets on. Nos 3 & 4 did training.
Two companies had hot baths.
2nd Lieut. I. J. V. B. Apley left for 3rd Bn.

4th Nov. 1915.
In billets at LAPUGNOY. A very foggy morning. Nos 2 & 4 Coy fired with smoke-helmets on, commencing at 11 a.m. No 2 Coy instructed in "wiring" by R.E.

5th Nov. 1915.
    In billets at LAPUGNOY. A fine day. Companies did Field Training

6th Nov 1915.
    In billets at LAPUGNOY. Cold and foggy with sharp frost in morning. A Battalion Parade and Drill at 11.0 a.m. The Band of the Regiment played in front of Battalion Headquarters from 1.45 p.m. to 3 p.m.

7th Nov. 1915.
    In billets at LAPUGNOY. A beautiful day. Church Parade by half Battalions. Captain H. A. Clive admitted to Hospital. (4th Field Ambulance.)

8th Nov. 1915.
    In billets at LAPUGNOY. A fine, bright day. Companies doing Field Training. Two Companies had hot baths.

9th Nov. 1915.
    In billets at LAPUGNOY. A fine morning but a wet afternoon. Companies engaged in field training and preparations for moving. Two Companies had hot baths.

10th Nov. 1915.
    A very wet morning. Battalion left billets at LAPUGNOY at 9.15 a.m. Joined the Brigade at CHOCQUES, marched via HINGES to billets between EPINETTE (North) and CROIX MARMEUSE (South) arriving at 1.15 p.m. Found 5th Bn. North Staffs Regt (T) still in Billets. They paraded at 3 p.m. and we then took over Billets. Billets good but scattered.

11th Nov. 1915.
    In billets as above. A fine morning but heavy rain after 4.0 p.m. Companies did field training.

12th Nov 1915.
    In billets as above.
    Rained all the previous night,

and very wet to day. C and q Bfr
inspected the Transport harness.
Training suspended owing to
inclement weather.

13th Nov 1915.
In Billets as above. A wet
morning. Companies doing Drill
and Training.

14th Nov 1915.
Fine and sunny with a sharp
frost. The Battalion moved to
fresh billets at LA GORGUE at 3.45 p.m.
arriving at 4.45 p.m. At about
5.30 p.m. it became known that a
man of No 3 Company, No 19480,
Pte R. Hayes had fallen into the
muddy river which flows past the
Company's billet. Capt & Adjt. Hon. H. R.
Bailey, No 13716, Sgt H. J. Thomas and
No 19516 Pte H. H. Grose made every
endeavour to effect a rescue in spite of
the cold and darkness of the night.
Unfortunately, their efforts were
unsuccessful. Companies did Drill
and Training in the morning.

15th Nov. 1915.

The body of Pte Hayes was recovered and was buried during the afternoon in the Roman Catholic Cemetery, LA GORGUE. A very fine day but cold, with frost at night. Companies did Drill and Training. In billets at LA GORGUE.

16th Nov. 1915.

In billets at LA GORGUE. Companies did Drill and Training. A fine morning, rained in afternoon, frost at night. Conference of Commanding Officers at Brigade Headquarters on Trench Warfare.

17th Nov. 1915

Selected N.C.O's and men attended a demonstration of poisonous gases and the efficacy of the smoke helmet. Heavy hail-storm about mid-day. Otherwise fine but cold. Companies did Drill and Training.

Lieut. Colonel G. D. Jeffreys resumed command of the Battalion this day.

18th Nov. 1915
In billets at LA GORGUE. Very wet.

19th Nov. 1915.
In billets as above. Very wet.

20th Nov. 1915.
The Brigade took over line of trenches opposite PIETRE. All in a very bad state, communication trenches flooded and front line breastworks crumbling and were not bullet proof. Country in a very wet state. Major Rt. Hon. Winston Churchill, who has just resigned from Government, arrived to be attached to the Battalion for instruction, and accompanied the Battalion to the Trenches. Relief completed about 7 p.m. Battalion Headquarters established behind ruined farm near RUE DE TILLELOY. Hard frost at night. The Battalion worked very hard on the line all night and improved it very much.
Casualties. Nil.

28th Nov. 1915.
 In Billets at RIEZ BAILLEUL. Took over PIETRE Line from Irish Guards at 7 p.m. A quiet night. Casualties 1 man slightly wounded.

29th Nov. 1915.
 In Line opposite PIETRE. A fairly quiet day. Rained hard and trenches were very wet. A quiet night.
 Casualties. Nil.

30th Nov. 1915.
 In Line opposite PIETRE. Enemy shelled a good deal but did little damage. Relieved by Irish Guards at 7 p.m. and marched to reserve Billets at RIEZ BAILLEUL.
 Casualties 3 men wounded and 3 slightly wounded.

J. S. Effay
Lieut. Colonel.
Comdg 2nd Bn Grenadier Guards.
30-11-1915.

21st Nov. 1915.
In Line opposite PIETRE. Hard frost. The Battalion again worked very hard on trenches all night. Enemy active and fired bursts of machine gun fire all night.
Casualties 1 killed and 2 wounded.

22nd Nov. 1915.
In line opposite PIETRE. Still freezing. Considerable improvement effected in front line. Relieved at 6 p.m. by Irish Guards, and marched to reserve billets at BOUT DEVILLE.
Casualties. 1 man killed.

23rd Nov. 1915.
In reserve at BOUT DEVILLE. Wet and muddy. Poor billets.

24th Nov. 1915.
In billets at BOUT DEVILLE. Took over PIETRE Line at 5.30 p.m from Irish Guards. A good deal of machine gun fire and some shelling during the night.
Casualties Nil.

25th Nov. 1915.
In line opposite PIETRE. Enemy shelled our trenches a good deal with field guns and 4.2 Howitzers during the afternoon and also shelled the trenches and sunken road intermittently throughout the night. Cold and raw with a little snow during the night.

26th Nov. 1915.
Enemy Howitzers shelled the line soon after dawn and at intervals during the morning, otherwise no incident during the day. Relieved at 7 p.m. by Irish Guards and marched to reserve billets at RIEZ BAILLEUL. Good billets.
Casualties for 25th & 26th. 1 N.C.O. and 1 man killed, 2 men died of wounds, 8 wounded and 1 slightly wounded

27th Nov. 1915.
In billets at RIEZ BAILLEUL.
Hard frost during the night.

1st Guards Brigade.

Guards Division.

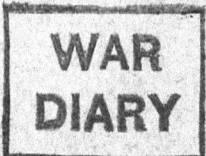

2nd BATTN. GRENADIER GUARDS.

DECEMBER

1915

On His Majesty's Service.

Army Form C. 2118.

WAR DIARY
or
INTELLIGENCE SUMMARY.

(Erase heading not required.)

Instructions regarding War Diaries and Intelligence Summaries are contained in F. S. Regs., Part II and the Staff Manual respectively. Title pages will be prepared in manuscript.

Hour, Date, Place	Summary of Events and Information	Remarks and references to Appendices
1st Dec. 1915.	In Billets at RIEZ BAILLEUL. Weather fine and mild.	
2nd Dec. 1915.	Weather fine and mild. The Battalion marched at 2 p.m. via PONT RIQUET to new billets south of MERVILLE, arriving about 5 p.m. Billets very much scattered. Rained at night.	
3rd Dec. 1915.	In Billets at MERVILLE. A stormy day but warm. Companies doing Drill and Training.	
4th Dec. 1915.	In Billets at MERVILLE. Wet day but warm. Companies doing Drill and Training. Half the Battalion had baths and used "Thresh Disinfector."	
5th Dec. 1915.	In Billets at MERVILLE. Fine and warm but rained at night. Companies doing Drill and Training.	
6th Dec. 1915.	In Billets at MERVILLE. A very stormy night, and high wind continued until about mid-day. Half the Battalion had baths and used "Thresh Disinfector."	

WAR DIARY or INTELLIGENCE SUMMARY.

Army Form C. 2118.

(Erase heading not required.)

Instructions regarding War Diaries and Intelligence Summaries are contained in F.S. Regs., Part II and the Staff Manual respectively. Title pages will be prepared in manuscript.

Hour, Date, Place	Summary of Events and Information	Remarks and references to Appendices
7th Dec. 1915.	In Billets at MERVILLE. Companies doing Drill and training. A fine morning but heavy rain in the afternoon.	
8th Dec. 1915.	In Billets at MERVILLE. A fine warm day. The Battalion marched at 9.30 a.m. to new billets at LAVENTIE arriving about 1 p.m. Took over by D. & Left half companies, and command of the 1st Guards Brigade, vice Brigadier General L. Feilding, accidentally wounded.	
9th Dec. 1915.	In billets at LAVENTIE. Very wet all day. Took over left Battalion Life Section of Front Line from 1st Bn. Irish Guards, from H.1 & e.9.e. to H.13 & 2.3, south east of PICANTIN. 1st Companies in the front line. Relief completed by 6.30 p.m. A quiet night. Orders received about 9.30 p.m. to clear about 150 yards of front line trenches at H.13 & 9.1 owing to the existence of a German mine. Casualties Nil.	Ref Map Sheet 36 N.W.

(73989) W4141—463. 400,000. 9/14. H.&J.Ltd. Forms/C. 2118/10.

WAR DIARY
or
INTELLIGENCE SUMMARY.
(Erase heading not required.)

Army Form C. 2118.

Hour, Date, Place	Summary of Events and Information	Remarks and references to Appendices
10th Dec. 1915	In front line as above. A fine day, but wet at night. "A" Company 16th Bn. Royal Welsh Fusiliers attached to the Battalion for instruction and was split up among Companies. Casualties Nil.	
11th Dec. 1915.	In front line as above. A fine day. Heavy wind blowing. It was proposed to shell the suspected German mine-shaft at N.14.C.1.8. but an heavy artillery but this would have entailed the clearing of some 500 yards of our front line. After a conference between Lieut Hanratty C.R.E. Guards Divn. Major Snow R.A. Comdg 2/5 Brigade and the Commanding Officer, it was decided to postpone the bombardment. Relief by 1st Bn. Irish Guards completed by 6.30 p.m. and Battalion marched to former billets at LAVENTIE. Heavy rain during the night. Lieut. & A.M. Banning admitted to Hospital. Other ranks wounded. Casualties.	

WAR DIARY
or
INTELLIGENCE SUMMARY.
(Erase heading not required.)

Army Form C. 2118.

Hour, Date, Place	Summary of Events and Information	Remarks and references to Appendices
12th Dec. 1915.	In billets at LAVENTIE. A fine day. A voluntary Divine Service was held in the goods shed, LAVENTIE Railway Station at which the Bishop of Khartoum officiated and held confirmation.	
13th Dec. 1915.	In billets at LAVENTIE. Lieut. Colonel J.D. Affleck resumed command of the Battn. The Battalion relieved 1st Bn. Wilts Regt. in trench line as before. Lieut. Hav. H.A.B. Parnell went out at 2.30 a.m. with a party of 11 other ranks from N.13,1.50. and entered the German trench line about N.13.c.2.8 and worked for about three hours along the German trench line 400 yards which they found unoccupied, nor could they find any trace of the supposed German mine shafts at N14.c.1.8. The party returned safely having accomplished its mission. A frosty night. Casualty. 2 men wounded, and 1 N.C.O. killed.	

WAR DIARY or INTELLIGENCE SUMMARY

Army Form C. 2118.

Hour, Date, Place	Summary of Events and Information	Remarks and references to Appendices
14th Dec. 1915.	In draw line as above. A fine frosty morning. The same patrol with the addition of one machine gunner, an officer and one other rank of the R.E. during Co. left our line about 12.30 a.m. and again entered the German lines at the same point and proceeded along the German draw line in an easterly direction for about 400 yds. It came upon a German post, which it surprised, killing two and taking one prisoner without firing a shot. Afterwards proceeding along the trench found a reserve party two with a view to attempt a rescue but were driven off by an enemy patrol. Our party lost one man, 9/12 19512, Pte C.R. Maiden, who was mortally wounded and had to be left in the German lines, otherwise the patrol returned safely. The mining Engineers reported that there was no German mine in the vicinity. Simultaneously with this patrol, a patrol from the 2nd Battn Coldstream Guards entered the German line at the same point as our patrol, and	

WAR DIARY
or
INTELLIGENCE SUMMARY.
(Erase heading not required.)

Army Form C. 2118.

Hour, Date, Place	Summary of Events and Information	Remarks and references to Appendices
14th Dec. 1915. (Continued)	proceeded along the German Line trenches for a distance of some 700 yards and found them unoccupied. Both patrols report that the German trenches are infinitely wetter than ours and that all the "dug-outs" they went into were full of water. Lieut. Hon. H. C. B. Parnell has been awarded the "Military Cross" and No.1027, L/Cpl. I. Lyons the Distinguished Conduct Medal for gallantry upon this occasion. Casualties. 1 man wounded + missing (Pte G. R. Jordan)	
15th Dec. 1915.	In trench line as above. Hanmer and four 2nd Lieut. H. D. Jeffreys again assumed command of the 1st Guard Brigade, vice Brigadier General Heyworth, proceeded to England. The Battalion was relieved by 1st Bn. Irish Guards and marched to billets at LAVENTIE. Casualties. Nil.	

Army Form C. 2118.

WAR DIARY
or
INTELLIGENCE SUMMARY.
(Erase heading not required.)

Instructions regarding War Diaries and Intelligence Summaries are contained in F.S. Regs., Part II. and the Staff Manual respectively. Title pages will be prepared in manuscript.

Hour, Date, Place	Summary of Events and Information	Remarks and references to Appendices
16th Dec. 1915.	In Billets at LAVENTIE. A fine warm day but no sun.	
17th Dec. 1915	In Billets at LAVENTIE. A fine morning, but rain in the afternoon. "A" Company, 16th Batn. Royal Welsh Fusiliers completed its attachment with the Battalion. The Battalion relieved 1st Bn Irish Guards as above. Orders were received during the evening not to patrol and not to provoke the enemy in any way as gas was being put into the line just south. Casualties Nil.	
18th Dec. 1915.	In Trench Line as above. A very foggy morning, and observation from front line quite impossible. Lieut. Colonel D. Davies M.P. and "A" Company, 14th Bn. Royal Welsh Fusiliers attached to the Battalion and visitors 20 glits up among Companies and also 20 cadets from the Cadets School, ST. OMER. These later attached for one night only. Casualties 1 was killed and 1 slightly wounded.	

WAR DIARY
or
INTELLIGENCE SUMMARY.
(Erase heading not required.)

Army Form C. 2118.

Hour, Date, Place	Summary of Events and Information	Remarks and references to Appendices
19th Dec. 1915	In Trenches line as above. A fine day. The enemy appear to be holding front line very lightly. Relieved by 1st Bn Irish Guards and marched to billets at LAVENTIE. Casualties 1 man killed and 1 wounded.	
20th Dec. 1915.	In Billets at LAVENTIE. A fine day. The Battalion left LAVENTIE at 1.15 p.m. and marched via LA GORGUE to billets south of MERVILLE, which they had previously occupied, arriving about 5 p.m.	
21st Dec. 1915.	In Billets at MERVILLE. Wet all day.	
22nd Dec. 1915.	In Billets at MERVILLE. Snow but heavy rain storms at intervals. Companies did Drill and Training.	
23rd Dec. 1915.	In Billets at MERVILLE. Heavy rain, especially in the evening. Companies did Drill and Training. Brigadier General came to R.6. 11th Coys inspected work going on for the improvements of Billets.	

WAR DIARY or INTELLIGENCE SUMMARY.

(Erase heading not required.)

Army Form C. 2118.

Hour, Date, Place	Summary of Events and Information	Remarks and references to Appendices
24th Dec. 1915	In Billets at MERVILLE. A fine morning, but rain during the afternoon. No 3 Coy had Christmas Dinner in the building formerly occupied by the Lahore Clearing Stn at 12 noon. No 2 Company had Dinner at 5 p.m. Drafts of 55 other ranks arrived.	
25th Dec. 1915.	In Billets at MERVILLE. Heavy rain in the morning. The Major General saw all Officers at Battalion Headquarters. Nos 1 & 4 Companies had Christmas Dinner in the Lahore Clearing Stn.	
26th Dec. 1915.	A fine bright morning. The Battalion marched at twelve noon via LAGORGUE and took over billets at RIEZ BAILLEUL from 3rd Bn Grenadier Guards arriving about 2 p.m. A' Coy, 15th Bn Royal Welsh Fusiliers and Lt Col. Bell and Headquarters attached to the Battalion for one night. The enemy shelled a point about 300 yds south of the moat southerly billets during the afternoon.	

Army Form C. 2118.

WAR DIARY
or
INTELLIGENCE SUMMARY.
(Erase heading not required.)

Instructions regarding War Diaries and Intelligence Summaries are contained in F.S. Regs., Part II. and the Staff Manual respectively. Title pages will be prepared in manuscript.

Hour, Date, Place	Summary of Events and Information	Remarks and references to Appendices
27th Dec. 1915.	In billets at RIEZ BAILLEUL. A wet morning but fine later. Companies doing Drill and Training. "A" Company 10th Bn. South Wales Borderers attached to the Battalion.	
28th Dec. 1915.	In Billets as above. Officers and selected N.C.O's attended a lecture and demonstration at LA GORGUE on "Bombing" by Captain Hockech - Westcoat. Companies doing Drills and Training. The Battalion relieved 1st Bn. Irish Guards in front line trenches Ebenezer Farm Section. Trenches in bad order and waterlogged. A few did dark night during relieve in both sides. 2nd Lieut. V.L.B.S. Yerbur joined the Battalion. Casualties Nil.	Batt HQ EBENEZER FARM. map 36. N.W. M.34.B.5.9 Line Held. SIGN POST LANE M.35.D.45 To M.29.D.5.9.
29th Dec. 1915.	A fine quiet morning, but dull later. In front line trenches as above. The Right group bombarded the German trenches from 10.00 a.m. to 10.12 a.m. causing considerable damage. A 9.2 gun bombarded a german trench house, the sixth and eighth shells were	

Army Form C. 2118.

WAR DIARY
or
INTELLIGENCE SUMMARY.
(Erase heading not required.)

Instructions regarding War Diaries and Intelligence Summaries are contained in F.S. Regs., Part II. and the Staff Manual respectively. Title pages will be prepared in manuscript.

Hour, Date, Place	Summary of Events and Information	Remarks and references to Appendices
29th Dec. 1915. (contd)	divide this. The block-house was demolished. Otherwise a quiet day. Casualties 1 man killed.	
30th Dec. 1915.	In trenches as above. A fine morning with some frost. A quiet day. The Battalion was relieved by 1st Bn. Irish Guards and marched to Billets at RIEZ BAILLEUL. 2nd Lieuts J. H. Hinchin, H. F. Bowen and N. M. Joslen joined Battalion. Casualties {1 man wounded.}	
31st Dec. 1915.	In Billets at RIEZ BAILLEUL. A fine morning. Bn. paraded in the afternoon. Battalion employed in cleaning clothes and saving smoke helmets.	

A S Dyer Glyn
Major
Comdg 2nd Bn. Grenadier Guards

1st Guards Brigade.
Guards Division.

2nd BATTAKION

GRENADIER GUARDS

JANUARY 1916.

War Diary

January, 1916.

2nd Battalion Grenadier Guards.

Army Form C. 2118

WAR DIARY
or
INTELLIGENCE SUMMARY
(Erase heading not required.)

Instructions regarding War Diaries and Intelligence Summaries are contained in F.S. Regs., Part II. and the Staff Manual respectively. Title Pages will be prepared in manuscript.

Place	Date	Hour	Summary of Events and Information	Remarks and references to Appendices
	1/1/16		In Billets at RIEZ BAILLEUL. Marched at 3.15 p.m. to relieve 1st Battalion Irish Guards in trenches, EBENEZER FARM Section, M.35 D4.3. to M.29 D5.9. Map 36 N.W. Casualties, 1 man slightly wounded.	
	2/1/16		In trenches as above. A quiet day. Casualties, 1 man killed and 1 wounded.	
	3/1/16		In trenches as above. Relieved by 1st Battalion Irish Guards and marched to Billets at RIEZ BAILLEUL. Casualties, 1 man killed and 1 wounded, also 1 slightly wounded who remained at duty.	
	4/1/16		In Billets at RIEZ BAILLEUL. The Battalion marched at 3.0 p.m. to relieve 1st Battalion Irish Guards in trenches as above. Worcesters of 10th Division on our right. Casualties, 2 men wounded.	
	5/1/16		In trenches as above. A quiet day. The Commanding Officer of the 10th Welsh Regiment attached. Casualties, 1 man killed.	
	6/1/16		In trenches above. Relieved by the 10th Welsh Regiment, 1½ hours late, as their platoons got hopelessly mixed up in the dark. The Battalion marched to Billets at RIEZ BAILLEUL. Casualties, 1 man wounded and 1 slightly wounded.	
	7/1/16		In Billets at RIEZ BAILLEUL. The Battalion marched at 11.30 a.m. to new billets at CALONNE, arriving about 2 p.m. En route, the billets occupied by the Welsh Guards and 1st Battalion Grenadier Guards, just south of MERVILLE, were passed.	

Army Form C. 2118

WAR DIARY
or
INTELLIGENCE SUMMARY

(Erase heading not required.)

Instructions regarding War Diaries and Intelligence Summaries are contained in F.S. Regs., Part II. and the Staff Manual respectively. Title Pages will be prepared in manuscript.

Place	Date	Hour	Summary of Events and Information	Remarks and references to Appendices
	7/1/16	(Continued)	The Billets at CALONNE were left in a very dirty condition by the Welsh Regiment.	
	8/1/16		In Billets at CALONNE.	
	9/1/16		In Billets at CALONNE. Companies doing Drill and Training.	
	10/1/16		In Billets at CALONNE. Companies doing Drill and Training. Lieut. Colonel C. Pereira assumed command of the Brigade and Lieut. Colonel G. D. Jeffreys resumed command of the Battalion.	
	11/1/16		In Billets at CALONNE. Companies doing Drill and Training.	
	12/1/16	10.45 a.m.	In Billets at CALONNE. The Battalion marched at to billets at ARREWAGE, in 3rd Corps area, about two miles north of MERVILLE.	
	13/1/16		In Billets at ARREWAGE. Companies doing Drill and Training.	
	14/1/16		In Billets at ARREWAGE. Companies doing Drill and Training. Lieut. Colonel G. D. Jeffreys assumed temporary command of the 3rd Battalion. Captain R.H.V. Cavendish,M.V.O. assumed temporary command of the Battalion, owing to Major A.St.I.Glyn being on leave.	
	15/1/16		In Billets at ARREWAGE. Companies doing Drill and Training.	
	16/1/16		In Billets at ARREWAGE. Companies doing Drill and Training.	
	17/1/16		In Billets at ARREWAGE. Companies doing Drill and Training.	

1875 Wt. W593/826 1,000,000 4/15 J.B.C. & A. A.D.S.S./Forms/C. 2118.

Army Form C. 2118

WAR DIARY
or
INTELLIGENCE SUMMARY
(Erase heading not required.)

Instructions regarding War Diaries and Intelligence Summaries are contained in F. S. Regs., Part II. and the Staff Manual respectively. Title Pages will be prepared in manuscript.

14 Div

Place	Date	Hour	Summary of Events and Information	Remarks and references to Appendices
	17/1/16	(Continued)	Lieut. Colonel G. D. Jeffreys appointed to command of 58th Infantry Brigade.	
	18/1/16		In Billets at Arrewage. Companies doing Drill and Training. Lieut. Colonel G. D. Jeffreys rode over and took leave of the Officers.	
	19/1/16		In Billets at ARREWAGE. Companies doing Drill and Training.	
	20/1/16		In Billets at ARREWAGE. Companies doing Drill and Training.	
	21/1/16		In Billets at ARREWAGE. Companies doing Drill and Training. 2nd Lieut. J. Arbuthnott joined the Battalion.	
	22/1/16		In Billets at Arrewage. Companies doing Drill and Training.	
	23/1/16		In Billets At ARREWAGE. Divine Service in the morning. Major A. St. Leger Glyn assumed temporary command of the Battalion on returning off leave. 2nd Lieut. D. Harvey joined the Battalion.	
	24/1/16		In Billets at ARREWAGE. Companies doing Drill and Training. Orders received to march tomorrow to Billets at RIEZ BAILLEUL.	
	25/1/16		The Battalion marched at 9.0 a.m. to RIEZ BAILLEUL, via MERVILLE and LA GORGUE, arriving about twelve noon. The Battalion occupied the same billets as on the previous occasion it was at RIEZ BAILLEUL. Two platoons of No. 3 Company garrisoned ROUGE CROIX east and west, and marched ahead of the Battalion.	

Army Form C. 2118

WAR DIARY
or
INTELLIGENCE SUMMARY
(Erase heading not required.)

Instructions regarding War Diaries and Intelligence Summaries are contained in F. S. Regs., Part II. and the Staff Manual respectively. Title Pages will be prepared in manuscript.

Place	Date	Hour	Summary of Events and Information	Remarks and references to Appendices
	26/1/16		In Billets at RIEZ BAILLEUL. The Battalion left billets at 4.0 a.m. to relieve 1st Battalion Irish Guards in trenches, Ebenezer Farm Section, M.35.D 4.8. to M.29 D 5.9, Map 36 N.W. A quiet night. A good deal of work done, viz, carrying up bombs, S.A.A., etc, in view of an expected attack by the enemy, tomorrow being the anniversary of the Kaiser's Birthday. Special precautions taken. Casualties, Nil.	
	27/1/16		In trenches as above. A very quiet day. The expected attack was not made, and there was nothing to suggest that the enemy intended making an attack. Our Artillery shelled the German Trenches from 5.0 a.m. onwards at intervals, but there was very little retaliation. The enemy sent over a few 5 inch shells which dropped on the LA BASSEE road Near ROUGE CROIX at 5.0 p.m. Relieved by Irish Guards and marched to Billets at RIEZ BAILLEUL. Casualties, Nil.	
	28/1/16		In Billets at RIEZ BAILLEUL.	
	29/1/16		In Billets at RIEZ BAILLEUL. The Battalion marched at 4.0 p.m. to relieve Irish Guards, 14th Battalion Welsh Regiment on our right and 2nd Battalion Coldstream Guards on left. Major C.R.C. de Crespigny, D.S.O. from the 1st Battalion, assumed command of the Battalion. Casualties, 3 men wounded and 1 slightly wounded. The latter remained at Duty.	

Army Form C. 2118

WAR DIARY
or
INTELLIGENCE SUMMARY
(Erase heading not required.)

Instructions regarding War Diaries and Intelligence Summaries are contained in F. S. Regs., Part II. and the Staff Manual respectively. Title Pages will be prepared in manuscript.

Place	Date	Hour	Summary of Events and Information	Remarks and references to Appendices
	30/1/16		In trenches as above. A thick mist all day, hardly a shot fired. Casualties, Nil.	
	31/1/16		In trenches as above. A quiet day. 14th Welsh Regiment on our right and 3rd Battalion Coldstream Guards on left. The Battalion relieved by Irish Guards and marched to Billets at RIEZ BAILLEUL. Casualties, 1 man killed, 1 wounded and 3 slightly wounded. The latter remained at Duty.	

A.S.dyer-glyn (?)
Major,
Commanding 2nd Battalion Grenadier Guards.

1st Guards Brigade.
Guards Division.

2nd BATTALION

GRENADIER GUARDS

FEBRUARY 1 9 1 6

2nd Battalion
Grenadier Guards.

War Diary.

February, 1916.

Vol XIX

Army Form C. 2118

WAR DIARY
or
INTELLIGENCE SUMMARY
(Erase heading not required.)

Instructions regarding War Diaries and Intelligence Summaries are contained in F. S. Regs., Part II. and the Staff Manual respectively. Title Pages will be prepared in manuscript.

Place	Date	Hour	Summary of Events and Information	Remarks and references to Appendices
	1-8-15		In Billets at RIEZ BAILLEUL. Companies doing drill and training.	
	2-8-15		In Billets at RIEZ BAILLEUL. The Battalion relieved 1st Battalion Irish Guards, passing ROUGE CROIX about 5.0 P.M., in Trenches, Ebenezer Farm section, M.35 & 4.8 to M.29 d 5.8, sup 36 N.W. A very quiet night. Casualties, Nil.	
	3-8-15		In Trenches as above. Lieut. Audrey of the Wilts Yeomanry attached for instruction. 10th South Wales Borderers on our right and Coldstream Guards on left. Casualties, 1 man killed.	
	4-8-15		In Trenches as above. A few small shells. Relieved by 1st Battalion Irish Guards and marched to billets at RIEZ BAILLEUL. Casualties, 1 man wounded.	
	5-8-15		In Billets at RIEZ BAILLEUL.	
	6-8-15		In Billets at RIEZ BAILLEUL. The Battalion relieved 1st Battalion Irish Guards in trenches as above. Casualties, Nil.	
	7-8-15		In Trenches as above. Rained during the night, and a few shells during the morning. The Battalion was relieved by the 2nd Battn. Scots Guards under Lieut. Colonel Lord Esme Gordon-Lennox and marched to billets at LA GORGUE. Casualties 1 man wounded.	

Army Form C. 2118

WAR DIARY

or

~~INTELLIGENCE SUMMARY~~

(Erase heading not required.)

Instructions regarding War Diaries and Intelligence Summaries are contained in F.S. Regs., Part II. and the Staff Manual respectively. Title Pages will be prepared in manuscript.

Place	Date	Hour	Summary of Events and Information	Remarks and references to Appendices
	8-2-16		In Billets at LA GORGUE. Companies doing Drill and Training.	
	9-2-16		In Billets as above. Companies doing Drill and Training.	
	10-2-16		In Billets as above. Companies doing Drill and Training.	
	11-2-16		In Billets as above. Rained heavily all day. The Battalion marched about 2.0 p.m. along the MERVILLE Road to a field just outside MERVILLE, where the Brigade was formed up for inspection by Field Marshal Lord Kitchener of Khartoum. The inspection was timed for 3.30 p.m. but we were kept standing in the rain until 4.15 p.m.	
	12-2-16		In Billets as above. Companies doing Drill and Training.	
	13-2-16		In Billets at LA GORGUE. The Band of the Coldstream Guards played in the Square.	
	14-2-16		The Battalion marched at 10.0 a.m. to Billets N.W. of MERVILLE about K.32. Map 36. Battalion H.Q. situated at COURTREFOIS FARM.	

WAR DIARY or INTELLIGENCE SUMMARY

(Erase heading not required.)

Army Form C. 2118

Instructions regarding War Diaries and Intelligence Summaries are contained in F.S. Regs., Part II. and the Staff Manual respectively. Title Pages will be prepared in manuscript.

Place	Date	Hour	Summary of Events and Information	Remarks and references to Appendices
	15-3-16		The Battalion marched at 7.50 a.m. to Billets at GODEWAERSVELDE, arriving about twelve noon. There was a tremendous wind during the whole march, but no man fell out. The Billets were much scattered and men were rather crowded. Orders for tomorrow's move received at 10.30 p.m.	
	16-3-16		The Battalion marched at 8.15 a.m. to a Camp of huts and tents, west of POPERINGHE, and about 800 yards south of the PROVEN-POPERINGHE road. Map reference, F.278.95, Sheet 27, 1/20000. There was a tremendous wind and heavy rain during the whole march. There is no road up to the Camp and all traffic has to come up by a small trench railway. The huts were insufficient to accommodate the whole battalion and some of the tents had to be used. Most of the Camp was under water and the mud was almost everywhere 1 foot deep.	
	17-3-16		In Camp as above. The whole day was spent in trying to clean up the Camp, putting down floor boards and endeavouring to make it habitable. A gale of wind and rain all day.	
	18-3-16		In Camp as above. No parades owing to the incessant rain. During the night aeroplanes or zeppelins dropped bombs on POPERINGHE, the explosion of which could be plainly heard from the Camp. Lt. Col. J.V. Campbell, D.S.O., Acting Brigadier came over during the afternoon, and also the Corps	

Army Form C. 2118

WAR DIARY
or
INTELLIGENCE SUMMARY
(Erase heading not required.)

Instructions regarding War Diaries and Intelligence Summaries are contained in F.S. Regs., Part II. and the Staff Manual respectively. Title Pages will be prepared in manuscript.

Place	Date	Hour	Summary of Events and Information	Remarks and references to Appendices
	18-2-16 (Continued)		Commander, Lord Cavan and Brigadier General Gathorne-Hardy.	
	19-2-16		In Camp as above. A 30 yards Rifle Range was used by No. 4 Company. A very cold day. An accident occurred in the morning when No. 14212 Private F. Drury was leading a horse, which fell and crushed Drury's leg against a trench board, and breaking his leg.	
	20-2-16		In Camp as above. A fine sunny morning. Hostile aeroplanes dropped bombs at POPERINGHE and neighbourhood between 7.15 a.m. and 8.45 a.m. No damage done. Voluntary Church Parade held in Barn at 11 a.m. Hard frost at night.	
	21-2-16		In Camp as above. Hostile aeroplanes threw several bombs during the night. One fell but did not explode about 400 yards from the Camp. A cold grey day. Companies did Training and Route marches.	
	22-2-16		In Camp as above. Snowing all the morning. A detachment of all ranks attended a demonstration of German liquid fire. No harm can happen anybody provided they keep their heads low down in the trench, as the liquid fire rises in the air about 6 or 8 yards from the nozzle of the apparatus. A small portable apparatus as shown has a range of about 30 yards and discharges fire for about 1½ hours, after which it requires refilling. Companies unable to train owing to the weather. A cold night with frost.	

Army Form C. 2118

WAR DIARY

or

~~INTELLIGENCE SUMMARY~~

(Erase heading not required.)

Instructions regarding War Diaries and Intelligence Summaries are contained in F.S. Regs., Part II. and the Staff Manual respectively. Title Pages will be prepared in manuscript.

Place	Date	Hour	Summary of Events and Information	Remarks and references to Appendices
	23-2-16		In Camp as above. Companies unable to train owing to the weather. More snow in the morning. More snow at night and bitterly cold.	
	24-2-16		In Camp as above. A fine bright morning but cold. The Brigadier held a conference at Battalion Headquarters on the subject of move to C.I.II.S. Hostile aeroplanes threw bombs at POPERINGHE and neighbourhood, one of which exploded just outside the Camp, forming a crater 8 feet across and 4 feet deep, otherwise no damage done. At 1.30 p.m. received orders to entrain at CASSEL at 8.30 a.m. on the 25th. A slight thaw during the afternoon. All horses roughed by 6 p.m. The Transport with 2 platoons of No. 1 Company marched at 11.45 p.m. via POPERINGHE and STEENVOORDE. A very sharp frost at night.	
	25-2-16		The Battalion marched at 2.30 a.m. via STEENVOORDE. A very hard frost all night. Arrived at foot of hill near CASSEL at 6.30 a.m. This hill was a sheet of ice, and the Battalion had to march on each side of the road in the snow. The hill down from CASSEL was equally bad. Baggage wagons skidded in to the ditch as did two Cookers. The latter were got out but the former had to be left. The shaft of a water cart was broken owing to the cart skidding into the ditch. The Battalion reached B.WINGHOVE Station at 7.40 a.m. The Transport had arrived at 7.0 a.m. All vehicles except Baggage wagons and whole Battalion entrained by 8.30 a.m. But the train did not start until after 9 a.m. The Battalion and Transport 1 in one train, which proceeded via ST. OMER and arrived at	

1875 Wt. W503/826 1,000,000 4/15 J.B.C. & A. A.D.S.S./Forms/C. 2118.

Army Form C. 2118

WAR DIARY or INTELLIGENCE SUMMARY

(Erase heading not required.)

Instructions regarding War Diaries and Intelligence Summaries are contained in F. S. Regs., Part II. and the Staff Manual respectively. Title Pages will be prepared in manuscript.

Place	Date	Hour	Summary of Events and Information	Remarks and references to Appendices
	25-2-16	(Continued)	CALAIS-COULOGNE Station at 11.30 a.m. The Battalion detrained and marched to No. 6 Large Rest Camp (C. Camp) about four kilometres out of the Town on the DUNKIRK ROAD and took over the Camp which had been occupied by the 4th Battalion Grenadier Guards. 1st Battalion Grenadier Guards, 2nd Battalion Scots Guards and 1st Battalion Welsh Guards were still in Camp on our arrival. Very cold all day, heavy snow in the evening and early night. One extra Blanket per man issued to the Battalion.	
	26-2-16		In No. 6 Large Rest Camp, CALAIS. A fine bright morning, and snow melting. The Battalion employed in cleaning up the Camp. 2nd Battalion Coldstream Guards arrived about 3 a.m. 3rd Battalion Coldstreams about 11.30 a.m. and 1st Battalion Irish Guards about 3 p.m. More snow in the evening.	
	27-2-1916		In Camp as above. A slight thaw in the morning. The Battalion marched across CANAL DE MARCK to the Sands East of BASSIN DE CHASSES and did Battalion Drill. Snow melting all day.	
	28-2-16		In Camp as above. Warmer with heavy rain in the evening. Battalion employed in Drill, Training and Bombing.	
	29-2-16		In Camp as above. Much warmer and snow practically disappeared. Companies employed in Drill, Training and Bombing. Forwarded list of names for the King's Birthday Honours Gazette.	

[signature]
Lieut. Colonel,
Commanding 2nd Battalion Grenadier Guards.

1st Guards Brigade.
Guards Division.

2nd BATTALION

GRENADIER GUARDS

MARCH 1916

War Diary.
2nd Battalion Grenadier Guards.
March 1916
Vol XX

Army Form C. 2118

WAR DIARY

INTELLIGENCE SUMMARY

(Erase heading not required.)

Instructions regarding War Diaries and Intelligence Summaries are contained in F. S. Regs., Part II. and the Staff Manual respectively. Title Pages will be prepared in manuscript.

Place	Date	Hour	Summary of Events and Information	Remarks and references to Appendices
	1-3-16		In No. 6 Large Rest Camp, CALAIS. Companies doing Drill and Training. Lieut. A.T.A. Ritchie accidentally sprained his knee and was admitted to Hospital. No. 16657, L/Cpl G. Turner was found drowned in the Canal, near the Fortifications.	
	2-3-16		In Camp as above. Companies carried out Bombing attacks in turn during the day.	
	3-3-16		In Camp as above. The Battalion route marched.	
	4-3-16		In Camp as above. No parades owing to the incessant rain.	
	5-3-16		The Battalion marched at 5.30 a.m. to CALAIS Station and entrained at 7.30 a.m. arriving at CASSEL, about 11.30 a.m. Battalion detrained, marched about 9 miles and took over Billets from the 4th Battalion Grenadier Guards, near HERZEELE. The 1st Battalion marched through our Billets during the afternoon.	
	6-3-16		In Billets at HERZEELE. Good billets, although somewhat scattered. Snowed nearly all day.	
	7-3-16		In Billets at HERZEELE. Companies did Drill and Training.	
	8-3-16		In Billets at HERZEELE. Companies did Drill and Training.	

Army Form C. 2118

WAR DIARY

~~INTELLIGENCE SUMMARY~~

(Erase heading not required.)

Instructions regarding War Diaries and Intelligence Summaries are contained in F.S. Regs., Part II. and the Staff Manual respectively. Title Pages will be prepared in manuscript.

Place	Date	Hour	Summary of Events and Information	Remarks and references to Appendices
	9-3-16		In Billets at HERZEELE. Companies did Drill and Training.	
	10-3-16		In Billets at HERZEELE. Companies did Drill and Training.	
	11-3-16		In Billets at HERZEELE. The Battalion marched via WORMHOUDT for inspection by French Officers.	
	12-3-16		In Billets at HERZEELE. Companies did Drill and Training.	
	13-3-16		In Billets at HERZEELE. Companies did Drill and Training.	
	14-3-16		In Billets at HERZEELE. Companies did Drill and Training.	
	15-3-16		The Battalion marched at 8.0 a.m. to Camp "M", near POPERINGHE, arriving about 11.0 a.m.	
	16-3-16		In Camp as above. Companies did Drill and Training.	
	17-3-16		In Camp as above. Companies did Drill and Training. Major A. St. Leger Glyn took command of the 1st Battalion, vice Lieut. Colonel G. Trotter, who took over a Brigade.	
	18-3-16		In Camp as above. The Battalion marched at 6.0 p.m. to POPERINGHE, where it entrained, and detrained close to the Asylum at YPRES. The train was stopped for a few	

1875 Wt. W593/826 1,000,000 4/15 J.B.C. & A. A.D.S.S./Forms/C. 2118.

Army Form C. 2118

WAR DIARY

INTELLIGENCE SUMMARY

(Erase heading not required.)

Instructions regarding War Diaries and Intelligence Summaries are contained in F.S. Regs., Part II. and the Staff Manual respectively. Title Pages will be prepared in manuscript.

Place	Date	Hour	Summary of Events and Information	Remarks and references to Appendices
	19-5-15.		minutes close to VLAMERTINGHE by shell fire. Marched from the Asylum to Line east of POTIJE Village to relieve a Battalion of the Essex Regiment, of the 71st Brigade, and part of the 1st Battalion Leicester Regiment. No. 3 Company took over left Sector, No. 4 took over right Sector, No. 1 Company in Support and No. 2 in Reserve. Battalion Headquarters situated in POTIJE WOOD. The Relief was completed about 10.0 p.m. The 1st Line Transport remained north of Road, midway between VLAMERTINGHE and POPERINGHE. 2nd Battalion Scots Guards on our right and 3rd Battalion Coldstream Guards on our left. An excellent night for relief - very little shooting and plenty of light. Casualties, 1 man killed, and 1 N.C.O. slightly wounded and remained at duty.	
	20-5-15		In Line as above. A few shells in the morning on our support line and Battalion Headquarters, otherwise a quiet day. The trenches were in very bad order, with parapets waist high only, and in no place were they bullet-proof, no communication trenches and no drainage or sanitary arrangements. It was evident that no work had been done on the line for some months. Casualties, 3 men wounded.	
			In Line as above. A quiet day. The Battalion worked very hard putting the trenches in good order - heightening and thickening the parapets. Casualties, 1 man killed, 1 man wounded and 1 slightly wounded, the latter remained at Duty.	

1875 Wt. W593/826 1,000,000 4/15 J.B.C. & A. A.D.S.S./Forms/C. 2118.

Army Form C. 2118

WAR DIARY

INTELLIGENCE SUMMARY

(Erase heading not required.)

Instructions regarding War Diaries and Intelligence Summaries are contained in F. S. Regs., Part II. and the Staff Manual respectively. Title Pages will be prepared in manuscript.

Place	Date	Hour	Summary of Events and Information	Remarks and references to Appendices
	21-3-16		In Line as above. A quiet day. Rained heavily, which hindered work considerably. No. 1 Company relieved No. 4 and No. 2 Company relieved No. 3 during the night. 2nd Battalion Scots Guards took over POTIJE Defences and KAAIE Salient Defences, and No. 3 Company went back to "dug-outs" near the Canal Bank, just north of YPRES. Casualties, 1 man wounded.	
	22-3-16		In Line as above. Rained heavily all day. A few small shells. Casualties, 1 man wounded.	
	23-3-16		In Line as above. The trenches are considerably improved, and it is now possible to walk along the entire line without being seen by the enemy, and all parapets are bullet-proof. During the afternoon, two places in the line held by No. 1 Company were blown in by field gun shells, fired by a gun about 500 yards away. Relieved by the 1st Battalion Irish Guards during the night. The Irish Guards arrived at YPRES by Train about 9.0 p.m. but, owing to their guides leading them wrongly, their Headquarters and No. 1 Company did not arrive until 11.30 p.m. The relief was completed and the Battalion entrained at the Asylum and arrived at "A" Camp, near VLAMERTINGHE about 3=0 a.m. This Camp consisted of huts. Casualties, Sgt Major H. Wood slightly wounded, but remained at Duty.	

Army Form C. 2118

WAR DIARY

INTELLIGENCE SUMMARY

(Erase heading not required.)

Instructions regarding War Diaries and Intelligence Summaries are contained in F. S. Regs., Part II. and the Staff Manual respectively. Title Pages will be prepared in manuscript.

Place	Date	Hour	Summary of Events and Information	Remarks and references to Appendices
	24-3-15		In Camp as above. Snow fell heavily during the early morning.	
	25-3-15		In Camp as above. Rained heavily during the day. The G.O.C. Division and the R.E. Brigadier inspected the Camp and decided to vacate it as the huts are in bad condition and the ground all round is a mud swamp.	
	26-3-15		In Camp as above. Divine Service in the morning. Rained all day.	
	27-3-15		In Camp as above. 1st Battalion Grenadier Guards about 800 yards away from us in Camp "B". An attack was made by the 5th Corps at ST. ELOI, preceded by heavy mine explosions, which were felt from our Camp. Heavy shelling all day. Commenced to rain about 2.0 p.m. and continued all night. The Battalion left Camp at 6.15 p.m. to relieve the 1st Battalion Irish Guards. Entrained at Q.G.b. to YPRES. Relief complete about 10.0 P.M. No. 1 Company on Right No. 2 Company on the Left, No. 3 in Support or "X" Line, and No. 4 Company in Reserve on the Canal Bank. Casualties, NIL.	
	28-3-15		In Line East of POTIJE Village. A quiet day. Casualties. 3 men wounded and 1 N.C.O slightly wounded, the latter remained at Duty.	

Army Form C. 2118

WAR DIARY

INTELLIGENCE SUMMARY

(Erase heading not required.)

Instructions regarding War Diaries and Intelligence Summaries are contained in F. S. Regs., Part II. and the Staff Manual respectively. Title Pages will be prepared in manuscript.

Place	Date	Hour	Summary of Events and Information	Remarks and references to Appendices
	29-3-16		In Line as above. During the Night, No. 4 Company relieved No. 1 on the Right and No. 3 relieved No. 2 on the Left. A quiet day. 1st Battalion Scots Guards on our Right and 3rd Battalion Coldstream Guards on our Left. Casualties, 2nd Lieut. H.G. Carter wounded, 1 N.C.O. and 1 man wounded.	
	30-3-16		In Line as above. We were heavily shelled by g15 guns for about 5 hours. The trenches of No. 4 Company were completely levelled for about 180 yards and also about 200 yards of the Support "X" Line. The Battalion was very fortunate in having very few casualties. This Bombardment was expected to be the prelude of an attack but no attack followed. Casualties, 1 N.C.O. killed, 10 N.C.Os and men wounded and 5 slightly wounded, the latter remained at Duty.	
	31-3-16		In Line as above. The enemy shelled the parts of the trenches which had been levelled all night and work upon them was almost impossible. The shelling ceased at Daybreak. A very quiet day ensued, and hardly a shot was fired by either side. 3rd Battalion Grenadier Guards on our right and 2nd Battalion Coldstream Guards on our left. Relieved by 1st Battalion Irish Guards. Relief completed about 10.0 p.m. Entrained at the Asylum, YPRES about 11.0 p.m. and arrived at Camp "C", near Vlamertinghe about 1.30 a.m. NOTE On next sheet.	

WAR DIARY

INTELLIGENCE SUMMARY
(Erase heading not required.)

Army Form C. 2118

Place	Date	Hour	Summary of Events and Information	Remarks and references to Appendices
			N O T E. Camp "A" situated at H.1.d.9.9. Camp "C" situated at G.6.a.8.9. Battalion Headquarters in POTIJE WOOD at I.4.a.9.6. The Right of the Line held by the Battalion was about I.5.b.1.3. The Left of the Line held by the Battalion was C.29.a.5.5. Map No. 28. 1/40000. BELGIUM. Lieutenant Colonel, Commanding 2nd Battalion Grenadier Guards.	

1st Guards Brigade.
Guards Division.

2nd BATTALION

GRENADIER GUARDS.

APRIL 1916

2nd BATTALION GRENADIER GUARDS.

WAR DIARY FOR THE MONTH

Ending 30th April, 1916.

Army Form. C. 2118

WAR DIARY
or
INTELLIGENCE SUMMARY
(Erase heading not required.)

Instructions regarding War Diaries and Intelligence Summaries are contained in F. S. Regs., Part II. and the Staff Manual respectively. Title Pages will be prepared in manuscript.

Place	Date	Hour	Summary of Events and Information	Remarks and references to Appendices
	1-4-16		In Camp "C", near VLAMERTINGHE. An excellent camp of huts in a wood. Battalion Brigade Reserve.	
	2-4-16		In Camp as above.	
	3-4-16		In Camp as above. Orders received for three platoons to work daily on line of posts running north from VLAMERTINGHE.	
	4-4-16		In Camp as above. The whole of the Brigade is now out of the line and in Divisional Reserve. The other three Battalions are billetted in POPERINGHE.	
	5-4-16		In Camp as above. A Battalion Concert was held at 6.0 p.m. in the Church Army Hut. The Concert was a great success. Captain E.N.E.M. Vaughan joined Battalion as 2nd in command.	
	6-4-16		In Camp as above.	
	7-4-16		In Camp as above.	
	8-4-16		In Camp as above.	
	9-4-16		In Camp as above. Divine Service held in the morning in the Church Army Hut.	
	10-4-16		The Battalion Marched from Camp at 6.30 p.m. by Companies and entrained at G.5.d (Map 28, "B" Series, Belgium and France) at 7.30 p.m., detrained at the Asylum, YPRES, and billetted in cellars and dug-outs in YPRES. No. 1 Company in dug-outs in the	

Army Form. C. 2118

Instructions regarding War Diaries and Intelligence Summaries are contained in F.S. Regs., Part II. and the Staff Manual respectively. Title Pages will be prepared in manuscript.

WAR DIARY or INTELLIGENCE SUMMARY

(Erase heading not required.)

Place	Date	Hour	Summary of Events and Information	Remarks and references to Appendices
	10-4-16 (Continued)		Ramparts, north of MENIN GATE, No. 2 Company in dugouts south of MENIN GATE, Battalion Headquarters and No. 3 Company in the cellars of CONVENT DES CARMES and No. 4 Company in various cellars between the CONVENT and the RAILWAY STATION. 2nd Lieut. J.S. Burton joined the Battalion.	
	11-4-16		In Billets as above. A quiet morning, but at about 6.30 p.m. a heavy bombardment in the north and "S.O.S." signal sent through from the 20th Division, which was being attacked, consequently, our relief was held up for 1½ hours. We left YPRES at 9.0 p.m. via MENIN GATE to relieve the 2nd Battalion Irish Guards in the Line between RAILWAY WOOD and the MENIN ROAD, I.11.b. and d, Map 28, Belgium and France. Battalion Headquarters situated in Schaubaive Farm (Rifleman's Farm) in I. 10. d. about 200 yards north east of the HALTE. No. 1 Company on the right, No. 2 on the left, No. 4 in the support line, and No. 3 partly in reserve trenches and partly in cellars on the MENIN-ROAD. Casualties, Nil.	
	12-4-16.		In Line as above. A very quiet day, which was chiefly spent in making ourselves acquainted with the new line, which appeared to be very bad, there being no continuous defensive line. A large gap on our left, between us and the Coldstream Guards and one on our right between us and the Canadians, whose left is on the MENIN ROAD. Casualties, 1 man wounded and died of wounds, 1 wounded and 1 slightly wounded. The latter remained at Duty.	

Army Form. C. 2118

WAR DIARY
or
INTELLIGENCE SUMMARY

(Erase heading not required.)

Instructions regarding War Diaries and Intelligence Summaries are contained in F.S. Regs., Part II. and the Staff Manual respectively. Title Pages will be prepared in manuscript.

Place	Date	Hour	Summary of Events and Information	Remarks and references to Appendices
	13-4-16		In Line as above. A few small shells around the HALTE. A German Mine reported to be underneath our Front Line. Casualties, 1 man killed, 1 wounded and 1 accidentally wounded.	
	14-4-16		In Line as above. During the night, No. 4 Company relieved No. 1, and No. 3 Company relieved No. 2. A very quiet day, cold and showery. Casualties, 1 man killed and 1 N.C.O. wounded.	
	15-4-16		In Line as above. A quiet day. A few small shells on the HALTE. Casualties, 1 wounded.	
	16-4-16		In Line as above. Relieved by the 1st Battalion Irish Guards, who left YPRES about midnight. Their right Company went astray and No. 4 did not arrive in YPRES until 4.0 a.m. 17th. Casualties, 2 men wounded.	
	17-4-16		In Cellars and dug-outs in YPRES as before. Lieut. M.H. Macmillan joined the Battalion. Casualties, 2 men slightly wounded but remained at Duty.	
	18-4-16		In YPRES as above. Casualties, 1 man slightly wounded, but remained at Duty.	

Army Form. C. 2118

WAR DIARY
or
INTELLIGENCE SUMMARY
(Erase heading not required.)

Instructions regarding War Diaries and Intelligence Summaries are contained in F. S. Regs., Part II. and the Staff Manual respectively. Title Pages will be prepared in manuscript.

Place	Date	Hour	Summary of Events and Information	Remarks and references to Appendices
	19-4-16		In YPRES as above. A few shells in the Town, no damage done to the Battalion. We left MENIN GATE at midnight to relieve the 1st Battalion Irish Guards in the Line. No. 3 Company on the left, No. 4 on the Right, No. 2 in support, and No. 1 in reserve. Casualties, 1 man slightly wounded, but remained at Duty.	
	20-4-16		In Line as above. A quiet day, but heavy sniping and machine gun fire during the night. Lieutenant T. Parker-Jervis joined the Battalion. Casualties, 2 men wounded.	
	21-4-16		In Line as above. 2nd Lieutenant J.C. Cornforth joined the Battalion. Rained heavily practically all day. no shooting on out front, but very heavy shooting to the north. 6th Division reported to have lost and retaken their trenches. Casualties, Nil.	
	22-4-16		In Line as above. No. 2 Company relieved No. 4 and No. 1 relieved No. 3. The wind was steadily veering round from west to south-east and the "Gas alert" was on all night. Rained heavily all day. German Mine again reported beneath out front line. Heavy shooting to the north – 6th Division reported counter-attacking. Casualties, Nil.	

Army Form. C. 2118

WAR DIARY
or
INTELLIGENCE SUMMARY

(Erase heading not required.)

Instructions regarding War Diaries and Intelligence Summaries are contained in F. S. Regs., Part II. and the Staff Manual respectively. Title Pages will be prepared in manuscript.

Place	Date	Hour	Summary of Events and Information	Remarks and references to Appendices
	23-4-15		In Line as above. A very hot and quiet day. An unusual number of German aeroplanes circling over the Canadian lines all day - no British areaoplanes appeared at all. 1st Battalion Irish Guards left YPRES at 11. 0 p.m. to relieve us. Our last Company arrived in YPRES about 2.45 a.m. Casualties, 2 men killed, 3 wounded, and 2 slightly wounded, the latter remained at Duty.	
	24-4-15		In cellars and dugouts in YPRES as before. During the day, the Germans sent a good many shells into the Town. Casualties, 1 man slightly wounded, who remained at Duty.	
	25-4-15		In YPRES. The Commanding Officer and Adjutant, with a party, visited ZILLEBEKE churchyard and repaired the graves of Officers and men of the Brigade of Guards and Household Cavalry, who were buried there in 1914.	
	26-4-15		Remained in YPRES. Very heavy shelling south of the MENIN ROAD on the Canadian lines and in the south eastern quarter of YPRES. The Battalion left by train at 9.0 p.m. from the Asylum, passing the 1st Battalion Grenadier Guards, and went back to billets near the Station in POPERINGHE.	
	27-4-15		In Billets at POPERINGHE. Excellent Billets. A very hot day. The Battalion paraded at 12.45 p.m. and marched to the Emergency Ground for inspection by	

Army Form. C. 2118

WAR DIARY
or
INTELLIGENCE SUMMARY
(Erase heading not required.)

Instructions regarding War Diaries and Intelligence Summaries are contained in F. S. Regs., Part II. and the Staff Manual respectively. Title Pages will be prepared in manuscript.

Place	Date	Hour	Summary of Events and Information	Remarks and references to Appendices
	27-4-16 (continued)		General Sir.Herbert C.O. Plumer, G.C.M.G., K.C.B., G.O.C. 2nd Army. After the inspection, we did Battalion Drill and marched past by platoons.	
	28-4-16		In Billets as above. A very hot day. Companies did Drill and Training. Many fatigues are found by the Battalion and a large number of N.C.Os and men are taken away for courses, Sniping, Bombing, etc.	
	29-4-16		In Billets as above. The Germans sent over a few 6 inch shells about 6.30 a.m—some falling among our billets. No. casualties. The officers had a football match with the officers of the Divisional Headquarters, result, 1 goal all.	
	30-4-16		In Billets as above. About 4.0.a.m. an enemy aeroplane came over and dropped bombs on POPERINGHE, one falling about 25 yards from Battalion Headquarters, and wounding two of our men with a Lewis Gun on anti-aircraft duty. A very hot day. The Officers of the Battalion played a team of N.C.Os at football in the afternoon.	

Major for Lieutenant Colonel,
Commanding 2nd Battalion Grenadier Guards.

1st Guards Brigade.
Guards Division.

2nd BATTALION

GRENADIER GUARDS.

MAY 1916

WAR DIARY FOR THE

MONTH ENDING 31st May, 1916.

2nd Battalion Grenadier Guards.

Army Form C. 2118

WAR DIARY

or

~~INTELLIGENCE SUMMARY~~

(*Erase heading not required.*)

Instructions regarding War Diaries and Intelligence Summaries are contained in F.S. Regs., Part II. and the Staff Manual respectively. Title Pages will be prepared in manuscript.

Place	Date	Hour	Summary of Events and Information	Remarks and references to Appendices
	1/5/16		In Billets at POPERINGHE. Companies did Drill and Training. A hot day.	
	2/5/16		In Billets as above. Companies did Drill and Training.	
	3/5/16		In Billets as above. Companies did Drill and Training. The Brigadier inspected billets during the morning. Officers and certain N.C.Os of the Battalion attended a "S.O.S." demonstration at Brigade Headquarters.	
	4/5/16		In Billets as above. Companies did Drill and Training. The Battalion entrained at 8.0 p.m. at POPERINGHE Station and detrained at the Asypum, YPRES. Went in to billets near the prison at YPRES for the night. Battalion Headquarters situated in the prison.	
	5/5/16		In Billets at YPRES. The Battalion relieved the 2nd Battalion Irish Guards in the Line, C.29.a.3.1. to C.28.a.5.8. Sheet 28, in front of WIELTJE. Battalion Headquarters situated in HASLARS FARMS. No. 1 Company on the right, No. 2 on the left, No. 3 in support, and No. 4 in reserve in LA BRIQUE Post. Casualties, NIL.	

Army Form C. 2118

WAR DIARY
or
INTELLIGENCE SUMMARY
(Erase heading not required.)

Instructions regarding War Diaries and Intelligence Summaries are contained in F.S. Regs., Part II. and the Staff Manual respectively. Title Pages will be prepared in manuscript.

Place	Date	Hour	Summary of Events and Information	Remarks and references to Appendices
	6/5/15		In the Line as above. Heavy shelling in the morning on the left Company. Our Artillery replied vigourously. The enemy shelled WIELTJE ROAD intensely from 7.45 p.m. to 1.0 a.m. Considerable damage was done to various transports. Casualties, Lieutenant Hon. B.B. Ponsonby and one man wounded, one horse killed and one wounded while bringing up rations. Other casualties, 3 N.C.Os and men killed and 6 wounded.	
	7/5/15		In the Line as above. Intermittent shelling during the day. Drizzling with rain most of the day. Casualties, 4 men wounded.	
	8/5/15		In the Line as above. A quiet day. Casualties, 4 men wounded.	
	9/5/15		In the line as above. Relieved by the 1st Battalion Irish Guards about midnight. There was shelling at intervals during the day. The Battalion marched to the same billets near the prison, YPRES. Casualties, 3 men wounded and 2 slightly wounded, the latter remained at Duty. 2nd Lieutenant G.A. Arbuthnot joined Battalion.	
	10/5/15		In billets at YPRES.	
	11/5/15		In Billets at YPRES. 1 man wounded (Shell-fire).	

Army Form C. 2118

WAR DIARY
or
INTELLIGENCE SUMMARY
(Erase heading not required.)

Instructions regarding War Diaries and Intelligence Summaries are contained in F. S. Regs., Part II. and the Staff Manual respectively. Title Pages will be prepared in manuscript.

Place	Date	Hour	Summary of Events and Information	Remarks and references to Appendices
	12/5/16		In Billets at YPRES.	
	13/5/16		In Billets at YPRES. Rained all day. The Battalion relieved the 1st Battalion Irish Guards about midnight. No. 4 Company on the right, No. 3 on the left, No. 1 in support, and No. 2 in reserve at LA BRIQUE post. Casualties, NIL.	
	14/5/16		In Line as above. A considerable amount of work was done in deepening the trenches and heightening the parapets, and a great deal of wiring was done by all Companies, the Battalion used 84 coils of barbed wire. Casualties, 1 man killed.	
	15/5/16		In Line as above. A few shrapnel round Battalion Headquarters. The enemy shelled our communication trenches. Casualties, 1 man wounded.	
	16/5/16		In Line as above. Enemy shelled WIELTJE FARM and trenches. Relieved by the 1st Battalion Irish Guards about midnight and marched to billets near the prison at YPRES. Casualties, 2nd Lieutenant J.S. Burton killed and 6 other ranks wounded.	
	17/5/16		In Billets at YPRES.	

Army Form C. 2118

WAR DIARY or INTELLIGENCE SUMMARY

(Erase heading not required.)

Instructions regarding War Diaries and Intelligence Summaries are contained in F.S. Regs., Part II. and the Staff Manual respectively. Title Pages will be prepared in manuscript.

Place	Date	Hour	Summary of Events and Information	Remarks and references to Appendices
	18/5/16		In Billets at YPRES. The Battalion entrained at the Asylum, Ypres at 9.20 p.m. detrained at POPERINGHE and marched to Camp "K" for the night, arrived at 11 p.m. This Camp is situated just off the PROVEN Road.	
	19/5/16		The Battalion formed up on Mass at 10.55 a.m. and marched at 11 a.m. to HOPOUTRE SIDING, arriving there about 12.15 p.m. Troops had dinner and entrained for ST. OMER, arriving at 5.45 p.m. and marched to billets at TATINGHEM, about four kilometres west of ST. OMER. An excessively hot day, but no men fell out. Billets are very clean and comfortable and the villagers were ready to assist in every possible way.	
	20/5-16.		In Billets at TATINGHEM. Companies did Drill and Training.	
	21/5/16.		In Billets as above. Companies did Drill and Training.	
	22/5/16.		In Billets as above. Companies did Drill and Training.	
	23/5/16		In Billets as above. Companies did Drill and Training.	
	24/5/16		In Billets as above. Companies did Drill and Training.	

WAR DIARY or INTELLIGENCE SUMMARY

(Erase heading not required.)

Army Form C. 2118

Instructions regarding War Diaries and Intelligence Summaries are contained in F. S. Regs., Part II. and the Staff Manual respectively. Title Pages will be prepared in manuscript.

Place	Date	Hour	Summary of Events and Information	Remarks and references to Appendices
	25/5/16		In Billets as above. A wet morning, which somewhat interfered with the Training.	
	26/5/16		In Billets as above. Companies did Drill and Training. The Second in Command, and the four Company Commanders went by bus from Brigade Headquarters to HEDIN, a distance of 55 kilometres, to view a STOKES GUN demonstration. The Major General and Brigadier General attended this demonstration.	
	27/5/16		In Billets as above. Companies did Drill and Training.	
	28/5/16		In Billets as above. Voluntary Divine Service was held in the morning which was well attended by the troops.	
	29/5/16		In Billets as above. Companies did Drill and Training. The Brigade Bombing School under the Brigade Bombing Officer gave a display - bombing up trenches and blowing in traverses for blocking purposes. The Major General, Brigadier General, and the Brigadier General, Commanding the 3rd Brigade, Commanding Officers and Seconds in Command of the 1st Brigade were present.	
	30/5/16		In Billets as above. A wet morning, but fine later. Companies did Drill and Training. The Battalion found one Company for Drill at the	

Army Form C. 2118

WAR DIARY
or
INTELLIGENCE SUMMARY

(Erase heading not required.)

Instructions regarding War Diaries and Intelligence Summaries are contained in F.S. Regs., Part II. and the Staff Manual respectively. Title Pages will be prepared in manuscript.

Place	Date	Hour	Summary of Events and Information	Remarks and references to Appendices
Second Army Central School of Instruction.	30/5/16 (continued)			
	31/5.16		In Billets as above. Companies did Drill and Training. From the 23rd May, several instructors have been found by the Battalion for Drill purposes at the Second Army Central School of Instruction at WISQUES. One Company did Drill at the Second Army School today.	

[signature]

Lieutenant Colonel,
Commanding 2nd Battalion Grenadier Guards.

1st Guards Brigade.
Guards Divisin

2nd BATALION

GRENADIER GUARDS.

AUGUST 1 9 1 6

WAR DIARY for the month

ending 30th August, 1916.

2nd Battalion Grenadier Guards.

Army Form C. 2118

WAR DIARY
or
INTELLIGENCE SUMMARY

(Erase heading not required.)

Instructions regarding War Diaries and Intelligence Summaries are contained in F.S. Regs., Part II. and the Staff Manual respectively. Title Pages will be prepared in manuscript.

Place	Date	Hour	Summary of Events and Information	Remarks and references to Appendices
	1/8/16		Billeting Party under Lieutenant H.F.C. Crookshank left at 5.0 a.m. The Battalion marched from NEUVILLETTE at 6.10 a.m. via DOULLENS to SARTON arriving about 10.15 a.m. after a dusty march. The Battalion did not carry great coats for the first time since the commencement of the campaign - these and steel helmets were conveyed by lorry. The Billets were left in a very dirty state by the 13th Battalion Royal Welsh Fusiliers.	
	2/8/16		In Billets at SARTON. A very hot day. Companies had bathing parade in the morning in the AUTHIE Stream.	
	3/8/16		In Billets at SARTON. Companies did Arm Drill and Physical Training in the morning and most of the Battalion bathed in the afternoon. A fine day.	
	4/8/16		In Billets at SARTON. Battalion marched at 5.0 a.m. for a route march, arriving back for breakfast at 7.30 a.m. A very hot day. All Captains rode over to a conference at Brigade Headquarters, VAUCHELLES, at 4.30 p.m.	
	5/8/16		In Billets at SARTON. Companies did Arm Drill and Physical Training. The Brigadier inspected the Transport during the morning. All bathing stopped, but horses are still allowed to water in the Stream. The Band of the Irish Guards played from 3.0 p.m. to 5.0 p.m.	

1875 Wt. W593/826 1,000,000 4/15 J.B.C. & A. A.D.S.S./Forms/C. 2118.

WAR DIARY or INTELLIGENCE SUMMARY

(Erase heading not required.)

Army Form C. 2118

Instructions regarding War Diaries and Intelligence Summaries are contained in F.S. Regs., Part II. and the Staff Manual respectively. Title Pages will be prepared in manuscript.

Place	Date	Hour	Summary of Events and Information	Remarks and references to Appendices
	6/8/16		In Billets at SARTON. Divine Service at 11.0 a.m.	
	7/8/16		In Billets at SARTON. No. 1 Company paraded for Drill at 8.0 a.m. under the Adjutant. Nos. 3 and 4 Companies route marched. No. 2 Company sent off two detachments of one Officer and fifty other ranks each for fatigue near DOULLENS. The Band of the Irish Guards played from 3.0 p.m. to 5.0 p.m.	
	8/8/16		In Billets at SARTON. No. 3 Company and the remainder of No. 2 Company paraded in the morning for Drill. The remainder of the Battalion did Training. The Battalion played a Football Match in the evening against the Welsh Gunners, and won, result one goal to nil. Warned that His Majesty The King comes to inspect us tomorrow.	
	9/8/16		In Billets at SARTON. His Majesty The King did not arrive. Companies did Drill and Training. A very hot day. In the Evening, the officers of the Battalion played the Officers of the 2nd Battalion Coldstream Guards at Football, result three goals all. 2nd Lieutenant R.E.H. Oliver slipped a cartilage in his knee and went to Hospital.	
	10/8/16		In Billets at SARTON. The Battalion marched at 3.55 p.m. via LOUVEN- COURT to huts in BERTRANCOURT. Rain fell early.	

Army Form C. 2118

WAR DIARY
or
INTELLIGENCE SUMMARY
(Erase heading not required.)

Instructions regarding War Diaries and Intelligence Summaries are contained in F. S. Regs, Part II. and the Staff Manual respectively. Title Pages will be prepared in manuscript.

Place	Date	Hour	Summary of Events and Information	Remarks and references to Appendices
	10/8/16 (Continued)		in the morning and laid the dust, but the road was very congested the whole way by elements of the 71st and 75th Brigades and many motor lorries. His Majesty The King and His Royal Highness The Prince of Wales passed us in a motor car just beyond MARIEUX. Arrived in Camp about 6.45 p.m.	
	11/8/16		The Billeting Party of the 3rd Battalion Grenadier Guards under Captain G. Rasch, D.S.O., came over early and took over from us. The Battalion moved off by Companies at intervals of one hour, commencing at 8.0 a.m. Order of March, Nos. 4, 1, 2, and 3 Companies. The Lewis Gun and Kit Limbers went on ahead at 5.30 a.m. Marched via BEAUSSART, MAILLY-MAILLET and VITERMONT, where guides of the 2nd Battalion Sherwood Foresters met us. We relieved this Battalion in the Right Sub Sector of the BEAUMONT-HAMEL line, 9.16 a. BEAUMONT Trench Map, 57 d., S.E., 1/10,000. Relief complete about 2.0 p.m. No. 4 Company on the Left, No. 2 on the Right, No. 1 in Left Support and No. 3 Company in Right Support. 3rd Battalion Coldstream Guards on our Left and the "Buffs" on our Right. The trenches were considerably better than any we have taken over since LOOS, and there are several deep "dugouts" in the Line. The enemy sent over a few heavy shells during the afternoon, but did little damage. Heavy fighting going on all the evening to the south of us, beyond THIEPVAL WOOD. Casualties, 1 N.C.O. killed, 4 men wounded, and 2 slightly wounded, the latter remained at Duty.	

Army Form C. 2118

WAR DIARY
or
INTELLIGENCE SUMMARY
(Erase heading not required.)

Instructions regarding War Diaries and Intelligence Summaries are contained in F. S. Regs., Part II. and the Staff Manual respectively. Title Pages will be prepared in manuscript.

Place	Date	Hour	Summary of Events and Information	Remarks and references to Appendices
	12/8/16		In the Line as above. No. 2 Company was heavily shelled with 4.5 shells in the morning, and, during the afternoon, some heavy shells fell around Battalion Headquarters and No. 1 Company. The Brigadier went round the Line at 10 a.m. Casualties, 2 men killed and 3 slightly wounded, the latter remained at Duty.	
	13/8/16		In the Line as above. Some promiscuous shelling, but little damage done. About 10.0 p.m. unexpected orders for relief arrived. Casualties, 5 N.C.Os and men slightly wounded, who remained at Duty.	
	14/8/16		In the Line as above. Lieutenant P. M. Walker and Billeting Party left at 5.0 a.m. We were relieved by the 1st Leicesters, commencing at 10.0 a.m. Relief complete about 1.30 p.m. Companies marched independently to Camp F.2 a, south west of BERTRANCOURT. We were caught by a heavy shower of rain on the way and the troops were wet through. Marched through BEAUSSART where the 4th Battalion Grenadier Guards were billeted, and reached Camp about 3.30 p.m. Casualties, NIL.	
	15/8/16		In Camp as above. A quiet day with heavy showers of rain. 2nd Lieutenant C.C. Cubitt and 2nd Lieutenant A. Hasler joined the Battalion.	

1875 Wt. W593/826 1,000,000 4/15 J.B.C. & A. A.D.S.S./Forms/C. 2118.

Army Form C. 2118

WAR DIARY
or
INTELLIGENCE SUMMARY
(*Erase heading not required.*)

Instructions regarding War Diaries and Intelligence Summaries are contained in F.S. Regs, Part II. and the Staff Manual respectively. Title Pages will be prepared in manuscript.

Place	Date	Hour	Summary of Events and Information	Remarks and references to Appendices
	16/8/16		We marched at 11.15 a.m. to COURCELLES, arriving in billets at 12.15 p.m. taking over from the 7th Battalion D.C.L. Infantry and K.O.Y.L. Infantry. Good billets but left in a dirty state and flies are abundant. On arrival, we organised baths, and two hundred men of Nos. 2 and 4 Companies had baths.	
	17/8/16		In Billets as above. The remainder of Nos. 2 and 4 Companies bathed in the morning, and No. 3 Company bathed during the afternoon. Fifty men of No. 1 Company were sent to Brigade Headquarters as a digging party at 8.30 a.m. and returned at midday. During the afternoon, No. 1 Company carried out a practice bombing attack under the Brigade Bombing Officer. Heavy showers during the day. The Battalion is now in Brigade Reserve. The 1st Battalion Irish Guards and 2nd Battalion Coldstream Guards being in the line.	
	18/8/16.		In Billets at COURCELLES. No. 1 Company had Bombing Instruction and practice bombing attack under the Brigade Bombing Officer from 8.0 a.m. to 12 noon. The remainder of the Battalion did Drill under Captains. No. 1 Company gave an open air concert in the evening.	

1875 Wt. W593/826 1,000,000 4/15 J.B.C. & A. A.D.S.S./Forms/C. 2118.

Army Form C 2118

WAR DIARY
or
INTELLIGENCE SUMMARY

(Erase heading not required.)

Instructions regarding War Diaries and Intelligence Summaries are contained in F.S. Regs, Part II. and the Staff Manual respectively. Title Pages will be prepared in manuscript.

Place	Date	Hour	Summary of Events and Information	Remarks and references to Appendices
	19/8/16		In Billets as above. Nos. 2 & 3 Companies had Bombing Instruction under the Brigade Bombing Officer in the morning and afternoon. No. 3 Company gave a concert in the evening.	
	20/8/16		In billets as above. We were relieved by the 17th Middlesex Regiment, 2nd Division. We marched at 11.0 a.m. via BERTRANCOURT and BUS, passing the relieving Battalion on the way, to the southernmost camp in BOIS DE WARNIMONT. A splendid position for a Camp, but no sanitary arrangements and a great scarcity of water. The Band of the Irish Guards played in the Camp during the afternoon.	
	21/8/16	10.0 a.m.	In Camp as above. No. 2 Company paraded under the Adjutant at The remainder of the Battalion did Drill and Training under Captains. 2nd Lieutenant D.W. Cassy joined the Battalion from Brigade Headquarters, where he had Signal Officer. The Brigadier visited the Commanding Officer during the morning.	
	22/8/16		In Camp as above. We marched at 8.30 a.m. for a route march, marching about ten miles. In the evening, the Officers of the Battalion played football with the Officers' Servants, and won, result two goals to nil. The Major General roade through the Camp during the day. 2nd Lieutenant D.W. Cassy posted to the 3rd Battalion and left during the afternoon.	

Army Form C. 2118

WAR DIARY
or
INTELLIGENCE SUMMARY

(Erase heading not required.)

Instructions regarding War Diaries and Intelligence Summaries are contained in F. S. Regs., Part II. and the Staff Manual respectively. Title Pages will be prepared in manuscript.

Place	Date	Hour	Summary of Events and Information	Remarks and references to Appendices
	23/8/16		We marched, second in the brigade, at 7.30 a.m. via SARTON to billets in BEAUVAL, arriving about midday. A hot march, but the Battalion went perfectly. Billets fair.	
	24/8/16		Marched at 7.40 a.m. to billets at FLESSELLES, arriving at mid-day, after a march of about ten miles. Billets very dirty and French Senegalese Troops scattered over the village. No water or sanitary arrangements. In the evening, the massed drums of the Brigade played "Retreat" in the centre of the village. Orders for tomorrow's move received very late.	
	25/8/16		Marched at 9.20 a.m. about 5 miles to CANAPLES and waited there about 1½ hours, entrained at 1.40 p.m 45 in a truck. The Billeting party under 2nd Lieutenant J. Arbuthnott and the 1st Line Transport proceeded by road, a distance of about twenty miles. The train passed through AMIENS about 3.45 p.m. and the Battalion detrained at MERICOURT, from where we marched about five miles to billets in MEAULTE, arriving about 8.15 p.m. A hot day and a long journey, which we could have accomplished more easily by road. Dirty billets and swarming with flies. A draft of twenty other ranks joined at MEAULTE and Lieutenant A.T.A. Ritchie joined on arrival of the Battalion at MEAULTE.	
	26/8/16		In Billets at MEAULTE. We sent 100 men at 8.0 a.m. to prepare Bombing Trenches under the Brigade Bombing Officer. The Commanding Officer went to a Conference at Brigade Headquarters at 6.45 p.m.	

1875 Wt. W593/826 1,000,000 4/15 J.B.C. & A. A.D.S.S./Forms/C. 2118.

WAR DIARY
or
INTELLIGENCE SUMMARY

(Erase heading not required.)

Army Form C. 2118

Instructions regarding War Diaries and Intelligence Summaries are contained in F. S. Regs., Part II. and the Staff Manual respectively. Title Pages will be prepared in manuscript.

Place	Date	Hour	Summary of Events and Information	Remarks and references to Appendices
	26/8/16 (Continued)		Rumours of an attack next week alongside the French at GUILLEMONT.	
	27/8/16		In Billets at MEAULTE. Rained hard all night and all the morning. At 7.0 a.m. 2nd Lieutenant D. Harvey and twelve other ranks proceeded to 186th Tunnelling Company, R.E. for attachment. No. 1 Company sent 100 men to load empty shell cases at the Railhead at 8.0 a.m. Three N.C.O's from the Royal Flying Corps arrived to be attached to the Battalion for Discipline. At 2.0 p.m. No. 2 Company sent 100 men for work under the Brigade Bombing Officer.	
	28/8/16		In Billets at MEAULTE. No. 2 Company paraded under the Adjutant in the morning. - No. 3 Company route marched. No. 1 Company paraded under its Captain for Drill. No. 4 Company used the Training Ground during the afternoon.	
	29/8/16		In Billets at MEAULTE. No. 4 Company paraded under the Adjutant in the morning. No. 3 Company used the Bombing Trenches in the morning. No. 1 Company used the assault trenches in the afternoon. No. 2 Company route marched. The Commanding Officer attended a Conference at Brigade Headquarters at 7.0 p.m. Rumours of a big attack tomorrow.	

Army Form C. 2118

WAR DIARY
or
INTELLIGENCE SUMMARY

(Erase heading not required.)

Instructions regarding War Diaries and Intelligence Summaries are contained in F.S. Regs., Part II. and the Staff Manual respectively. Title Pages will be prepared in manuscript.

Place	Date	Hour	Summary of Events and Information	Remarks and references to Appendices
	30/8/15		In Billets at MEAULTE. Rained in torrents all day - no work possible.	
	31/8/15		In Billets at MEAULTE. Nos 3 & 4 Companies each sent away working parties of one hundred other ranks. No. 1 Company used the Bombing Trenches. Headquarter Officers and one Officer per Company attended a demonstration of communication between areoplanes and troops in the morning. About 5.0 p.m. orders came in to move at once, which were cancelled about 3.15 p.m. when we were ordered to move tomorrow. About 3.30 p.m. orders to move during the evening received, to dig for the 20th Division. We marched at 6.30 p.m. leaving the Main road just outside MEAULTE,-proceeded over the hills along a very bad track to about F.25.b.7.8. south west of BOIS GAFFET. We arrived about 8.45 pm and bivouacked about 500 yards from the Headquarters of the 20th Division, who supplied us with one hundred bivouacs. The Transport and Lewis Gun Carts proceeded by road and arrived half an hour earlier than the Battalion.	

Lieutenant Colonel,

Commanding 2nd Battalion Grenadier Guards.

1st Guards Brigade.
Guards Division.

2nd BATTALION

GRENADIER GUARDS.

SEPTEMBER 1916

2nd Battalion Grenadier Guards.   1st Gds Bde.

WAR DIARY OF THE
ABOVE BATTALION FOR
THE MONTH OF
September, 1916.

Army Form C. 2118

WAR DIARY
or
INTELLIGENCE SUMMARY

(Erase heading not required.)

Instructions regarding War Diaries and Intelligence Summaries are contained in F.S. Regs., Part II. and the Staff Manual respectively. Title Pages will be prepared in manuscript.

Place	Date	Hour	Summary of Events and Information	Remarks and references to Appendices
	1/9/16		In bivouacs south west of BOIS CAFTET. No. 1 Company and half of No. 2 Company marched from Camp at 8.0 a.m. under Captain A.F.R Wiggins to clear the trenches in BERNAFY WOOD. No. 4 Company under Captain G.G.F. Harcourt-Vernon also went up to carry material. Both these parties returned at about 4.30 p.m. No. 3 Company and the remainder of No. 2 Company left Camp at 7.0 p.m. for digging. Heavy shelling everywhere along the front, but no shells came near our Camp. Colonel Heywood, G.S.O. 1 of the Division Major Ellice, Commanding 7th Entrenching Battalion and his Adjutant came over during the afternoon. Casualty, one man slightly wounded, who remained at Duty.	
	2/9/16		In bivouacs as above. No. 3 Company and half of No. 2 Company arrived back in Camp at 3.15 a.m. No. 4 Company and the remainder of No. 2 Company went up to dig in BERNAFY WOOD at 8.0 a.m. No. 1 Company as a carrying party left at 9.0 a.m. No. 3 Company and the remainder of No. 2 Company went up to dig at 7.0 p.m. Casualty, one man slightly wounded, who remained at Duty.	
	3/9/16		One Officer and one hundred other ranks of No. 4 Company paraded to repair the road, near CARNOY at noon, one hour's work.	

Army Form C. 2118

WAR DIARY
or
INTELLIGENCE SUMMARY

(Erase heading not required.)

Instructions regarding War Diaries and Intelligence Summaries are contained in F.S. Regs., Part II. and the Staff Manual respectively. Title Pages will be prepared in manuscript.

Place	Date	Hour	Summary of Events and Information	Remarks and references to Appendices
	3/9/16 (Continued)		The Battalion marched at 3.30 p.m. and returned to our old billets in MEAULTE, arriving there about 5.0 p.m.	
	4/9/16		In Billets at MEAULTE. At 9.30 a.m., all Captains rode a short way out from MEAULTE to watch a scheme between the 3rd Battalion Coldstream Guards and areoplanes. At 4.30 p.m. Lieutenant T. Parker-Jervis and twenty five other ranks from each Company paraded for fatigue at GROVE TOWN Supply Siding. Grenadier Boxing Contest at VILLE commenced at 4.0 p.m.	
	5/9/16		In Billets at MEAULTE. No. 1 Company used the Bombing Trenches in the morning. At 2.30 p.m. the Battalion paraded on the Training Area to practice the Assault. Battalion under four hours' notice to move. Orders received to move at short notice after 5.0 a.m. on the 6th.	
	6/9/16	2.15 a.m. 8.30 a.m. 8.30 a.m.	In Billets at MEAULTE. Orders cancelled to two hours' notice at Cancelled again to four hours notice at No. 1 Company sent off a party of one hundred other ranks under Lieutenant P.M. Walker for fatigue at GROVE TOWN Supply Siding at No. 4 Company used the assault trenches in the morning. No. 3 Company used the Training rea E.28 E.29 in the afternoon.	

Army Form C. 2118

WAR DIARY
or
INTELLIGENCE SUMMARY

(Erase heading not required.)

Instructions regarding War Diaries and Intelligence Summaries are contained in F.S. Regs., Part II. and the Staff Manual respectively. Title Pages will be prepared in manuscript.

Place	Date	Hour	Summary of Events and Information	Remarks and references to Appendices
	6/9/16		No. 2 Company paraded under the Adjutant in the morning. Four hours' notice cancelled.	
	7/9/16		In Billets at MEAULTE. The Battalion paraded for Training on the K.5 area at 9.30 a.m. The Divisional Commander, G.S.O.1 and the Brigadier were present. The Brigadier inspected our Billets at 11.45 a.m.	
	8/9/16		In Billets at MEAULTE. The Battalion paraded at 8.30 a.m. for a Brigade Field Day practising Brigade Attack.	
	9/9/16		In billets at MEAULTE. No. 2 Company used the Bombing Trenches in the morning. Nos. 1 and 3 Companies used the Training Ground in the afternoon. No. 4 Company paraded for Drill under the Adjutant in the morning. GINCHY reported taken and the 3rd Brigade is moving up with our 1st and 4th Battalions to relieve those troops.	
	10/9/16		The Battalion marched at 8.45 a.m. to CARNOY and bivouacked about 1500 yards from our old bivouacs at twelve noon. Rumours that the 4th Battalion Grenadier Guards attacked at dawn and the Welsh Guards were heavily counter-attacked as they were relieving during the night.-- Colonel E.G. Trotter's Grave located close to our bivouacs. --	

1875 Wt. W593/826 1,000,000 4/15 J.B.C. & A. A.D.S.S./Forms/C. 2118.

Army Form C. 2118

WAR DIARY
or
INTELLIGENCE SUMMARY

(Erase heading not required.)

Instructions regarding War Diaries and Intelligence Summaries are contained in F.S. Regs., Part II. and the Staff Manual respectively. Title Pages will be prepared in manuscript.

Place	Date	Hour	Summary of Events and Information	Remarks and references to Appendices
	10/9/16 (Continued)		No cover proved for the troops until 10.0 p.m. when 25 bivouacs arrived. A very cold night and the troops had no great coats - only waterproof sheets. During the evening, a few large shells fell in the Camp of the 3rd Battalion Coldstream Guards on the opposite hill. Sgt P. Casey, of this Battalion, was hit by a flying splinter.	
	11/9/16		In bivouacs at CARNOY. Rumoured in the Battalion that the big attack is on the 15th inst, and that we shall be in it. At 10.35 a.m. orders arrived that we move into the line tomorrow night. At 6.0 p.m. a conference of Commanding Officers at Brigade Headquarters, when we were informed the plan of attack.	
	12/9/16		We moved from our bivouacs by platoons at 6.30 pm via BERNAFAY WOOD TRONES WOOD and GUILLEMONT, and relieved the 2nd Battalion Scots Guards on the North and Eastern sides of GINCHY. Battalion Headquarters in a dug out in GUILLEMONT. A very difficult relief owing to shelling and the broken state of the ground. 3rd Battalion Grenadier Guards on our right. Lieut. Hon. M.E.H. Towneley-Bertie wounded, two N.C.Os and one man killed, seven N.C.Os and men wounded, and one man slightly wounded, who remained at Duty.	

Army Form C. 2118

WAR DIARY
or
INTELLIGENCE SUMMARY
(Erase heading not required.)

Instructions regarding War Diaries and Intelligence Summaries are contained in F.S. Regs., Part II. and the Staff Manual respectively. Title Pages will be prepared in manuscript.

Place	Date	Hour	Summary of Events and Information	Remarks and references to Appendices
In the Line at GINCHY.	13/9/16		Heavy shelling all day and our trenches much knocked about.	
	14/9/16,) 15/9/16,) and 16/9/16.)		As per attached narrative by Lieutenant Colonel C.R.C. de Crespigny, D.S.O., On the 15th Sept., we had the following casualties in Officers :-	
			Captain M.K.A. Lloyd, Killed.	
			2/Lieut. A. Hasler, Wounded, 15/9/16.	
			Died, 16/9/16	
			2/Lieut. J. Arbuthnott, Wounded, 15/9/16.	
			Died, 16/9/16.	
			Captain H.C.C. Viscount Lascelles, Wounded.	
			Lieutenant T. Parker-Jervis, Wounded.	
			Lieutenant M.H. Macmillan, Wounded.	
			Lieut. A.T.A. Ritchie, Wounded.	
			Lieut. H.F.C. Crookshank, Wounded.	
			2/Lieutenant T.W. Minchin, Wounded.	
			2/Lieutenant N.M. Jesper, Wounded.	
			2/Lieutenant D. Harvey, Wounded.	
			2/Lieutenant C.C. Cubitt Wounded.	
			Captain G.U.F. Harcourt-Vernon and Captain J.A. Andrews, R.A.M.C., attached to Battalion, were slightly wounded, but remained at duty. During the operations of 13th, 14th, 15th and 16th September, we had the following casualties in Non-Commissioned Officers and men :-	
			Killed, 98	A draft of fifty other ranks arrived on 16th.
			Died of Wounds, 16	
			Wounded, 232	
			Missing, 13	
			Total 359	

Army Form C. 2118

WAR DIARY
or
INTELLIGENCE SUMMARY
(Erase heading not required.)

Instructions regarding War Diaries and Intelligence Summaries are contained in F.S. Regs., Part II. and the Staff Manual respectively. Title Pages will be prepared in manuscript.

Place	Date	Hour	Summary of Events and Information	Remarks and references to Appendices
	17/9/16		About 3.0 a.m. we were relived by the 15th K.R.R. and went back to the Camp at the Citadel, near FRICOURT. The Battalion had a rendez-vous at the South end of BERNAFAY WOOD, where the cookers met us and provided a hot meal. Message as attached received from the Army Commander. The Battalion slept all day.	
	18/9/16		In Camp as above. The Battalion rested all day. We were informed we would be required to attack again shortly. Attached message received from the Brigadier General. Lieutenant R.B.B. Wright joined. Lieutenant P.M. Walker admitted hospital.	
	19/9/16		In Camp as above. Day spent in re-organizing and checking casualties. A very wet day.	
	20/9/16		The Battalion left Camp at 6.45 p.m. by Companies at intervals of one hundred yards and marched to BERNAFAY WOOD, which we reached about 9.0 p.m. A bad march owing to mud and congestion of traffic. No shelter of any description provided by the Staff for the troops, although it is common knowledge we attack again on the 25th. 2nd and 3rd Battalions Coldstream Guards took over the Front and Support Lines in the Brigade area, and 1st Battalion Irish Guards in bivouacs at GINCHY.	

Army Form C. 2118

WAR DIARY
or
INTELLIGENCE SUMMARY
(Erase heading not required.)

Instructions regarding War Diaries and Intelligence Summaries are contained in F.S. Regs, Part II. and the Staff Manual respectively. Title Pages will be prepared in manuscript.

Place	Date	Hour	Summary of Events and Information	Remarks and references to Appendices
	20/9/16 (Continued)		Pouring with rain all night and the men dug themselves in in shell-holes where they could. A disgraceful piece of Staff work.	
	21/9/16		In BERNAFAY WOOD. Weather cleared a little in the morning and we were able to collect some corrugated iron and sacks, with which to erect bivouacs, but the bulk of the Battalion is still in the open. Several heavy shells fell close to the Battalion during the evening. 2nd and 3rd Battalions Coldstream Guards side-stepped into battle position. Lieutenants M.A. Knatchbull-Hugessen and F.H.G. Layland-Barratt and draft of 71 other ranks arrived.	
	22/9/16 23/9/16		In BERNAFAY WOOD. Quiet days. Several fatigues found of about fifty men each to carry rations, water, ammunition, etc., to the front line. Weather has improved during the past few days. A draft of 192 other ranks joined on 22nd Sept.	
	24/9/16		Companies moved off at intervals of two hundred yards at 7.50 p.m. to take up our battle position, relieving the 2nd Battalion Coldstream Guards in the front line, opposite LES BOEUFS Village with our right on the GINCHY-LES BOEUFS Road. In the front Line, No. 2 on the right, No. 1 on left In the Support Line, No. 4 on right and No. 3 on left. The Support Line was a narrow assembly trench about 150 yards to the rear of the front line, dug by the Coldstream Guards the previous night.	

1875 Wt. W593/326 1,000,000 4/15 J.B.C. & A. A.D.S.S./Forms/C. 2118.

WAR DIARY
or
INTELLIGENCE SUMMARY

(Erase heading not required.)

Army Form C. 2118

Instructions regarding War Diaries and Intelligence Summaries are contained in F. S. Regs., Part II. and the Staff Manual respectively. Title Pages will be prepared in manuscript.

Place	Date	Hour	Summary of Events and Information	Remarks and references to Appendices
	24/9/16 (Continued)		The relief was complete about 1.0 a.m. the 25th. Heavy shelling during the whole relief.	
	25/9/16 and 26/9/16		As per attached narrative by Lieutenant Colonel G.R.C. de Crespigny D.S.O. During these operations, we had the following casualties in Officers :-	
			Captain A.K.S. Cuningham, Killed, 25/9/16.	
			Lieut. Hon. W.A.D. Parnell, Killed, 25/9/16.	
			Lieut. M.A. Knatchbull-Hugessen, Killed, 25/9/16.	
			2/Lieut. G.A. Arbuthnot, Killed, 25/9/16.	
			Captain G.C.T. Harcourt-Vernon, Wounded, 25/9/16.	
			Captain W.H. Beaumont-Nesbitt, Wounded, 25/9/16.	
			Lieutenant A.F. Irvine, Wounded, 25/9/16.	
			Lieutenant H.G. Wiggins, Wounded, 25/9/16.	
			Lieutenant R.B.B. Wright, Wounded, 25/9/16.	
			2/Lieutenant K. Terrell joined 25/9/16	
			We had the following casualties in Non-Commissioned Officers and men :-	
			Killed, 67	
			Wounded, 175	
			Died of Wounds, 11	
			Missing, 77	
			Total, 330	
			We were relieved on the night of the 26th by the 2nd Battalion Irish Guards, relief being complete about 10.0 p.m. We marched back to the Citadel Camp, stopping on the way at the South end of	

Army Form C. 2118

WAR DIARY
or
INTELLIGENCE SUMMARY
(Erase heading not required.)

Instructions regarding War Diaries and Intelligence Summaries are contained in F.S. Regs., Part II. and the Staff Manual respectively. Title Pages will be prepared in manuscript.

Place	Date	Hour	Summary of Events and Information	Remarks and references to Appendices
	25/9/16 and 26/9/16. (Continued)		BERNAFAY WOOD for hot food provided by our cookers. We arrived in Camp at 4.0 a.m. the 27th. A draft of 14 other ranks arrived. Attached message received.	
	27/9/16		In Camp as above. The Battalion slept all day.	
	28/9/16		In Camp as above. Day spent in re-organizing and checking casualties. A party left at 9.0 a.m under the Adjutant and recovered the bodies of Captain A.K.S. Cuninghame, Lieutenant M.A. Knatchbull-Hugessen and 2/Lieut. G.A. Arbuthnot. The remains of these officers were buried in the Cemetery close to the Camp before we marched off. Attached message received from the Brigadier. The Battalion moved at 6.30 p.m. about one mile down the Valley to the Camp of the 7th Entrenching Battalion.	
	29/9/16		In the Camp of the 7th Entrenching Battalion. A very wet day. 2/Lieut. Lawson Johnston went up to the Bowle and buried the bodies of 2/Lieut Parnell and 2/Lieut 35 O.R. A Billeting Party under Captain A.F.R. Wiggins left at 10 a.m. for MORLANCOURT. Another Billeting Party under 2/Lieutenant A.McW. Lawson-Johnston left at noon for AUMONT.	
	30/9/16		The Battalion marched at 1.50 p.m. for MORLANCOURT where we billetted for the night.	

W.R. ……… Captain,
Commanding 2nd Battalion Grenadier Guards.

Narrative of events from Sept. 13th -17th, 1916.

On 13th Sept. the Battalion was holding the Northern Sector of the GINCHY Line. Orders were received that we were to straighten the Line by an attack that night in order to form a good jumping off place for the big attack on the 15th. No. 4 Company was detailed for this and No. 2 Company were ordered to protect their left flank and join up with them. The operation was a difficult one as the left of the attack had to advance further than the right in order to form a line facing N.E; there was also a bright moon which showed up our attacking party very plainly. Thirty or forty shrapnel were fired at the German trench just north of the Orchard, but did very little good and the Germans were on the alert and met No. 4 Company under 2/Lieut. T.W. Minchin, with heavy rifle and machine gun fire causing some casualties. The party cleared the Orchard killing some Germans who were in shell-holes and dug in, a line to the edge of the Orchard, after a fruitless attempt to push on. They were shot at heavily the whole time but completed their trench before morning.

On the 14th the whole of the Battalion Front was bombarded all day by 4.5 and 5.9 shells and the line was much knocked about and the Companies all rather shaken. We were relieved that night by the 2nd and 3rd Battalions Coldstream Guards and went into bivouac in shell holes a few hundred yards behind GINCHY where rations were given out and rum issued. A bitterly cold night and no great coats.

At 6.20 a.m. on 15th, our bombardment began and we moved off in two lines of platoon blobs. The German barrage dropped before we reached GINCHY and we went through the middle of it, on the whole losing extraordinarily few men, considering the intensity of the fire. At about 6.40 a.m. we halted in GINCHY, luckily the bulk of the barrage was on the south edge but we lost a good many men and Captain M.K.A. Lloyd.

About twenty minutes later we decided to push on out and clear of GINCHY and remain for a short time in shell holes. We saw nothing of the Coldstream Battalions. At 7.20 a.m. we moved on towards our objective with our Right on the Sunken Road. We came at once under machine gun fire from our left front and after a while rifle fire from our right and a good many men went down including several officers. The left Companies were held up by rifle fire from the GREEN LINE, which appeared to be held strongly from about T.8.d.3.8 to T.8.a.8.4. The right Companies pushed on into the GREEN LINE and our right was in touch with some of the 3rd Battalion Grenadier Guards, 2nd Guards Brigade; who were attempting to stop the Germans from turning their right flank. One platoon of No. 1 Company and a machine gun was rushed over and succeeded in forming a defensive flank and preventing the Germans, of whom there were a considerable number, from working up behind us. The Division on our right had apparently failed and the Germans were very thick in their trenches and were shooting hard at us. We lost the bulk of our casualties during this period. The centre of the Battalion then rushed a part of the GREEN LINE and bayoneted all Germans they found. The left were unable to get on. Almost as soon as the centre got in the Germans began bombing down the trench very strongly having three or four men throwing our bombers could not stop them and Company Sgt Major J. Norton who was lying out by the wire with some men rushed them and stopped the attack for the time. All available bombs were then collected and a party began to work up the trench but was met by a furious bomb attack and driven back some way, most of the bombers being knocked out. We were forced back some way and to relieve the pressure, as the men were rather overwhelmed by the shower of bombs, and all British Bombs had been finished, Captain G.C.F. Harcourt-Vernon organized and led a bayonet charge over the top, killing the bombing party and driving the remainder back, 40 or 50 of whom surrendered.

Our bombing party worked north along the trench until the Germans broke and ran and across the open towards the BLUE LINE. Having cleared the trench for some way we began to consolidate. Two small parties of Germans tried to enter the trench on the left but were dealt with by our Lewis Guns.

During the evening our troops retired from the BLUE LINE across our front followed at not more than a hundred yards by a large body of Germans. They were shot at and lay down in the grass. As it was getting dark it was difficult to see them and fire was ordered to be withheld in the hopes that they would attack and as they were being continually reinforced.

Nothing happened, however, during the night.

On the 16th we were very heavily shelled for most of the day from the front and direct enfilade from the left. We were shot at continuously from our right rear, but this eased after our snipers has killed a good many.

We were relieved on the 17th about 2.0 a.m. by the 15th K.R.R.

19/9/16.

(Sd) C. de Crespigny,
Lieutenant Colonel,
Commanding 2nd Battalion Grenadier Guards.

G.B. 682   17th Sept.

Following from General Rawlinson begins AAA

Please convey to the Guards Division my congratulations and best thanks for their successful attacks on 15th and 16th September AAA The gallantry and vigour they displayed in capturing the enemy's second and third systems of defence deserves the highest praise.

2nd Battalion Grenadier Guards.

    As your Brigadier I wish to say in a few words how deeply I appreciate the gallant work done by you in the recent operations at GINCHY.

    On the 12th September you took over GINCHY Trenches and the following night you drove the Germans out of GINCHY ORCHARD; this work caused you one hundred casualties, but by your fine work you cleared the ground for the advance on 15th September and ensured that it would not be held up at the very beginning.

    On 15th September your first advance was through a heavy artillery barrage but owing to the splendid discipline of your Regiment, you went through it as if on parade.

    Your opportunity came later on when you cleared trenches at the point of the bayonet having run out of bombs and when you charged a trench strongly held and in the face of machine gun fire.

    You have shown the Germans what they have to expect when they meet the pick of the British Army.

    In the near future you may be called upon to do as much again and I know that you will not fail.

(Sd) G.E. PEREIRA, Brigadier General Commanding 1st Guards Brigade.

In the Field,
18th September, 1916.

NARRATIVE of events from 24th - 26th Sept. 1916.

On the night of Sept. 24th the Battalion moved from BERNAFAY WOOD, where we had been in Bivouac, and relieved the 2nd Battalion Coldstream Guards in the front line, our right being on the GINCHY-LES BOEUFS road, and the Battalion after relief being formed up in our Assembly Area - Two Companies and H.Q., in the front line and two Companies in the Support Line 150 yards behind. A good deal of shelling was going on during the relief but we only had a few casualties.

The morning of Sept. 25th was a very bad one for us as the trenches were very narrow and the men shoulder to shoulder almost unable even to sit down. It was quite impossible to lie down.

At 12.35 p.m. our barrage opened and we advanced in two waves of two Companies each. The Germans evidently knew that an attack was imminent as within one minute they began putting heavy shell into the waves and at the same time a terrific barrage was opened on our front line.

About 12.35½ our leading Companies caught up our barrage and lay down. About 12.39 or 12.40 p.m. the first objective was gained with a certain amount of difficulty as our Artillery had entirely failed to cut a single strand of the wire: While the Companies were cutting it and making their way through the Germans picked off almost all our Officers with the rifle and caused us some casualties by throwing bombs. Many Germans were killed in this Line and a nice bag of prisoners made, also a Machine Gun was captured. Some Germans who were lying shell holes in "No Man's Land" were also killed.

At 1.35 p.m. we moved forward to the edge of the Village of LES BOEUFS, killing more Germans who emerged from dugouts in the Sunken Roads and taking some prisoners. All dugouts were bombed and no doubt many Germans were killed that way, as one or two were seen to be full of dead.

Two Companies pushed rather too far into LES BOEUFS and were forced back by our own Artillery Fire.

At 2.35 p.m. we advanced through the Village meeting with little opposition and taking a few more prisoners. We gained the Eastern edge of the Village and consolidated. The Germans were seen retiring over the next hill in small parties and ones and twos; some loss was inflicted on them.

While we were consolidating we were sniped at heavily by a few Germans in a trench in the hollow to our immediate front, causing us some casualties.

During the evening the Village was severely shelled by heavy guns but except for a few stray shells, the front line was left alone. Sniping and shelling continued all night and the next morning.

During the afternoon of 26th we were heavily shelled. The Germans could be seen counter-attacking about half a mile to our left and also digging in all along the ridge to our front.

During the whole of the operations we were ably and closely supported by Captain Verelst and the 2nd Battalion Coldstream Guards.

The observation from the front of the Village was perfect but no Artillery lines or observation posts were fromed up to the time we were relieved on the night of the 26th by the 2nd Battalion Irish Guards.

The dash and gallantry of the Infantry was magnificent in spite of large numbers of recent drafts and totally untrained men being in the ranks, but the co-operation of the Artillery was remarkable for its absence and a great deal of ammunition was uselessly expended on ground where no Germans were, and places where Germans could be seen were left untouched.

I should like to record my thanks to the 2nd Battalion Coldstream Guards for the admirable way in which they supported me.

(Sd) C. de Crespigny, Lieut. Colonel,
Commanding 2nd Battalion Grenadier Guards.

26/9/16.

2nd Battalion Grenadier Guards.

You have again maintained the high traditions of the 1st Guards Brigade when called upon a second time in the Battle of the Somme. For five days previous to the assault the 2nd and 3rd Battalions Coldstream Guards held the trenches under constant heavy shell fire and dug many hundred yards assembly and communication trenches, this work being constantly interrupted by the enemy's artillery. The 2nd Bn. Grenadier Guards and 1st Bn. Irish Guards though under shell fire in their bivouacs were kept clear of the trenches until the evening of 24th September and were given the task of carrying by assault all the objectives to be carried by this Brigade. Nothing deterred them in this attack not even the fact that in places the enemy wire was still intact and the enemy strongly posted there; this wire was cut in the face of rifle and machine gun fire and in spite of all resistance and heavy losses the entire main enemy defensive line was captured.

Every Battalion in the Brigade carried out its task to the full.

The German 52nd Reserve Division which includes the 238th 239th and 240th Regiments and which opposed you for many weeks at YPRES left the salient on the 18th September. You have now met them in the open, a worthy foe, but you have filled their trenches with their dead and have driven them before you in headlong flight.

I cannot say how proud I am to have had the honour of commanding the 1st Guards Brigade in this Battle, a Brigade which has proved itself to be the finest in the British Army.

The Brigade is now under orders for rest and training and it must now be our object to keep up to the high standard of efficiency and those who have come to fill our depleted ranks will strive their utmost to fill worthily the places of those gallant officers and men who have laid down their lives for a great cause.

(Signed) G. E. PEREIRA,
Brigadier General,
Commanding 1st Guards Brigade.

28th September, 1916.

B.M.X. 166   25th Sept.

Following received from Corps Commander AAA
Hearty thanks and sincere congratulations to you all AAA
A very fine achievement splendidly executed.

B.M.X. 167   25th Sept.

G.O.C. and all ranks of 2nd (Second) Guards Brigade wish to
congratulate 1st and 3rd Guards Brigades on their splendid
success today.

B.M.X. 168.   25th Sept.

Following from 14th Corps begins AAA
Army Commander sends his best congratulations to all ranks
on their great successed.

B.M.X. 169   26th Sept.

Following from Army Commander begins. AAA
Please convey to Guards Division my thanks and admiration
for the excellent manner in which they carried out their
attacks today AAA Ends.

1st Guards Brigade.
Guards Division.

2nd BATTALION

GRENADIER GUARDS.

OCTOBER 1 9 1 6

Army Form C. 2118

October 1916   2nd Bn Grenadier Guards   Vol 27

WAR DIARY
or
INTELLIGENCE SUMMARY
(Erase heading not required.)

Instructions regarding War Diaries and Intelligence Summaries are contained in F. S. Regs., Part II. and the Staff Manual respectively. Title Pages will be prepared in manuscript.

Place	Date	Hour	Summary of Events and Information	Remarks and references to Appendices
	1/10/16		The Battalion left MORLANCOURT at 9.40 a.m. and proceeded by buses, lent by the French Government, to AUMONT, arriving about 6.0 p.m. after a long and dusty journey. The First Line Transport proceeded by road. Excellent billets.	
	2/10/16		In Billets at AUMONT. No parades possible owing to the incessant downpour of rain. First Line Transport rejoined Battalion. 2nd Lieut. W.H.S. Dent joined the Battalion.	
	3/10/16		In Billets at AUMONT. Nos. 1 and 2 Companies route marched. Nos. 3 and 4 Companies paraded for Drill under the Adjutant at 9.30 a.m. Bombing Practice was also carried out.	
	4/10/16		In Billets at AUMONT. Nos. 3 and 4 Companies route marched and trained. Nos. 1 and 2 Companies paraded for Drill under the Adjutant at 9.30 a.m. Instruction in Bombing and Lewis Gunnery was also carried out. Received notification that G.O.C. in Chief, under authority granted by His Majesty The King, has awarded decorations as under, to Officers, Non-Commissioned Officers and men of this Battalion.	

Army Form C. 2118

WAR DIARY
or
INTELLIGENCE SUMMARY
(Erase heading not required.)

Place	Date	Hour	Summary of Events and Information	Remarks and references to Appendices
	4/10/16 (Continued)		DISTINGUISHED SERVICE ORDER. Captain Hon. W.R. Bailey. Captain G.C.F. Harcourt-Vernon. 2nd Lieutenant T.W. Minchin. MILITARY CROSS. Lieutenant P.M. Walker. Captain J.A. Andrews, R.A.M.C., attached to Battn DISTINGUISHED CONDUCT MEDAL. 9797, CSM Snook F. 16318, L/C Fincham J. 13372, Pte Clarke W. 15570, " Gardiner H. MILITARY MEDAL. 14362, Sgt Sharp G. 15317, " Gambrill W.F. 12813, L/Cp Jeanes J.V. 15821, L/C Dewick H.B. 16243, Pte Roper W.A. 14105, " Wilson G. 19111, " Jeffreys C.J. 14116, " Gipson J. 18379, " Millins F.J. The undermentioned have also been awarded the MILITARY MEDAL during the recent operations.	

Army Form C. 2118

WAR DIARY
or
INTELLIGENCE SUMMARY
(Erase heading not required.)

Instructions regarding War Diaries and Intelligence Summaries are contained in F.S. Regs., Part II. and the Staff Manual respectively. Title Pages will be prepared in manuscript.

Place	Date	Hour	Summary of Events and Information	Remarks and references to Appendices
	4/10/16 (Continued)		15353, A/S Adderley P. 10697, Sgt Bosworth J. 17225, L/C Hayes A. 17551, L/C Duddy J. 14356, L/C Williams W. 18191, L/C Greenhalf W. 14165, Pte Saunders J. 17129, " Tomkinson T. 16400, " Bryant W. 17545, " Jones A. 18473, L/C Ryder J. 23280, Pte Dighton W. 15507, " Rockley A.	
	5/10/16		In Billets at AUMONT. Companies paraded under Captains for Drill at 9.30 a.m. The Battalion paraded in a field at the South end of the village at 11.45 a.m. when Major General G.P.T. Feilding, C.B., D.S.O., Commanding Guards Division presented medal ribbons for the decorations recently awarded. Captain E.O. Stewart joined the Battalion.	
	6/10/16		In Billets at AUMONT. Nos. 3 and 4 Companies route marched. Nos. 1 and 2 Companies paraded for Drill under the Adjutant at 9.30 a.m. No. 1 Company fired on the Range. Instruction in Bombing and Lewis Gunnery was also carried out. Lieut. Hon. F.H. Manners, Lieut. F.A.M. Browning, 2nd Lieut. R.A.W. Bicknell and 2nd Lieut. J.H. Jacob joined the Battalion.	

Army Form C. 2118

WAR DIARY
or
INTELLIGENCE SUMMARY

(Erase heading not required.)

Instructions regarding War Diaries and Intelligence Summaries are contained in F. S. Regs., Part II. and the Staff Manual respectively. Title Pages will be prepared in manuscript.

Place	Date	Hour	Summary of Events and Information	Remarks and references to Appendices
	7/10/16		In Billets at AUMONT. The Battalion used the Baths at HORNOY during the day, and received new underclothing. No. 1 Company paraded for Drill under the Adjutant at 9.30 a.m. No. 2 Company paraded for Physical Drill and Bomb-Throwing. No. 3 Company fired on the Range from 1.30 p.m. No. 2 Company detailed a party of one N.C.O. and twenty men for fatigue under the Divisional Gas Officer. 2nd Lieut. E.W. Seymour joined the Battalion.	
	8/10/16		In Billets at AUMONT. Divine Services in the morning. The attached message from the G.O.C., Fourth Army circulated through Guards Division.	
	9/10/16		In Billets at AUMONT. Nos. 1 and 2 Companies route marched. No. 3 Company paraded for one hour's Drill under the Adjutant at 9.30 a.m. and from 11.0 a.m. to 11.45 a.m. for Bomb Throwing and Musketry. This Company finished firing on the Range during the afternoon. No. 4 Company used the Range during the morning. N.C.O's and men who joined with drafts on the 16th and 22nd September paraded at 9.30 a.m. for a demonstration by the Divisional Gas Officer.	

Army Form C. 2118

WAR DIARY
or
INTELLIGENCE SUMMARY

(Erase heading not required.)

Instructions regarding War Diaries and Intelligence Summaries are contained in F. S. Regs., Part II. and the Staff Manual respectively. Title Pages will be prepared in manuscript.

Place	Date	Hour	Summary of Events and Information	Remarks and references to Appendices
	10/10/16		In Billets at AUMONT. Nos. 3 and 4 Companies route marched. No. 2 Company used the Range. No. 1 Company paraded for Physical Training, Musketry, Bombing, and Arm Drill under its Captain. The First Line Transport inspected by the Brigadier and A.D.V.S. Captain Hon. W.R. Bailey, D.S.O., granted temporary rank of Major as Second in Command of the Battalion.	
	11/10/16		In Billets at AUMONT. No. 4 Company paraded for one hour's Drill at 9.30 a.m. and from 11.0 a.m. to 11.45 a.m. for Musketry and Bombing. No. 3 Company used the Range. Nos. 1 and 2 Companies paraded at 8.30 a.m. under Captain A.F.R. Wiggins for Field Work. The Band of the Irish Guards played here during the afternoon.	
	12/10/16		In Billets at AUMONT. The Battalion used the Baths at HORNOY during the day. Nos. 3 and 4 Companies paraded for Drill under the Adjutant at 9.30 a.m. 2nd Lieut. W.H.S. Dent transferred to the 1st Guards Brigade Trench Mortar Battery, vice Lieut. T.A. Combe, who rejoined the Battalion. Captain G.F.A. Walker, M.C., 2nd Lieut. J.D.C. Wilton and a draft of 92 other ranks joined the Battalion.	

WAR DIARY
or
INTELLIGENCE SUMMARY

(Erase heading not required.)

Army Form C. 2118

Instructions regarding War Diaries and Intelligence Summaries are contained in F. S. Regs., Part II. and the Staff Manual respectively. Title Pages will be prepared in manuscript.

Place	Date	Hour	Summary of Events and Information	Remarks and references to Appendices
	12/10/16. (Continued)		Notification received that the following further decorations have been awarded to Officers, Non-Commissioned Officers and men of this Battalion. **MILITARY CROSS.** Captain W.H. Beaumont-Nesbitt. Lieut. F.H.G. Leyland-Barratt. 2nd Lieut. A.McW. Lawson-Johnston. **DISTINGUISHED CONDUCT MEDAL.** 23919, L/C Barber F. 15418, Pte Roberts J.	
	13/10/16		In Billets at AUMONT. Nos. 1, 2, and 3 Companies route marched. No. 4 Company fired on the Range. The draft, which joined the Battalion yesterday, paraded under the Adjutant for Drill at 9.30 a.m.	
	14/10/16		In Billets at AUMONT. The Battalion paraded at 9.30 a.m. for an Advanced Guard Scheme. Nos. 1 and 2 Companies formed the van guard, and Nos. 3 and 4 Companies formed the main guard. The area chosen for this scheme was the country on each side of the main road between AUMONT and HORNOY. Captain A.F.R. Wiggins left the Battalion for the Central Training Camp, HAVRE.	

Army Form C. 2118

WAR DIARY
or
INTELLIGENCE SUMMARY
(Erase heading not required.)

Instructions regarding War Diaries and Intelligence Summaries are contained in F.S. Regs., Part II. and the Staff Manual respectively. Title Pages will be prepared in manuscript.

Place	Date	Hour	Summary of Events and Information	Remarks and references to Appendices
	15/10/16		In Billets at AUMONT. Divine Services in the morning. The "Foden" Disinfecting Lorry allotted to the Battalion, commencing work at 11.0 a.m. and finishing at 5.0 p.m.	
	16/10/16		In Billets at AUMONT. No. 2 Company route marched. Nos. 1, 3 and 4 Companies paraded at 9.30 a.m. for an out-post scheme in the area south west of AUMONT. Captain I.St. C. Rose, Captain Lord F.T. Blackwood, D.S.O., and 2nd Lieut. Lord I.B.G.T. Blackwood joined the Battalion. Lieutenant A.H. Penn joined the Battalion as Adjutant vice Major Hon. W.R. Bailey, D.S.O.	
	17/10/16		In Billets at AUMONT. The Battalion used the Baths at HORNOY during the day. No. 1 Company fired on the Range from 1.30 p.m. No. 3 Company practised Bombing. No. 4 Company route marched.	
	18/10/16		In Billets at AUMONT. No. 3 Company used the Range. No. 2 Company practised an outpost scheme. No. 1 Company route marched. No. 4 Company paraded for Drill and Bombing.	
	19/10/16		In Billets at AUMONT. No. 3 Company fired on the Range. No. 1 Company paraded for Drill. Nos. 2 and 4 Companies were at the disposal of	

1875 Wt. W593/826 1,000,000 4/15 J.B.C. & A. A.D.S.S./Forms/C. 2118.

Army Form C. 2118

WAR DIARY
or
INTELLIGENCE SUMMARY

(Erase heading not required.)

Instructions regarding War Diaries and Intelligence Summaries are contained in F.S. Regs., Part II. and the Staff Manual respectively. Title Pages will be prepared in manuscript.

Place	Date	Hour	Summary of Events and Information	Remarks and references to Appendices
	19/10/16 (Continued)		Company Commanders. A draft of one Hundred N.C.O's and men joined the Battalion.	
	20/10/16		In Billets at AUMONT. No. 1 Company used the Brigade Bombing Ground. No. 2 Company paraded for Drill at 9.30 a.m. No. 3 Company route marched. No. 4 Company did Drill and Training.	
	21/10/16		In Billets at AUMONT. No. 1 Company was at the disposal of its Captain. No. 2 Company route marched. No. 3 Company practised the construction of wire entanglements. No. 4 Company fired on the Range. The Band of the Irish Guards played here during the afternoon.	
	22/10/16		In Billets at AUMONT. Divine Services in the morning. The Officers of the Battalion played the Sergeants at football, result, Sergeants won, three goals to one.	
	23/10/16		In Billets at AUMONT. No. 1 Company practised extended order drill, the early stages of the attack and fire control. No. 2 Company paraded for a Kit Inspection in the morning and used the Brigade Bombing Ground in the afternoon. No. 3 Company paraded for Drill at 9.30 a.m. No. 4 Company practised an outpost scheme.	

Army Form C. 2118

WAR DIARY
or
INTELLIGENCE SUMMARY
(Erase heading not required.)

Instructions regarding War Diaries and Intelligence Summaries are contained in F.S. Regs., Part II. and the Staff Manual respectively. Title Pages will be prepared in manuscript.

Place	Date	Hour	Summary of Events and Information	Remarks and references to Appendices
	24/10/16		In Billets at AUMONT. The Battalion route marched.	
	25/10/16		In Billets at AUMONT. The Battalion paraded under the Commanding Officer at 9.30 a.m. in a field south west of AUMONT, for Drill.	
	26/10/16		In Billets at AUMONT. The Battalion paraded under the Commanding Officer at 9.30 a.m. in a field south west of AUMONT, for Drill. The undermentioned Officers took part in a tactical scheme under the Brigade Major. Captain E.O. Stewart. Captain C.F.A. Walker, M.C. Captain Lord F. Blackwood, D.S.O. Captain C.N. Newton. The Adjutant, 2nd Lieut. Lord B. Blackwood.	
	27/10/16		In Billets at AUMONT. No. 1 Company practised an outpost scheme between the villages of BELINCOURT and DROMESNIL at 9.30 am No. 2 Company used the Range during the morning. No. 3-Company paraded for Kit Inspection and Lectures during the morning, and used the Brigade Bombing Ground during the afternoon. No. 4 Company paraded for Drill at 9.30 a.m. Instruction in Bombing and Lewis Gunnery was continued.	

Army Form C. 2118

WAR DIARY
or
INTELLIGENCE SUMMARY

(Erase heading not required.)

Instructions regarding War Diaries and Intelligence Summaries are contained in F.S. Regs., Part II. and the Staff Manual respectively. Title Pages will be prepared in manuscript.

Place	Date	Hour	Summary of Events and Information	Remarks and references to Appendices
	28/10/16		In Billets at AUMONT. No. 1 Company practised an outpost scheme between the villages of SELINCOURT and DROMESNIL at 9.30 a.m. No. 2 Company paraded for Drill at 9.30 a.m. Nos. 3 and 4 Companies practised the attack from artillery formation between AUMONT and MERICOURT. Captain T.St.C. Rose and one Non-Commissioned Officer per Company attended a one day course of instruction in wiring at Brigade Headquarters.	
	29/10/16		In Billets at AUMONT. Divine Services (Voluntary) in the morning. Very wet morning, but fine later. Received notification that Captain G.N. Newton has been awarded the Military Cross.	
	30/10/16		In Billets at AUMONT. The Battalion paraded in a field southwest of AUMONT, and practised for the inspection by His Royal Highness the Duke of Connaught, A.G., on 1st November.	
	31/10/16		In Billets at AUMONT. The Battalion paraded at 8.45 am and marched to a field between DROMESNIL and FRESNEVILLE, where the Division was assembled under Major General G.P.T. Feilding, C.B., D.S.O., to rehearse tomorrow's inspection.	

R.B. ——
Major
Lieutenant Colonel,
Commanding 2nd Battalion Grenadier Guards.

Fourth Army No. 373 (G)

Guards Division.

It is only since the reports have come in that it has become clear that the gallantry and perseverance of the Guards Division in the Battles of the 15th and 25th September were paramount factors in the success of the operations of the Fourth Army on those days.

On the 15th September, especially, the vigorous attack of the Guards in circumstances of great difficulty, with both flanks exposed to the enfilade fire of the enemy, reflects the highest credit on all concerned, and I desire to tender to every officer, N.C.O., and man my congratulations and best thanks for their exemplary valour on that occasion. Their success established the Battlefront of the XIV Corps well forward on the high ridge leading towards MORVAL and LES BOEUFS, and made the assault of these villages on the 25th a feasible operation.

On the 25th September the attack of the hostile trenches in front and North of LES BOEUFS was conducted with equal gallantry and determination. In this attack the Division gained all the objectives allotted to them, and I offer to all concerned my warmest thanks and gratitude for their fine performance.

(Signed) H. Rawlinson,
General,
Commanding Fourth Army.

H.Q., Fourth Army,
8th October, 1916.

1st Guards Brigade.
Guards Division.

2nd BATTALION

GRENADIER GUARDS.

NOVEMBER 1 9 1 6

3rd Bn. Grenadier Gds. Army Form C. 2118.

November 1916 Vol 28

WAR DIARY
or
INTELLIGENCE SUMMARY
(Erase heading not required.)

Place	Date	Hour	Summary of Events and Information	Remarks and references to Appendices
	1/10		In Billets at AUMONT. The Battalion marched at 8.45 a.m. to a field between DROMESNIL and FRESNEVILLE where the Battalion was formed up for Review by His Royal Highness the Duke of Connaught, K.G. the Colonel of the Regiment.	
	2/10		In Billets at AUMONT. No 1 Company practised an attack from artillery formation between AUMONT and MERICOURT. No 2 Company fired on the Range. No 3 Company practised an attack and rearguard action between SELINCOURT and DROMESNIL. No 4 Company paraded for drill under the Adjutant. Instruction in Bombing and Lewis Guns, continued.	
	3/10		In Billets at AUMONT. The Battalion practised woodfighting during the morning.	

Army Form C. 2118.

WAR DIARY
or
INTELLIGENCE SUMMARY.
(Erase heading not required.)

Instructions regarding War Diaries and Intelligence Summaries are contained in F.S. Regs., Part II. and the Staff Manual respectively. Title pages will be prepared in manuscript.

Place	Date	Hour	Summary of Events and Information	Remarks and references to Appendices
	3/7/16	(con)	2nd Lieut. E.H. Seymour and one Non-Commissioned Officer per Company attended a course of Instruction in Bayonet Fighting, Instruction in Barting and Lewis Gunnery continued.	
	4/7/16		In Billets at AUMONT. The Battalion route marched. Instruction in Barting and Lewis Gunnery continued.	
	5/7/16		In Billets at AUMONT. Divine Service in the morning.	
	6/7/16		In Billets at AUMONT. The Battalion went to bathe at HORNOY during the day. No 1 Company had Company and Platoon Drill in the morning from 11 a.m. to 12 noon. No 2 Company fired on the Range.	

Army Form C. 2118.

WAR DIARY
or
INTELLIGENCE SUMMARY.
(Erase heading not required.)

Instructions regarding War Diaries and Intelligence Summaries are contained in F. S. Regs., Part II. and the Staff Manual respectively. Title pages will be prepared in manuscript.

Place	Date	Hour	Summary of Events and Information	Remarks and references to Appendices
	6/10	(10a)	N° 4 Company paraded for Drill at 9 a.m. Instruction in Bombing and Lewis Gunnery continued. Captain J. St. C. Rose transferred to 3rd Battalion.	
	7/10		In billets at AUMONT. N° 4 Company used the Bombing grounds during the morning. N° 1, 2, and 3 Companies practised an attack. Instruction in Bombing and Lewis Gunnery continued. Orders received for leaving the present billets on 10th inst.	
	8/10		In billets at AUMONT. The 1st Line Transport left AUMONT at 9.15 am to proceed by road to the 14th Corps area. Companies were at the disposal of Company Commanders.	

WAR DIARY or INTELLIGENCE SUMMARY

Army Form C. 2118.

Instructions regarding War Diaries and Intelligence Summaries are contained in F. S. Regs., Part II. and the Staff Manual respectively. Title pages will be prepared in manuscript.

(Erase heading not required.)

Place	Date	Hour	Summary of Events and Information	Remarks and references to Appendices
	9/10		In Billets at AUMONT. The Battalion route marched. Instruction in Lewis Gunnery continued.	
	10/10		The Battalion left AUMONT by buses and by the french Government at 10. a.m. and delivered at a point between TREUX and MERICOURT at 4 p.m. and marched via MEAULTE to the Citadel Camp, arriving at 7 p.m. The journey to the Camp was a frightful condition owing to mud & many breakdowns.	
	11/10		In Camp at the Citadel. Day spent in cleaning arms and clothes.	
	12/10		In Camp at the Citadel. Voluntary Divine Service in the morning. The Battalion paraded at 2.30 p.m. and marched to	

WAR DIARY
or
INTELLIGENCE SUMMARY.

(Erase heading not required.)

Army Form C. 2118.

Instructions regarding War Diaries and Intelligence Summaries are contained in F. S. Regs., Part II. and the Staff Manual respectively. Title pages will be prepared in manuscript.

Place	Date	Hour	Summary of Events and Information	Remarks and references to Appendices
	12/7/16 (con)		"H.1" Camp near MONTAUBAN, arriving about 4 p.m. Roads and cross country tracks very much cut up and muddy which made marching very difficult. The huts in this Camp are the best encountered by this Battalion.	
	13/7/16		In "H.1." Camp. Batteries at disposal of Company Commanders	
	14/7/16		In "H.1" Camp. Day spent in drawing and repairing Camp. A party of 34 O.R. & 6 O.P. was proceeded to Brigade Headquarters as a Working Reconnaissance Line 9 & D Kilcen.	
	15/7/16		The Battalion marched at 1.30 p.m. to Camps "A" and "B" at TRONES WOOD, arriving about 3.30 p.m.	

Army Form C. 2118.

WAR DIARY
or
INTELLIGENCE SUMMARY
(Erase heading not required.)

Instructions regarding War Diaries and Intelligence Summaries are contained in F.S. Regs., Part II. and the Staff Manual respectively. Title pages will be prepared in manuscript.

Place	Date	Hour	Summary of Events and Information	Remarks and references to Appendices
	15/10	(a.m.)	No one except waterproof shelters erected over shell-holes. A very short post at night. 1st Bn Grenadier Guards in adjoining Camp.	
			In Camps "A" and "B"	
	16/10		The morning spent in cleaning Camp and collecting salvage — tents, ammunition etc, which was very plentiful. The Battalion marched at 2 p.m. to relieve the 1st Bn Coldm Gds Guards holding the made Right Sector between LES BOEUFS and GUEUDECOURT. No communication trenches, but a good relief owing to the frosty condition of the ground. N⁰ˢ 1 and 3 Companies in the front line, N⁰ 4 in Supports and N⁰ 2 in Reserve. The front line held by succession of small posts connected up by Battalion Headquarters at T 30. B 37. Trench Map France 57 & 8H. Edition 4a. Casualties during relief Nil. Working parties had 2 men killed and 2 men wounded by	

T2134. Wt. W708—776. 500000. 4/15. Sir J.C. & S.

WAR DIARY
or
INTELLIGENCE SUMMARY

(Erase heading not required.)

Army Form C. 2118.

Place	Date	Hour	Summary of Events and Information	Remarks and references to Appendices
	16/16 (cont)		the officers of a battalion being one Lieut & 20 killed & wounded.	
	17/16		In the line as above. Still cold and hazy. A very trying time — no communication with the front Companies possible by day. Difficulties of getting up rations and troops regiments very great. Very little shelter for the bulk of the men — a good deal of shelling. Casualties, nil.	
	18/16		In the line as above. Snow fell during the early morning, changing to sleet, rain and a thaw later. One of the worst trying days the battalion has experienced during the campaign, owing to the sea of mud caused by the sudden thaw. Difficulties of maintaining rations and supplies much increased	

WAR DIARY
or
INTELLIGENCE SUMMARY

Army Form C. 2118.

Place	Date	Hour	Summary of Events and Information	Remarks and references to Appendices
	18/7		had been carefully laid down way owing to the impossibility of distinguishing them. A considerable amount of clothing, particularly air raid 2 & No 3 Company's drab Casualties. 4 men killed, 2 wounded and 1 chap of wounded, the later remained at duty.	
	19/7		As the line was much as above. Much shelling along the front line & No 1 Company who particularly for which no having to fat casualties. The Battalion was relieved during the evening by the 2nd Batn Irish Guards. A long and difficult relief and was absolutely exhausted. The Battalion marched to H.1. Camp, MONTAUBAN, the last to arrive having about 6.2 am 20th. Hot food and dry canteen (for few) provided for the men as arrived in Camp.	

T.2134. Wt. W708—776. 500000. 4/15. Sir J. C. & S.

WAR DIARY
or
INTELLIGENCE SUMMARY.

(Erase heading not required.)

Army Form C. 2118.

Instructions regarding War Diaries and Intelligence Summaries are contained in F. S. Regs., Part II. and the Staff Manual respectively. Title pages will be prepared in manuscript.

Place	Date	Hour	Summary of Events and Information	Remarks and references to Appendices
	19/7/16		Captain B. St Newton M.C. slightly wounded but remained at Duty. 2 men wounded and 3 slightly wounded, the latter remained at Duty. 2 men "missing".	
	20/7/16		In "H.1" Camp, MONTAUBAN. The Battalion slept until midday. The remainder was spent in cleaning clothes, rifles and equipment which were plastered with mud.	
	21/7/16		The Battalion marched from "H.1" Camp at 9.30 a.m. to billets in MEAULTE arriving about 12.30 p.m.	
	22/7/16		In Billets at MEAULTE. The Battalion was employed in cleaning equipment and billets. The latter were very dirty. Captain B. St Newton admitted to Hospital.	

WAR DIARY
or
INTELLIGENCE SUMMARY

(Erase heading not required.)

Army Form C. 2118.

Place	Date	Hour	Summary of Events and Information	Remarks and references to Appendices
	22/7/16		In billets at MEAULTE The Battalion practiced Bayonet Drill and Arm Drill under Company arrangements	
	24/7/16		In Billets at MEAULTE The Battalion paraded for Brigade Billiard and Arms Drill at 9 a.m. A draft of 80 other ranks joined in the evening.	
	25/7/16		In Billets at MEAULTE The Brigadier inspected the Battalions Billets at 10 a.m. No 1 Company practiced Bombing and Lewis Gunnery No 2 Company practiced Bombing and Arm Drill No 3 Company found a party of 50 other ranks for road improvements. The remainder of the Company did Physical Drill Bayonet fighting & No 4 Company route marched.	

Army Form C. 2118.

WAR DIARY
or
INTELLIGENCE SUMMARY.
(Erase heading not required.)

Instructions regarding War Diaries and Intelligence Summaries are contained in F. S. Regs., Part II. and the Staff Manual respectively. Title pages will be prepared in manuscript.

Place	Date	Hour	Summary of Events and Information	Remarks and references to Appendices
	26/6		In Billets at MEAULTE. Snow service in the morning. No. 4 Company found a party of 50 other ranks for road improvement.	
	27/6		In Billets at MEAULTE. No. 1 Company found a party of 55 other ranks for road improvement. The remainder of the Battalion did P.T. & prac. drill. Bayonet fighting, etc. No. 2 Company received lewis Gunnery and Bombing. No. 3 Company route marched. No. 4 Company practised Bombing and rail drill.	
	28/6		In Billets at MEAULTE. The Battalion used the baths at VILLE during the day. No. 2 Company found the party for road improvement.	

Army Form C. 2118.

WAR DIARY
or
INTELLIGENCE SUMMARY.
(Erase heading not required.)

Instructions regarding War Diaries and Intelligence Summaries are contained in F.S. Regs, Part II. and the Staff Manual respectively. Title pages will be prepared in manuscript.

Place	Date	Hour	Summary of Events and Information	Remarks and references to Appendices
	28/7/16		No. 3 Company practised Company and Arm Drill.	
	29/7/16		In Billets at MEAULTE. No. 3 Company found the party for Road improvement (55 other ranks). The remainder of the Company practised Physical Drill and Bayonet fighting. No. 2 Company practised Company and Arm Drill. No. 1 Company route marched. Part of No. 4 Company had instruction in Lewis Gunnery the remainder of the Company was at the disposal of the Company Commander.	
	30/7/16		In Billets at MEAULTE. No. 4 Company found the party for road improvements the remainder of the Company practised Physical Drill and Bayonet fighting	

Army Form C. 2118.

WAR DIARY
or
INTELLIGENCE SUMMARY.
(Erase heading not required.)

Instructions regarding War Diaries and Intelligence Summaries are contained in F. S. Regs., Part II. and the Staff Manual respectively. Title pages will be prepared in manuscript.

Place	Date	Hour	Summary of Events and Information	Remarks and references to Appendices
	30/6 (con)		No. 2 Company route marched.	
			No. 1 and 3 Companies practised Company Drill.	

W Noel
Maj/r Lieutenant Colonel,
Comdg 2nd Bn. Grenadier Guards.

1st Guards Brigade.
Guards Division.

2nd BATTALION

GRENADIER GUARDS.

JULY 1916

------2nd Battalion Grenadier Guards.------

WAR DIARY FOR THE

MONTH ENDING

---31st July, 1916.---

Army Form C. 2118.

WAR DIARY
or
INTELLIGENCE SUMMARY
(Erase heading not required.)

Instructions regarding War Diaries and Intelligence Summaries are contained in F. S. Regs., Part II. and the Staff Manual respectively. Title Pages will be prepared in manuscript.

Place	Date	Hour	Summary of Events and Information	Remarks and references to Appendices
	1/7/16		In Camps "G" and "P", (A.15.a.8.4. and A.15.d.5.4 Sheet 28 respectively). Companies did Drill and Training.	
	2/7/16		In Camps as above. Companies did Drill and Training.	
	3/7/16		In Camps as above. Companies did Drill and Training in the morning, and, in the afternoon, played a cricket match against the Cyclist Battalion, which was quartered in a neighbouring Camp.	
	4/7/16		In Camps as above. Very heavy rain and no training possible. The Commanding Officer and Adjutant rode over to a Brigade Conference, where they received information concerning future operations.	
	5/7/16		In Camps as above. Inspection by the Corps Commander, Lieutenant General F.R. the Earl of Cavan, G.B., M.V.O., put off owing to the bad state of the ground. The relief was also postponed for twenty four hours.	
	6/7/16		In Camps as above. The Corps Commander inspected the Battalion in a field near Camp "P" at 10 a.m. The turnout of the Battalion could not have been better and the men looked magnificent. After the inspection, the Corps Commander addressed the Battalion,	

Army Form C. 2118.

WAR DIARY
or
INTELLIGENCE SUMMARY

(Erase heading not required.)

Instructions regarding War Diaries and Intelligence Summaries are contained in F. S. Regs., Part II. and the Staff Manual respectively. Title Pages will be prepared in manuscript.

Place	Date	Hour	Summary of Events and Information	Remarks and references to Appendices
	6/7/16 (Continued)		congratulating the men on their smartness and hinting at operations in the near future, and said he knew the Battalion would do as well in the future as it had done in the past. Major E.N.E.M. Vaughan left the Battalion on transfer to the 1st Battalion Grenadier Guards. The Battalion marched at 8.0 p.m. to relieve the 1st Battalion Grenadier Guards on the Canal Bank, south of Bridge 4, C.25.D.2.4, Sheet 28. During the night, the 4th Battalion Grenadier Guards had an enterprise against Canadian Dugouts occupied by the enemy, which was a failure. Casualties, NIL.	
In Dugouts on the Canal Bank.	7/7/16		The Battalion left at 6.30 p.m. to relieve the 4th Battalion Grenadier Guards in the line, (Irish Farm) C.21, A, B and D, Sheet 28. Relief complete by 1.0 a.m. No. 4 Company on the left No. 2 in the Centre, No. 1 on the Right, and No.3 in support. Battalion Headquarters situated in the "X" Line, close to Irish Farm. This is one of the worst positions we have taken over, and the other Brigades have evidently not attempted to remedy it in any way. The trenches were all very shallow, full of water and not joined up. There are not any communication trenches. Casualties, NIL.	
In the Line as above.	8/7/16		During the morning, the enemy sent a few small shells on No. 4 Company, and seven or eight	

2449 Wt. W14957/M90 750,000 1/16 J.B.C. & A. Forms/C.2118/12.

Army Form C. 2118.

WAR DIARY
or
INTELLIGENCE SUMMARY

(Erase heading not required.)

Instructions regarding War Diaries and Intelligence
Summaries are contained in F.S. Regs., Part II.
and the Staff Manual respectively. Title Pages
will be prepared in manuscript.

Place	Date	Hour	Summary of Events and Information	Remarks and references to Appendices
	8/7/16 (Continued)		5" shells round Irish Farm. A very hot day. During the afternoon, a German aeroplane dropped a bomb about 500 yards from Battalion Headquarters the bomb fell near the Headquarters of the 3rd Battalion Coldstream Guards, who are on our left. Casualties, 4 men wounded and 1 slightly wounded the latter remained at Duty. 2nd Lieutenant A. McW. Lawson-Johnston joined the Battalion.	
	9/7/16		In the Line as above. Comparatively a quiet day. Casualties, 6 N.C.Os and men wounded, and Captain A.K.S. Cunningname slightly wounded.	
	10/7/16		In the line as above. A quiet day. Captain and Adjutant Hon. W.R. Bailey, Sergeant Major H. Wood and five N.C.Os and men left at 4.0 p.m. to join the British Detachment ordered to proceed to PARIS for the 14th July Fete. Casualties, 2 men wounded.	
	11/7/16		In the Line as above. The Battalion was relieved by the 1st Battalion Irish Guards, commencing at 10.0 p.m. and returned to dugouts on the Canal Bank, as before. Owing to the noise made by the Irish Guards, the enemy sent over some field gun shells, which caused some casualties in the relieving Battalion. Casualties, 6 N.C.Os and men wounded.	

Army Form C. 2118.

WAR DIARY
or
INTELLIGENCE SUMMARY

(Erase heading not required.)

Instructions regarding War Diaries and Intelligence Summaries are contained in F. S. Regs., Part II. and the Staff Manual respectively. Title Pages will be prepared in manuscript.

Place	Date	Hour	Summary of Events and Information	Remarks and references to Appendices
	12/7/16		In dugouts on the Canal Bank. Captain H.G.C. Viscount Lascelles joined the Battalion as Second in Command. Casualties, 1 man (attached 1st Guards Brigade T.M. Battery) killed and 1 wounded.	
	13/7/16		On the Canal Bank. During the night, a party of 200 men was out digging. Casualties, 1 man wounded.	
	14/7/16		On the Canal Bank. During the night, a party of 200 men was out digging. Casualties, 1 man killed and 2 men wounded.	
	15/7/16		On the Canal Bank. The Battalion relieved the 1st Battalion Irish Guards leaving the Canal Bank at 10.0 p.m. A quiet relief. Casualties, NIL.	
	16/7/16		In the line as before. A quiet day. During the night, Lieutenant A.F. Irvine reconnoitred Canadian Dugouts with a small patrol. Casualties, NIL.	
	17/7/16		In the Line. The centre Company was shelled during the morning. During the night, Lieut. A.F. Irvine took out a patrol and Lieut. T. Parker-Jervis also took out a patrol, but neither party managed to secure a German, although the information obtained was very useful. Casualties, 1 man wounded.	

2449 Wt. W14957/M90 750,000 1/16 J.B.C. & A. Forms/C.2118/12.

Army Form C. 2118.

WAR DIARY
or
INTELLIGENCE SUMMARY

(Erase heading not required.)

Instructions regarding War Diaries and Intelligence Summaries are contained in F.S. Regs., Part II. and the Staff Manual respectively. Title Pages will be prepared in manuscript.

Place	Date	Hour	Summary of Events and Information	Remarks and references to Appendices
	18/7/16		In the Line. Patrols went out under the same officers as the previous night. A very quiet day. Captain Hon. W.R. Bailey and party returned from the PARIS Review during the evening. Casualties, 4 men wounded.	
	19/7/16		In the Line. During the night, Lieutenant M.H. MacMillan went out on a reconnoitring patrol with two men. A German sentry threw a bomb, wounding one man and slightly wounding Lieut. MacMillan in the head and back. This officer remained at Duty. Lieut. A.F. Irvine took out a strong patrol to examine the wire in front of Canadian Dugouts, and, on their return, were bombed by a patrol from No. 1 Company, but no damage was done. Captain A.F.R. Wiggins, laid out on Admiral's Road, but saw no enemy patrol. About 11.0 a.m. there was heavy artillery fire on our left by our guns, to which the enemy replied on the Goldstream's line with heavy Minenwerfer. During the afternoon, No. 3 Company was shelled by Field Guns, which ceased when our artillery retaliated. Relieved by the 1st Battalion Irish Guards, relief completed by 12.30 a.m. and returned to Canal Bank. There is a great difference in the line now, and the Companies have done a tremendous amount of work. The Major General and the Brigadier have congratulated the Battalion on the great improvement to the line. Two platoons of No. 4 Company went to FRASCATI POST. Casualties, 4 men wounded.	

Army Form C. 2118.

WAR DIARY
or
INTELLIGENCE SUMMARY

(Erase heading not required.)

Instructions regarding War Diaries and Intelligence Summaries are contained in F. S. Regs., Part II. and the Staff Manual respectively. Title Pages will be prepared in manuscript.

Place	Date	Hour	Summary of Events and Information	Remarks and references to Appendices
	20/7/16		In dugouts on the Canal Bank. A quiet day. Casualties, NIL.	
	21/7/16		On the Canal Bank. During the night, 200 men were out digging under the R.E. Casualties, 1 man wounded.	
	22/7/16		In dugouts on the Canal Bank. The Battalion left at 9.45 p.m. to relive the 1st Battalion Irish Guards in the Line as before. No. 3 Company on the left, No. 4 Centre, No. 1 on the right, and No. 2 in support. Relief complete about 11.30 p.m. Rations were sent up to LA BRIQUE and carried up from there, so as not to delay the relief. Very heavy artillery fire all night a long way to the south. Captain M.K.A. Lloyd joined the Battalion. Casualties, NIL.	
	23/7/16		In the Line. A quiet night on our front. No. 1 Company had two listening patrols out all night, but did not see any Germans. The trenches were handed over to us in a very bad state. There was a good "gassing" Breeze all day in the enemy's favour. The Major General and Brigadier went round the whole of our line about 9.30 a.m. The Major General was much struck at the improvement in the line. From 12 noon to 12.30 p.m. the "X" Line and Battalion Headquarters were shelled by a 6 inch gun on the Railway somewhere in front of RAILWAY WOOD. One dugout was blown in and one man of the advanced	

Army Form C. 2118.

WAR DIARY
or
INTELLIGENCE SUMMARY

(*Erase heading not required.*)

Instructions regarding War Diaries and Intelligence Summaries are contained in F. S. Regs., Part II. and the Staff Manual respectively. Title Pages will be prepared in manuscript.

Place	Date	Hour	Summary of Events and Information	Remarks and references to Appendices
	23/7/16 (Continued)		platoons of the Irish Guards killed. Otherwise a quiet day. 3rd Battalion Coldstream Guards on our left and the Sherwood Foresters on our right. Orders received that the Division will be relieved 27th-29th inst, and rumours we are bound for the south. Casualties, 1 man slightly wounded, who remained at Duty.	
	24/7/16		In the Line. A very quiet day. Coldstreams badly knocked about by aerial torpedoes. Almost all our big shells fired in retaliation were "blind". 2nd Lieutenant G.A. Arbuthnot was out all night with five snipers, but did not see any of the enemy. No. 1 Company sent out two patrols under N.C.Os, who did not see any of the enemy, but heard a good deal of work going on. About 10 a.m. the 6 inch gun fired a few shells on the "X" Line, but did not do any damage. The remainder of the day was quiet. At 2.0 p.m. No. 10371, Sergeant J. Lyon, of No. 1 Company, went in to "No man's Land" and came in about 8.0 p.m. bringing with him a German flag, which he had taken from a tree opposite WIELTJE, and he also gained some good information. Casualties, 2 wounded and 1 slightly wounded, the latter remained at Duty.	
	25/7/16		In the Line. A very quiet day. The Brigadier came up about 4.0 p.m. with the Brigade Major of the 4th Division and went round the line. The Battalion Snipers had a good day.	

Army Form C. 2118.

WAR DIARY or INTELLIGENCE SUMMARY

(Erase heading not required.)

Instructions regarding War Diaries and Intelligence Summaries are contained in F.S. Regs., Part II and the Staff Manual respectively. Title Pages will be prepared in manuscript.

Place	Date	Hour	Summary of Events and Information	Remarks and references to Appendices
	25/7/16 (Continued)		The 1st Battalion Irish Guards relieved us, commencing at 9.45 p.m. - relief complete by 12.30 a.m. The Battalion returned to dugouts on the Canal Bank. No. 2 Company leaving two advanced platoons in the "X" Line. Casualties, 1 man wounded.	
	26/7/16		In dugouts on the Canal Bank. About 10.30 a.m. the enemy fired a few small shells (shrapnel) killing one man. 2nd Lieutenant G.A. Arbuthnot and billeting party left at 12 noon for Camp "K". Advanced party of Lieutenant M.H. Macmillan and Drill Sergeant went on to HERZEELE. Relieved by the 1st Battalion Royal Warwicks about 9.30 p.m. The Battalion marched at 11.30 p.m. to the Asylum Siding, YPRES, waiting therefor two hours before entraining, detrained at L5 Central, west of POPERINGHE, and marched to Camp "K", all in Camp by 2.45 a.m.	
	27/7/16		Battalion left Camp "K" at 2.5 p.m. and marched via JAN DER BIETZEN, WATOU, and HOUTKERQUE to billets round HERZEELE. Companies in good billets, but very scattered. Battalion Headquarters in HERZEELE. A very hot and dusty march.	
	28/7/16		In Billets round HERZEELE. Three Companies bathed in the afternoon and received new underclothing. A very hot day.	

Army Form C. 2118.

WAR DIARY
or
INTELLIGENCE SUMMARY
(Erase heading not required.)

Instructions regarding War Diaries and Intelligence Summaries are contained in F. S. Regs., Part II. and the Staff Manual respectively. Title Pages will be prepared in manuscript.

Place	Date	Hour	Summary of Events and Information	Remarks and references to Appendices
	29/7/16		In Billets as above. No. 1 Company had baths in the morning. The Divisional Disinfector commenced going round Companies at 6.0 a.m. for the purpose of cleaning Service Dress. Billeting Party under 2nd Lieutenant G.A. Arbuthnot left at 2.30 p.m. to entrain at PROVEN en route for ST. POL.	
	30/7/16		No. 1 Company and the 1st Line Transport left Billets at 12.30 a.m. for PROVEN. The remainder of the Battalion marched at 2.45 a.m. viz HOUTKERQUE to PROVEN, arriving at the place of entrainment at 5.30 a.m. where the troops had breakfasts. The train left at 6.0 a.m. via HAZEBROUCK for ST. POL, arriving at the latter place about noon. We proceeded from St. POL to BOUQUEMAISON by motor lorries and marched to billets in NEUVILLETTE, where we arrived at 3.0 p.m. The billets were rather bad and very close, but the weather is very hot, and the men are mostly sleeping in the open.	
	31/7/16		In Billets at NEUVILLETTE. A very hot day. Companies had inspections of feet, rifles and smoke helmets. Captain C.N. Newton, Leicestershire Yeomanry, T.F. and five other ranks joined the Battalion.	

C.E. Corkran? Lieutenant Colonel
Commanding 2nd Battalion Grenadier Guards.

1st Guards Brigade.
Guards Division.

2nd BATTALION

GRENADIER GUARDS.

JUNE 1916

---2nd Battalion Grenadier Guards.---

-----W A R   D I A R Y-----

for the month ending 30th June, 1916.

Army Form C. 2118.

WAR DIARY
or
INTELLIGENCE SUMMARY

(Erase heading not required.)

Instructions regarding War Diaries and Intelligence Summaries are contained in F. S. Regs., Part II. and the Staff Manual respectively. Title Pages will be prepared in manuscript.

Place	Date	Hour	Summary of Events and Information	Remarks and references to Appendices
	1-6-16		In Billets at TATINGHEM. Companies did Drill and Training.	
	2-6-16		In Billets at TATINGHEM. Companies did Drill and Training.	
	3-6-16		In Billets at TATINGHEM. Companies did Drill and Training.	
	4-6-16		In Billets at TATINGHEM. Companies did Drill and Training.	
	5-6-16		In Billets at TATINGHEM. Companies did Drill and Training.	
	6-5-16		In Billets at TATINGHEM. A very wet day. We heard that the Canadians had lost HOOGE and OBSERVATION RIDGE.	
	7-6-16		The Battalion left TATINGHEM at 8.0 a.m. and marched to St. SYLVESTRE, via FORT ROUGE and STAPLE, arriving at 3.0 p.m. A hot day and long march, some men were rather foot-sore, but none were left behind.	
	8-6-16		Left ST. SYLVESTRE at 8.0 a.m. and marched to Camp "M", near POPERINGHE,-arriving at 11.30 a.m 2nd Lieut. J. Arbuthnott and forty other ranks detached to WATOU for Examining Posts. No. 2 Company left by the 9.30 p.m. train from POPERINGHE to billet in BRIELEN, as a permanent night fatigue for Cable Laying.	

2449 Wt. W14957/Mgo 750,000 1/16 J.B.C. & A. Forms/C.2118/12.

Army Form C. 2118.

WAR DIARY
or
INTELLIGENCE SUMMARY

(Erase heading not required.)

Instructions regarding War Diaries and Intelligence Summaries are contained in F. S. Regs., Part II. and the Staff Manual respectively. Title Pages will be prepared in manuscript.

Place	Date	Hour	Summary of Events and Information	Remarks and references to Appendices
	9-6-16		In Camp as above.	
	10-6-16		In Camp as above. No. 4 Company found a Fatigue Party of one hundred men to construct huts near Corps Headquarters.	
	11-6-16		In Camp as above. No. 1 Company constructing huts near Corps Headquarters. A wet day. 2nd Lieutenant E.G. Stirling joined.	
	12-6-16		In Camp as above. A very wet day with a good deal of wind. No. 3 Company found a party of one hundred and fifty men to billet for the night near ELVERDINGHE for cable laying. No. 2 Company still at BRIELEN. Nos.-1 and 4 Companies left Camp at 8.30 p.m. in motor lorries for cable laying near ST. JEAN.	
	13-6-16		In Camp as above. Nos. 1 and 4 Companies arrived back at Camp about 3.0 a.m. Pouring with rain. No. 3 Company returned from ELVERDINGHE during the evening, as, owing to the construction of the huts, billetting there was almost impossible this weather.	
	14-6-16		In Camp as above. Nos. 1 and 4 Companies were on Cable laying fatigue.	

2449 Wt. W14957/M90 750,000 1/16 J.B.C. & A. Forms/C.2118/12.

Army Form C. 2118.

WAR DIARY
or
INTELLIGENCE SUMMARY

(Erase heading not required.)

Instructions regarding War Diaries and Intelligence Summaries are contained in F. S. Regs., Part II. and the Staff Manual respectively. Title Pages will be prepared in manuscript.

Place	Date	Hour	Summary of Events and Information	Remarks and references to Appendices
	14/6/16 (Continued)		Captain E.W.M. Grigg, G.S.O.3, of the Division, gave a lecture on "Intelligence" at Battalion Headquarters at 2.30 p.m. Casualties, one man of No. 2 Company killed.	
	15-6-16		In Camp as above. Nos. 3 and 4 Companies on Cable laying fatigue. No. 2 Company returned from BRIELEN about 4.0.a.m. Weather improving. Captain G.G.F. Harcourt-Vernon, Lieut. H.F.C. Crookshank, Lieut. Hon. M.E.H. Towneley, Bertie and 2nd Lieut. R.E.H. Oliver and four other ranks joined the Battalion. 2nd Lieut. J. Arbuthnott and forty other ranks rejoined from WATOU.	
	16-6-16		In Camp as above. A fine day. The Battalion left Camp at 7.45 p.m. and marched via POPERINGHE to billets in ELVERDINGHE. No. 1 Company billeted in Camp "J", (A.8.b.8.7., Sheet 28). Nos. 2, 3, and 4 Companies arrived at new billets about 10.30 p.m. Battalion Headquarters situated in the CHATEAU, ELVERDINGHE.	
	17-6-16.		In Billets at ELVERDINGHE.	

Army Form C. 2118.

WAR DIARY
or
INTELLIGENCE SUMMARY
(Erase heading not required.)

Instructions regarding War Diaries and Intelligence Summaries are contained in F. S. Regs., Part II. and the Staff Manual respectively. Title Pages will be prepared in manuscript.

Place	Date	Hour	Summary of Events and Information	Remarks and references to Appendices
	18-6-16		In Billets as above. Divine Service was held in the morning. Nos. 3 and 4 Companies left billets at 9.30 p.m. to relieve two Companies of the 3rd Guards-Bde on the CANAL BANK, east of BRIELEN. No. 1 Company move from Camp "J" and took over the billets, which had been occupied by No. 3 Company. Lieutenant P.M. Walker joined the Battalion.	
	19-6-16		In Billets as above.	
	20-6-16		In Billets as above. The Battalion relieved the 1st Battalion Irish Guards, commencing at midnight in the LANCASHIRE FARM line, C.13 d - C.14 d, Sheet 28, N.W. No. 3 Company on the right, No. 2 in the Centre, and No. 4 on the left, and No. 1 in support with one platoon on the CANAL BANK, near Battalion Headquarters. Coldstream Guards on our left, and Welsh Guards on our right. Battalion Headquarters, C.19.c. Casualties, NIL.	
	21-6-16		In the Line as above. A quiet day. A few small shells on the CANAL Banks, and our right Company. Casualties, NIL.	

Army Form C. 2118.

WAR DIARY
or
INTELLIGENCE SUMMARY
(Erase heading not required.)

Instructions regarding War Diaries and Intelligence Summaries are contained in F. S. Regs., Part II. and the Staff Manual respectively. Title Pages will be prepared in manuscript.

Place	Date	Hour	Summary of Events and Information	Remarks and references to Appendices
	22-6-16		In the Line as above. Heavy sniping and machine gun fire all night. A quiet day. Casualties, 1 N.C.O killed and one man wounded.	
	23-6-16		In the Line as above. Heavy sniping and machine gun fire during the night, which was effectually stopped by fifty rounds from the Stokes Guns of the Brigade. Casualties, one man wounded.	
	26-6-16		In the Line as above. Our Artillery commenced a bombardment at 9.0 a.m. - heavy guns on KRUPP FARM and to the north of it, field guns cutting the wire in several places on the enemy's front. The enemy retalliated on our front line and on the Coldstream support Companies on the CANAL BANK to the north of us. Relieved by the 1st Battalion Irish Guards, relief commencing at 10 p.m. Nos. 1 and 2 Companies went into "dug-outs" on the CANAL BANK. Battalion Headquarters, Nos. 3 and 4 Companies marched to ELVERDINGHE. Casualties, 1 N.C.O killed, 4 men wounded and 3 slightly wounded, the latter remained at Duty. Some delay was caused during the relief owing to our limbers being blocked by artillery wagons.	
	25-6-16		In Billets and dugouts as above. Leave granted to men to bathe in the Lake in the grounds of the Chateau. The enemy dropped six "Universal" shells over the lake. One man was	

Army Form C. 2118.

WAR DIARY
or
INTELLIGENCE SUMMARY
(Erase heading not required.)

Instructions regarding War Diaries and Intelligence Summaries are contained in F. S. Regs., Part II. and the Staff Manual respectively. Title Pages will be prepared in manuscript.

Place	Date	Hour	Summary of Events and Information	Remarks and references to Appendices
	26-6-16		very slightly hit. During the evening, a field gun shells fell round the Chateaus	
	27-6-16		In Billets and dugouts as above. A quiet day. A few small shells fell in the grounds of the Chateau during the evening.	
			In Billets and dugouts as above. A very wet morning. The Battalion was relieved by the 1st Battalion Coldstream Guards. Headquarter and Nos. 3 and 4 Companies marched at 10 p.m. to Camp "G" (A.16.a.8.4., Sheet 28) arriving about 11.30 p.m. Roads very bad for marching. The relief of Nos. 1 and 2 Companies delayed until 12.30 a.m. They arrived at Camp "P" (A.15.d.5.4.) about 3.15 a.m.	
	28-6-16		In Camps as above. Weather improving.	
	29-6-16		In Camps as above. Companies did Drill and Training.	
	30-6-16		In Camps as above. Companies did Drill and Training.	

Lieutenant Colonel,
Commanding 2nd Battalion Grenadier Guards.

1st Brigade.
Guards Division.

2nd BATTALION

GRENADIER GUARDS.

DECEMBER 1 9 1 6

WAR DIARY or INTELLIGENCE SUMMARY.

Army Form C. 2118.

2nd Grenadier Guards.

December 1916.

Place	Date	Hour	Summary of Events and Information	Remarks and references to Appendices
	1/12/16		In billets at MEAULTE. No.1 Coy detailed a party of 25 men for road improvements. No. 2 and Coys practised Arm and Company Drill. No. 3 Coy route marched. Company next detailed 9 of N.C.O's and men to undergo Brigade Bombing Test.	
	2/12/16		The Battalion marched at 9.15 a.m. via BRAY to trench camp No. 108, BRONFAY arriving about noon.	
	3/12/16		In trench camp 108. Divine service in the morning.	
	4/12/16		The Battalion marched at 12 noon to trench camp 15 just north west of BRONFAY (about 500 yards from Camp 108).	

Army Form C. 2118.

WAR DIARY
or
INTELLIGENCE SUMMARY.
(Erase heading not required.)

Instructions regarding War Diaries and Intelligence Summaries are contained in F.S. Regs., Part II. and the Staff Manual respectively. Title pages will be prepared in manuscript.

Place	Date	Hour	Summary of Events and Information	Remarks and references to Appendices
	5/7/16		In Camp 12. Companies practised Company and Arm Drill and Musketry.	
	6/7/16		The Battalion marched at 1.30 p.m. to MALTZHORN Camp, near TRONESWOOD, arriving about 4.30 p.m. Camp consisted of tents - ground in a bad state owing to lack of drainage.	
	7/7/16		In MALTZHORN Camp. Battalion employed in cleaning and draining Camp and laying trench boards.	
	8/7/16		The Battalion marched at 1.30 p.m. to COMBLES to relieve 1st Bn. Coldstream Guards, one Company in dugouts at HAIEWOOD, the remainder of the Battalion in dugouts in and	

Army Form C. 2118.

WAR DIARY
or
INTELLIGENCE SUMMARY.
(Erase heading not required.)

Instructions regarding War Diaries and Intelligence Summaries are contained in F. S. Regs., Part II. and the Staff Manual respectively. Title pages will be prepared in manuscript.

Place	Date	Hour	Summary of Events and Information	Remarks and references to Appendices
	8/12/16 (con)		about COMBLES. A party of 200 men was found for fatigue during the night. The 1st Guards Brigade is now in the Right group under command of Br Genl Lord Henry Seymour, D.S.O., 4th & 6th and Guards Brigade much rain during the night.	
	9/12/16		In COMBLES. The battalion did four hours work in the morning. Relieved 1st Bn Irish Guards in SAILLY-SAILLISEL- sector right Sector of the Division. A very long and difficult relief. No. 2 and 4 Companies in the front line, No. 3 in support near the Battalion HQ, No. 1 in Reserve with Battalion Headquarters in the Prairie. Trenches in a very bad state, the front line was most continuous and water was knee-deep in the trenches Casualties Nil.	

Army Form C. 2118.

WAR DIARY
or
INTELLIGENCE SUMMARY.
(Erase heading not required.)

Instructions regarding War Diaries and Intelligence Summaries are contained in F. S. Regs., Part II. and the Staff Manual respectively. Title pages will be prepared in manuscript.

Place	Date	Hour	Summary of Events and Information	Remarks and references to Appendices
	10/7/16		In the line as above. Improvement of trenches carried on as far as possible, but rain rendered it impossible to make any appreciable improvement. Enemy shelled left of front line, causing some casualties. Casualties, one N.C.O. and one man killed.	
	11/7/16		In the line as above. Relieved by 2nd Bn. Irish Guards. All ranks much exhausted by the condition of the trenches and the heavy fatigues which preceded the tour in the trenches. The Battalion rendez-voused at HAIE WOOD and marched to MALTZHORN Camp, the last men arriving in the early morning of 12th. Casualties, 2 men killed and 3 wounded.	

T2134. Wt. W708-776. 500000. 4/15. Sir J. C. & S.

Army Form C. 2118.

WAR DIARY
or
INTELLIGENCE SUMMARY.
(Erase heading not required.)

Instructions regarding War Diaries and Intelligence Summaries are contained in F. S. Regs., Part II. and the Staff Manual respectively. Title pages will be prepared in manuscript.

Place	Date	Hour	Summary of Events and Information	Remarks and references to Appendices
	12/2/16		In Camp at MALTZHORN. Many men suffering from bad feet as a result of the condition of the trenches. The Battalion marched at 2 p.m. to St I Camp MONTAUBAN, men who were unable to march followed in lorries in charge of an Officer Lieut. (A.D.) Buchanan Jones.	
	13/2/16		In St. I Camp. The day was spent in cleaning arms, equipment and clothing and inspection of feet.	
	14/2/16		Battalion marched at 1 p.m. to COMBLES, relieving 1st Bn Coldstream Guards. Bn. Hd.Qrs. to Reserve Coy. 1st Grand Bois took command of the Right Group. The Battalion found two parties of 60 men each for carrying Casualties. Nil.	

Army Form C. 2118.

WAR DIARY
or
INTELLIGENCE SUMMARY.
(Erase heading not required.)

Instructions regarding War Diaries and Intelligence Summaries are contained in F. S. Regs., Part II. and the Staff Manual respectively. Title pages will be prepared in manuscript.

Place	Date	Hour	Summary of Events and Information	Remarks and references to Appendices
In COMBLES	15/9/16		300 N.C.O's and men detailed for fatigue. The Dug-outs at HAIE WOOD heavily shelled soon after 9 a.m. causing two casualties. Battalion relieved 1st Bn Irish Guards, commencing at 4 p.m. 1st Bn. 1st and 2 Coys in Front Line, No. 2 in Support and No. 4 in Reserve. Trenches almost as bad as before in spite of work during the intervening periods. Casualties, 1 man killed and 2 wounded.	
	16/9/16		In Line as before. Considerable improvements made to supports line and other trenches by making a foundation of timber and rubble from SAILLY. Reserve Company was carrying trench stores during most of the night. Casualties, one man wounded.	

Army Form C. 2118.

WAR DIARY
or
INTELLIGENCE SUMMARY.
(Erase heading not required.)

Instructions regarding War Diaries and Intelligence Summaries are contained in F. S. Regs., Part II. and the Staff Manual respectively. Title pages will be prepared in manuscript.

Place	Date	Hour	Summary of Events and Information	Remarks and references to Appendices
	17/7/16		In line as before. Intermittent rain during the day. Relieved by 2nd Br Irish Guards. A letter relief owing to progress of new line of trench boards from HAIE WOOD towards the Chateau. B[att].n H[ea]d[quarters] was considerably shelled during the relief. Casualties, 1 man killed and 2 men wounded (N[o]. 4 Coy) Battalion marched to TRONES WOOD and entrained there for PLATEAU SIDING and marched from there to French Camp 15, BRONFAY. The last Company arriving at 4.30 a.m. Day spent in resting and inspection of feet.	
	19/7/16		In Camp 15. Day spent in cleaning arms, equipment and clothing.	

WAR DIARY
or
INTELLIGENCE SUMMARY.

(Erase heading not required.)

Army Form C. 2118.

Place	Date	Hour	Summary of Events and Information	Remarks and references to Appendices
	20/7/16		Battalion entrained at PLATEAU SIDING at 1 p.m. for TRONES WOOD and marched from there to COMBLES. One Company is now moved from dug-outs in village of COMBLES to a new line of trenches, which is in course of construction in front of the village. Three hours work done by N$\underline{o}$ 2 Coy on improvement of these trenches. One line of trench boards now complete from HAIE WOOD to support line, and another line now in QUARRY WOOD to support line almost complete.	
			———————//———————	
	21/7/16		In COMBLES. N$\underline{o}$ 1 and 3 Coys on fatigue carrying trench boards to the Chateau. Battalion relieved 1st Irish Guards starting from HAIE WOOD at 4 p.m. — a record relief which was complete by 6.45 p.m. Casualties Nil	
			———————//———————	

Army Form C. 2118.

WAR DIARY
or
INTELLIGENCE SUMMARY.
(Erase heading not required.)

Instructions regarding War Diaries and Intelligence Summaries are contained in F. S. Regs., Part II. and the Staff Manual respectively. Title pages will be prepared in manuscript.

Place	Date	Hour	Summary of Events and Information	Remarks and references to Appendices
	22/7/16		In Line as before. Very little hostile fire and we improved our trenches a good deal, though the sodden condition of the ground made work extremely difficult. The front line still held by isolated parties of trenches. Casualties Nil.	
	23/7/16		In Line as before. Relieved by 2nd Bn. Irish Guards. We were considerably shelled in SAILLY. No. 2 Coy having 1 man killed and 1 man wounded. Entrained at TRONES WOOD for the PLATEAU as before and marched to Camp 15. The better state of the weather has done much to improve the condition of the men, and the Battalion marched back to Camp very well, without any stragglers.	

Army Form C. 2118.

WAR DIARY
or
INTELLIGENCE SUMMARY.
(Erase heading not required.)

Instructions regarding War Diaries and Intelligence Summaries are contained in F. S. Regs., Part II. and the Staff Manual respectively. Title pages will be prepared in manuscript.

Place	Date	Hour	Summary of Events and Information	Remarks and references to Appendices
	24/12/16		In Camp 15. Day spent in cleaning arms, equipment and clothing and inspection of feet.	
	25/12/16		In Camp 15. Divine Service in morning. The Army Commander, Corps Commander, Divisional Commander and Prince of Wales attended also band of Welsh Guards. Christmas Dinner for the men postponed until the Battalion is out of the line.	
	26/12/16		The Battalion proceeded to COMBLES arriving at the PLATEAU at 1 p.m. for TRONES WOOD and marching from there to COMBLES. Brig. Gen. C. E. Pereira left Brigade to take command of 2nd Division.	

T.2134. Wt. W708-776. 50r000. 4/15. Sir J. C. & S.

Army Form C. 2118.

WAR DIARY
or
INTELLIGENCE SUMMARY.
(Erase heading not required.)

Instructions regarding War Diaries and Intelligence Summaries are contained in F.S. Regs., Part II. and the Staff Manual respectively. Title pages will be prepared in manuscript.

Place	Date	Hour	Summary of Events and Information	Remarks and references to Appendices
	27/9		In COMBLES. Relieved 1st Bn. Irish Guards in the line commencing at 4.15 p.m. Relief complete by 7.30 p.m. One of the first fine days since the Battalion has been in this portion of the line.	
	28/9		In the line as before. A fine morning, but a heavy mist in the afternoon. A great deal of movement carried out during the day. Heavy rain at night. A quiet day. Casualties, Nil.	
	29/9		In the line as before. A dull day. Our artillery carried out a bombardment for 45 minutes in the afternoon with field and heavy guns. The enemy made very little retaliation.	

T1134. W₁ W708—776. 500000. 4/15. Sir J. C. & S.

WAR DIARY or INTELLIGENCE SUMMARY.

Army Form C. 2118.

(*Erase heading not required.*)

Place	Date	Hour	Summary of Events and Information	Remarks and references to Appendices
	29/12 (con)		Relieved by 2nd Bn. Irish Guards and marched to TRONES WOOD, where we entrained for the PLATEAU and moved from thence to Camp 15. Owing to defects railway arrangements the Battalion did not reach Camp until 1. to 6 a.m. on morning of 30th. Casualties, NIL	
	30/12		In Camp 15, BRONFAY. Day spent in rest and cleaning arms clothing and equipment. Brig Gen J.D. Jeffrys C.M.G. assumed command of 1st Guards Bde.	
	31/12		In Camp 15. Divine Service in the morning.	

W R Bailey Major,
Comdg 2nd Bn. Grenadier Guards

2nd Bn Grenadier Guards
January 1917.

WAR DIARY
or
INTELLIGENCE SUMMARY
(Erase heading not required.)

Army Form C. 2118

Instructions regarding War Diaries and Intelligence Summaries are contained in F. S. Regs., Part II. and the Staff Manual respectively. Title Pages will be prepared in manuscript.

Place	Date	Hour	Summary of Events and Information	Remarks and references to Appendices
	1/1/17		In Camp 15, BRONFAY. The Battalion, less No. 4 Company, paraded at 9.30 a.m and marched via BRAY to MEAULTE, occupying billets at the north end of the village. On the whole, billets are better than during our last stay here. No. 4 Company proceeded to the CITADEL Camp for fatigue.	
	2/1/17		In Billets at MEAULTE. Day spent in cleaning arms, equipment and clothing. Lieutenant J.C. Cornforth joined Battalion.	
	3/1/17		In Billets at MEAULTE. Companies paraded for Drill, Musketry, Bombing and Lewis Gun Instruction.	
	4/1/17		In Billets at MEAULTE. Companies paraded for Drill, Bombing and instruction in Lewis Gunnery.	
	5/1/17		In Billets at MEAULTE. Companies paraded for Drill, Musketry, Bombing and instruction in Lewis Gunnery. No. 2 Company proceeded to the CITADEL to relieve No.4 Company on fatigue.	
	6/1/17		In Billets at MEAULTE. One Officer and ninety other ranks from No. 3 Company proceeded on fatigue, part at the CITADEL and the remainder at MONTAUBAN. The Officer Commanding 9th Squadron, R.F.C., lectured Officers and Platoon Sergeants of the Brigade in the evening.	

WAR DIARY
or
INTELLIGENCE SUMMARY

Army Form C. 2118

2nd Bn Grenadier Guards
January 1917

Place	Date	Hour	Summary of Events and Information	Remarks and references to Appendices
	1/1/17		In Camp 15, BRONFAY. The Battalion, less No. 4 Company, paraded at 8.30 a.m and marched via BRAY to MEAULTE, occupying billets at the north end of the village. On the whole, billets are better than during our last stay here. No. 4 Company proceeded to the CITADEL Camp for fatigue.	
	2/1/17		In Billets at MEAULTE. Day spent in cleaning arms, equipment and clothing. Lieutenant J.C. Cornforth joined Battalion.	
	3/1/17		In Billets at MEAULTE. Companies paraded for Drill, Musketry, Bombing and Lewis Gun Instruction.	
	4/1/17		In Billets at MEAULTE. Companies paraded for Drill, Bombing and Instruction in Lewis Gunnery.	
	5/1/17		In Billets at MEAULTE. Companies paraded for Drill, Musketry, Bombing and Instruction in Lewis Gunnery. No. 2 Company proceeded to the CITADEL to relieve No.4 Company on fatigue.	
	6/1/17		In Billets at MEAULTE. One Officer and ninety other ranks from No. 3 Company proceeded on fatigue, part at the CITADEL and the remainder at MONTAUBAN. The Officer Commanding 9th Squadron, R.F.C., lectured Officers and Platoon Sergeants of the Brigade in the evening.	

Army Form C. 2118

WAR DIARY
or
INTELLIGENCE SUMMARY
(Erase heading not required.)

Instructions regarding War Diaries and Intelligence Summaries are contained in F.S. Regs., Part II. and the Staff Manual respectively. Title Pages will be prepared in manuscript.

Place	Date	Hour	Summary of Events and Information	Remarks and references to Appendices
	7/1/17		In Billets at MEAULTE. Voluntary Divine Services in the morning. The Battalion was allotted the Baths at VILLE, clean clothes were provided.	
	8/1/17		In Billets at MEAULTE. Companies did Drill and Training. No. 2 Company returned from the CITADEL and went into billets vacated by a Company of the 2nd Battalion Coldstream Guards, which relieved No. 2 Company on fatigue.	
	9/1/17		In Billets at MEAULTE. Nos. 1 and 2 Companies paraded for Drill. No. 3 Company route marched. No. 4 Company found a party of forty men for fatigue, making horse standings. The remainder of the Company practised Bombing under Lieutenant J.C. Cornforth, and Lewis Gunnery. The Drums paraded for Brigade practice. Captain E.O. Stewart proceeded to MAUREPAS as Camp Commandant.	
	10/1/17		In Billets at MEAULTE. One Officer and one hundred and thirty other ranks of No. 3 Company proceeded to the PLATEAU RAILHEAD on fatigue, unloading and sorting live ammunition, etc. One Sergeant and fifty other ranks from No. 1 Company on fatigue in MEAULTE. Lieut. Hon. F.H. Manners and seventeen other ranks proceeded to join the Guards Division Works Battalion. A four days' course of GYMNASTIC INSTRUCTION and BAYONET FIGHTING under S/M Tooth, of the Army	

1875 Wt. W593/826 1,000,000 4/15 J.B.C. & A. A.D.S.S./Forms/C. 2118.

Army Form C. 2118

WAR DIARY
or
INTELLIGENCE SUMMARY
(Erase heading not required.)

Instructions regarding War Diaries and Intelligence Summaries are contained in F.S. Regs., Part II. and the Staff Manual respectively. Title Pages will be prepared in manuscript.

Place	Date	Hour	Summary of Events and Information	Remarks and references to Appendices
	10/1/17 (cont.)		Gymnastic Staff, was commenced. A party of six Officers and twenty four other ranks attended a demonstration of the employment of contact areoplane at the 9th Squadron Areodrome, MORLANCOURT.	
	11/1/17		In Billets at MEAULTE. One Sergeant and fifty other ranks of No. 1 Company on fatigue in MEAULTE. The remainder of the Company practixed Musketry and received instruction in the use of Gas Helmets. No. 4 Company paraded for Drill and No. 2 Company route marched.	
	12/1/17		In Billets at MEAULTE. The Brigadier inspected the billets of the Battalion in the morning. No. 1 Company proceeded to a Camp near BERNAFAY WOOD for work on the DECAUVILLE Railway. No. 4 Company practised Musketry and received instruction in the use of Gas Helmets. Men of No. 2 Company, clear of Duty, cleared and repaired Bombing Trenches in MEAULTE.	
	13/1/17		In Billets at MEAULTE. Part of No. 2 Company on fatigue. The remainder of the Company practised Musketry and Bombing. No. 4 Company route marched.	
	14/1/17		In Billets at MEAULTE. Divine Services in the morning. No. 3 Company returned to Billets at MEAULTE on completion of fatigue at PLATEAU RAILHEAD.	

Army Form C. 2118

WAR DIARY
or
INTELLIGENCE SUMMARY

(Erase heading not required.)

Instructions regarding War Diaries and Intelligence Summaries are contained in F.S. Regs., Part II. and the Staff Manual respectively. Title Pages will be prepared in manuscript.

Place	Date	Hour	Summary of Events and Information	Remarks and references to Appendices
	15/1/17		In Billets at MEAULTE. No. 2 Company practised Musketry, Bombing and Lewis Gunnery. No. 3 Company Paraded for Arm and Company Drill. No. 4 Company on fatigue.	
	16/1/17		In Billets at MEAULTE. Nos. 2 and 4 Companies practised Arm and Company Drill. No. 3 Company route marched. No. 4 Company practised Lewis Gunnery. A party of twenty two other ranks attended a demonstration in Flying at the 9th Squadron Areodrome. Three inches of snow fell during the night.	
	17/1/17		In Billets at MEAULTE. No. 3 Company on fatigue. No. 4 Company practised Musketry and had Kit Inspection in the morning. No. 2 Company route marched. No. 4 Company marched at 12.30 p.m. to relieve No. 1 Company on fatigue. No. 1 Company returned to MEAULTE arriving about 6.0 p.m. 2nd Battalion Grenadier Guards and 3rd Battalion Coldstream Guards gave a joint concert in the Y.M.C.A. Hut, MEAULTE, at which the Corps Commander and Brigadier attended. A successful concert.	
	18/1/17		In Billets at MEAULTE. The Battalion used the Baths at VILLE. No. 2 Company on fatigue. No. 3 Company practised Lewis Gunnery and Bombing. No. 1 Company cleaned arms, clothes and equipment and held kit inspection.	

Army Form C. 2118

WAR DIARY
or
INTELLIGENCE SUMMARY
(Erase heading not required.)

Instructions regarding War Diaries and Intelligence Summaries are contained in F. S. Regs, Part II. and the Staff Manual respectively. Title Pages will be prepared in manuscript.

Place	Date	Hour	Summary of Events and Information	Remarks and references to Appendices
	19/1/17		In Billets at MEAULTE. The Battalion used the Baths at VILLE. No. 1 Company practised Bombing and Lewis Gunnery. Part of No. 2 Company on fatigue. The remainder of the Company practised Musketry and Bombing. No. 3 Company practised Lewis Gunnery and Bayonet Fighting.	
	20/1/17		In Billets at MEAULTE. No. 1 Company route marched. No. 2 Company paraded for Drill and practised Bombing. No. 3 Company paraded for Bombing and Drill. Draft of thirty six N.C.Os and men joined Battalion.	
	21/1/17		In Billets at MEAULTE. Divine Services in the morning.	
	22/1/17		In Billets at MEAULTE. Captain C.F.A. Walker, M.C., Lieut. A.T.A. Ritchie, M.C., and Lieut. A.McW. Lawson-Johnston, M.G., attended a lecture by Colonel Foulkes, D.S.O, at the 30th Division Anti-Gas School. Five N.C.Os were detailed by Nos. 1, 2 and 3 Companies to undergo a Course of Instruction in-Bayonet Fighting under S/M Tooth of the Army Gymnastic Staff. Thirty N.C.Os and men attended a Lecture on Gas by the Divisional Gas Officer. Thirty six other ranks from No. 1 Company paraded for Instruction in Lewis Gunnery. The remainder of the Company practised Bombing. This Company also drilled under the Adjutant. Nos. 2 and 3 Companies route marched.	

Army Form C. 2118.

WAR DIARY
or
INTELLIGENCE SUMMARY
(Erase heading not required.)

Instructions regarding War Diaries and Intelligence Summaries are contained in F. S. Regs., Part II. and the Staff Manual respectively. Title Pages will be prepared in manuscript.

Place	Date	Hour	Summary of Events and Information	Remarks and references to Appendices
	22/1/17 (Con)		The Corps Commander and Brigadier inspected Lewis Gun Traversing Tripod invented by the Pioneers of this Battalion.	
	23/1/17		In Billets at MEAULTE. No. 1 Company route marched. No. 2 Company had lecture on Gas and practised Gas Helmet Drill, and had Kit Inspection. No. 3 Company practised Bombing and Drill.	
	24/1/17		In Billets at MEAULTE. No. 1 Company paraded for Drill and practised Bombing. No. 2 Company practised Musketry and Bayonet Fighting. No. 3 Company route marched. Captain G.C.F. Harcourt-Vernon, D.S.O., joined the Battalion. The Brigadier inspected the six Canadian N.C.Os attached to the Battalion for instructional purposes, in Drill during the morning. A telegram from the Brigade was received at 11.30 a.m. saying that the Battalion would be sent to PRIEZ FARM by eighteen busses and ten lorries at 8.0 a.m. tomorrow.	
	25/1/17		Freezing hard. The Battalion, less No. 4 Company, paraded in great coat order at 8.50 a.m. At 9.40 a.m. three lorries arrived, at 10.0 a.m. six lorries arrived, and at 10.40 a.m. seven busses arrived. No other of the promised vehicles arrived, and, as a result, a large part of the Battalion had to march. Proceeded via FRICOURT, CARNOY,	

2449 Wt. W14957/Mgo 750,000 1/16 J.B.C. & A. Forms/C.2118/12.

Army Form C. 2118.

WAR DIARY
or
INTELLIGENCE SUMMARY

(Erase heading not required.)

Instructions regarding War Diaries and Intelligence Summaries are contained in F. S. Regs., Part II. and the Staff Manual respectively. Title Pages will be prepared in manuscript.

Place	Date	Hour	Summary of Events and Information	Remarks and references to Appendices
	25/1/17 (Con)		and MARICOURT to relieve the 1st Battalion Grenadier Guards at PRIEZ FARM, between COMBLES and RANCOURT. Accomodation in dugouts. No. 4 Company proceeded to a Camp at MAUREPAS.	
	26/1/17		At PRIEZ FARM. A fine day, but freezing hard. Battalion spent the day in improving dugouts.	
	27/1/17		At PRIEZ FARM. Fine but very cold. Work continued on dugouts. The filling of sandbags very difficult, as frost is nearly two feet into the ground. Shelled in the morning, not heavily, but very unluck-ily. One shell falling among our cookers. Casualties, 2 killed, 3 wounded and 1 slightly wounded, the-latter remained at Duty. One watercart was also blown up. 2 other men slightly wounded during the day.	
	28/1/17		At PRIEZ FARM. Still bitterly cold. 120 N.C.Os and men on fatigue carrying material at night.	
	29/1/17		The Battalion was relieved by the 3rd Battalion Coldstream Guards at 11.30 a.m. and marched to BILLON CAMP, near MARICOURT. A good camp consist-ing of large French Huts. Great difficulties in obtaining water, as all water supplies are frozen up.	

Army Form C. 2118.

WAR DIARY
or
INTELLIGENCE SUMMARY

(Erase heading not required.)

Instructions regarding War Diaries and Intelligence Summaries are contained in F. S. Regs., Part II. and the Staff Manual respectively. Title Pages will be prepared in manuscript.

Place	Date	Hour	Summary of Events and Information	Remarks and references to Appendices
In BILLON CAMP.	30/1/17		Frost still holding. No. 4 Company on fatigue demolishing old dugouts. The remainder of the Companies at the disposal of Company Commanders.	
In BILLON CAMP.	31/1/17		Frost still holding, some snow during the night. Battalion on fatigue with the exception of No. 4 Company, which practised arm and Company Drill.	

Lieutenant Colonel,

Commanding 2nd Battalion Grenadier Guards.

WAR DIARY
or
INTELLIGENCE SUMMARY.

(Erase heading not required.)

Army Form C. 2118.

2nd Bn. Grenadier Guards

February 1917

Place	Date	Hour	Summary of Events and Information	Remarks and references to Appendices
	1/2/17		In BILLON CAMP. Captain G.C.F. Harcourt-Vernon, D.S.O., Captain J.N. Buchanan attended a lecture by the Divisional Gas Officer on the use of the Small Box Respirator at 2.30 p.m. Battalion employed on various fatigues during the day.	
	2/2/17		In BILLON CAMP. One Sergeant and thirty men of No. 1 Company on fatigue cutting trees for fuel supply. Twelve other ranks from this Company received instruction in Lewis Gunnery. The remainder of the Company at the disposal of the Company Commander. No. 2 Company practised Physical Training under Company Sergeant Major Atherton, of the Army Gymnastic Staff, from 9.a.m. to 9.30 a.m. for the remainder of the morning, the Company was at the disposal of the Company Commander. No. 3 Company practised Musketry from 9. a.m. to 9.30 a.m. and from 9.30 a.m. to 10.0 a.m. practised Physical Training under Company Sergeant Major Atherton. For the remainder of the morning, this Company was at the disposal of the Company Commander. No. 4 Company practised Bombing and Company Drill Each Company detailed one N.C.O. and twenty four men for work under the Camp Commandant from 2.0 p.m. to 4.0 p.m.	

Army Form C. 2118.

WAR DIARY
or
INTELLIGENCE SUMMARY.
(Erase heading not required.)

Instructions regarding War Diaries and Intelligence Summaries are contained in F. S. Regs., Part II. and the Staff Manual respectively. Title pages will be prepared in manuscript.

Place	Date	Hour	Summary of Events and Information	Remarks and references to Appendices
	3/2/17		In BILLON CAMP. No. 1 Company found a party of one Officer and one hundred other ranks for work under the Camp Commandant from 9.0 a.m. to 12 noon. No. 2 Company practised Bombing from 9.a.m. to 10 a.m. and practised the attack from trenches at 10.15 a.m. No. 3 Company practised Lewis Gunnery and Arm and extended drill. No. 4 Company practised Physical Drill from 9.0 a.m. to 9.30 a.m. under Company Sergeant Major Atherton, and, for the remainder of the morning, was at the disposal of the Company Commander. No. 4 Company detailed a party of one Officer and one hundred other ranks for work under the Camp Commandant from 2.0 p.m. to 4.30 p.m.	
	4/2/17		In BILLON CAMP. Divine Services in the monring.	
	5/2/17		In BILLON CAMP. Companies practised Physical and Arm Drill from 9.0 a.m. to 9.30 a.m. Companies practised a Drill Attack at 10.0 a.m. from the trenches at the north east corner of BILLON WOOD.	
	6/2/17		In BILLON CAMP. No. 1 Company detailed one Officer and seventy other ranks for work on the Decauville Railway. No. 2 Company detailed one Officer and one hundred other ranks for work under the Camp Commandant from 9.0 a.m. to 12 noon.	

Army Form C. 2118.

WAR DIARY
or
INTELLIGENCE SUMMARY.
(Erase heading not required.)

Instructions regarding War Diaries and Intelligence Summaries are contained in F. S. Regs., Part II. and the Staff Manual respectively. Title pages will be prepared in manuscript.

Place	Date	Hour	Summary of Events and Information	Remarks and references to Appendices
	6/2/17 (Con)		No. 3 Company detailed a similar party for work from 2.0 p.m. to 4.30 p.m. No. 4 Company detailed party of twenty other ranks for work on the traverses of the Brigade Bombing Ground. All N.C.Os and men clear of fatigue were at the disposal of Company Commanders. The Battalion used the Divisional Baths at BRONFAY. Clean clothes were provided.	
	7/2/17		In BILLON CAMP. Nos. 1 and 2 Companies used the Practice trenches from 9. a.m. to 10.15 a.m. Nos. 3 and 4 Companies used the Practice Trenches from 10.15 a.m. to 11.30 a.m. Officers and N.C.Os of and above the rank of Platoon Sergeants attended a lecture by the Medical Officer on the use of the Small Box Respirator.	
	8/2/17		In BILLON CAMP. Company Commanders and the Adjutant proceeded to MAUREPAS for a lecture on Military Law by the D.A.A.G. and Court Martial Officer, Fourth Army, neither of whom put in an appearance.- The whole morning wasted. The Battalion used the Divisional Baths at BRONFAY The remainder of Companies not on fatigue practised Arm Drill and received instruction in the use of the new Small Box Respirator, recently issued. The Corps Commander appointed 6th, 7th and 8th February as "Ratting Days" for the XIV Corps. The Battalion catching the largest number of rats to receive an extra ration of rum. This Battalion captured 386 rats during the three days and secured the coveted prize.	

Army Form C. 2118.

WAR DIARY
or
INTELLIGENCE SUMMARY.
(Erase heading not required.)

Instructions regarding War Diaries and Intelligence Summaries are contained in F.S. Regs., Part II. and the Staff Manual respectively. Title pages will be prepared in manuscript.

Place	Date	Hour	Summary of Events and Information	Remarks and references to Appendices
	9/2/17		In BILLON CAMP. The Battalion used the Baths at BRONFAY. Many fatigues were found, chiefly in the improvement of Camp. Practice in the use of the Small Box Respirator continued.	
	10/2/17		The Battalion cleared BILLON CAMP by 8.30 a.m. and marched via MARICOURT to MAUREPAS RAVINE, taking over the Camp vacated by the 1st Battalion Welsh Guards. One Company in NISSEN Huts and the remainder of the Battalion in tents, both of which are much warmer than the large French huts at BILLON.	
	11/2/17		In Camp at MAUREPAS. The Battalion paraded during the morning for the new French foot-Bathing treatment, which consists principally of washing with a soap consisting of Talc and Camphor. Relieved the 1st Battalion Grenadier Guards in the Line with the right of the Battalion on RANCOURT village and 3rd Battalion Coldstream Guards on the left. Marched via COMBLES and met guides at PRIEZ FARM at 6.15 p.m. The line consists of a series of posts on the forward slope of the hill between PERONNE—BAPAUME Road and ST. PIERRE VAAST WOOD. Nos. 1 and — Companies in the Front Line and Nos. 3 and 4 Companies in Reserve, also in posts. Posts are dry and fairly well revetted. A fairly good relief, which was completed by 8. p.m. Casualties Nil.	

Army Form C. 2118.

WAR DIARY
or
INTELLIGENCE SUMMARY.
(Erase heading not required.)

Instructions regarding War Diaries and Intelligence Summaries are contained in F. S. Regs., Part II. and the Staff Manual respectively. Title pages will be prepared in manuscript.

Place	Date	Hour	Summary of Events and Information	Remarks and references to Appendices
	12/2/17		In Line as above. Much warmer. The Major General and Brigadier inspected parts of the line during the day. Ground still very hard, but a good deal of improvement was carried out on the revetting of trenches, etc. Casualties, NIL.	
	13/2/17		In Line as above. A fine day. A warm sun, which melted some of the snow, making the surface of the ground muddy, but the ground is still frozen to a depth of about 15". A very quiet day. A German areoplane was brought down opposite Left Reserve Company. Inter-Company relief in the evening, No. 4 relieving No. 1 and No. 3 relieving No. 2. Casualties, NIL.	
	14/2/17		In Line as above. A fine day. Not much work was possible owing to the frozen state of the ground, but a number of shelters of wood and corrugated iron were erected in the various posts. Fairly heavy enemy shelling took place from 7.30 p.m. to 8.0 p.m. extending from BAPAUME ROAD back to the Reserve Line. Telephone wire on the Decauville line was broken in places, but no other damage was sustained. Casualties, NIL.	

Army Form C. 2118.

WAR DIARY
or
INTELLIGENCE SUMMARY.
(Erase heading not required.)

Instructions regarding War Diaries and Intelligence Summaries are contained in F. S. Regs., Part II. and the Staff Manual respectively. Title pages will be prepared in manuscript.

Place	Date	Hour	Summary of Events and Information	Remarks and references to Appendices
	15/2/17		In Line as above. A fine day. Much aerial activity, one British machine shot down.	
		5.0	Left Reserve Company was shelled with 4.2's and shells about 5.0 p.m.	
		6.0 p.m.	Relieved by the 1st Battalion Irish Guards at A good relief. The Battalion marched back to Camp at MAUREPAS. The Decauville Line running from the road to the Junction of Reserve Companies made the supply of material and rations very convenient during the tour in the Line. Casualties, one man wounded.	
	16/2/17		In Camp at MAUREPAS. The Battalion paraded for foot-bathing in the morning. This treatment appears to have had good effect on the feet of the men during the last tour in the trenches. The large ammunition dump at the Plateau Railhead was blown up by bombs dropped from a German aeroplane during the early morning, explosions continued throughout the day. Thaw began with a little rain.	
	17/2/17		In Camp at MAUREPAS. Thaw continued making the Camp very muddy. Most of the day spent in draining and cleaning Camp. Lieut. A.T.A. Ritchie, M.C., proceeded to the Headquarters, Fourth Army to receive Legion d'Honneur (Chevalier) from General Nivelle.	

WAR DIARY
or
INTELLIGENCE SUMMARY.

(Erase heading not required.)

Army Form C. 2118.

Instructions regarding War Diaries and Intelligence Summaries are contained in F. S. Regs., Part II. and the Staff Manual respectively. Title pages will be prepared in manuscript.

Place	Date	Hour	Summary of Events and Information	Remarks and references to Appendices
	17/2/17 (Sun)		Lieutenant R.E.H. Oliver joined the Battalion.	
	18/2/17		In Camp at MAUREPAS. Divine Services in the morning. The Brigadier lectured all Officers on "Trench Discipline." Thaw continued.	
	19/2/17		In Camp at MAUREPAS. The Battalion paraded for foot-bathing in the morning. Relieved the 1st Battalion Irish Guards in the line in the evening. Lieut. A.McW. Lawson-Johnston, M.C., in temporary command of No. 4 Company, as Captain Lord F.T. Blackwood, D.S.O., remainded behind with details in MAUREPAS. A fairly good relief, although progress was slower than the last relief owing to the increased mud.	
	20/2/17		In the Line as before. A quiet day. The Battalion found one hundred other ranks out of the two Reserve Companies to dig a Support Line. Progress was slow owing to the intense darkness of the night and the great number of shell-holes encountered, most of which are now filled with water. Casualties, one man killed.	

Army Form C. 2118.

WAR DIARY
or
INTELLIGENCE SUMMARY.
(Erase heading not required.)

Instructions regarding War Diaries and Intelligence Summaries are contained in F. S. Regs., Part II. and the Staff Manual respectively. Title pages will be prepared in manuscript.

Place	Date	Hour	Summary of Events and Information	Remarks and references to Appendices
	21/2/17		In Line as above. A misty morning. The Battalion on our right, belonging to the 40th Division, was found to have abandoned the Headquarters of the Company adjoining us on the right and also a considerable amount of trench adjoining it. No intimation was given of their intention of doing so, and the trenches left in a state of indescribable filth and material of every kind was abandoned. A heavy barrage was put down by the enemy, which extended from the front to the Reserve Line. Lieut. A.McW. Lawson-Johnston, M.C., and Lieut. R. Terrell were wounded by the same shell. No other casualties. The two Reserve Companies again found one hundred other ranks for digging the Support Line. Inter-Company relief took place late at night.	
	22/2/17		In the Line. A misty morning. Obtained permission from Brigade Headquarters to carry on with the Support Line under cover of the mist instead of by night. Great progress was made with the Support Line and with two Communication Trenches running to the Front Posts. A New line of duck-boards was laid down to assist the relief of the Right Front Company. Information received in the evening that Lieut. A.McW. Lawson-Johnston, M.C., died of wounds at the 2/2nd London Hospital, GROVETOWN at 1.p.m.	

Army Form C. 2118.

WAR DIARY
or
INTELLIGENCE SUMMARY.
(Erase heading not required.)

Instructions regarding War Diaries and Intelligence Summaries are contained in F. S. Regs., Part II. and the Staff Manual respectively. Title pages will be prepared in manuscript.

Place	Date	Hour	Summary of Events and Information	Remarks and references to Appendices
	23/2/17		In Line as above. Mist in the morning, under cover of which work on the Support Line was continued. A great amount of work has been done during the past two days. The 21st Battalion Middlesex Regiment relieved the Battalion on our Right, the relief took twelve hours, and was still in progress at 8.30 a.m. Patrols sent out from our Right Front Company found that their Front Line was held only by small posts at wide intervals, we, therefore, proceeded to wire our Right Front. The Battalion was relieved by the 1st Battalion Irish Guards at 7.p.m. A heavy barrage commenced about 8.0 p.m. from the Right Flank and extended to our Front Companies. Relief was completed without a casualty, and the Battalion marched to Camp at MAUREPAS.	
	24/2/17		In Camp at MAUREPAS. The Battalion paraded for foot-bathing during the afternoon. The remains of Lieut. A.McW. Lawson-Johnston, M.C. interred in the Officers' Cemetery, GROVETOWN. A party of Officers and N.C.Os from the Battalion attended the funeral.	
	25/2/17		In Camp at MAUREPAS. Divine Services in the morning.	

Army Form C. 2118.

WAR DIARY
or
INTELLIGENCE SUMMARY.
(Erase heading not required.)

Instructions regarding War Diaries and Intelligence Summaries are contained in F. S. Regs., Part II. and the Staff Manual respectively. Title pages will be prepared in manuscript.

Place	Date	Hour	Summary of Events and Information	Remarks and references to Appendices
	26/2/17		The Battalion marched at 10.0 a.m. via MARICOURT to Camp 107, BILLON, vacated by the 3rd Battalion Grenadier Guards, arriving about noon.	
	27/2/17		In BILLON CAMP. No. 1 Company detailed a party of one Officer and eighty other ranks for road making. No. 2 Company marched at 1.30 p.m. to the BRIQUETERIE for fatigue. This Company is billeted at the BRIQUETERIE. No. 3 Company was at the disposal of the Company Commander. No. 4 Company detailed one Officer and eighty other ranks for work on the Decauville Line.	
	28/2/17		In BILLON CAMP. No. 3 Company detailed one Officer and one hundred other ranks for fatigue at the PLATEAU Ammunition Railhead. Nos. 1 and 4 Companies used the Divisional Baths at BRONFAY. Clean clothes were provided. When not bathing, Companies practised Platoon Drill.	

Lieutenant Colonel,
Commanding and Battalion Grenadier Guards.

Army Form C. 2118.

2nd Bn. Grenadier Guards

March 1917

Vol 32

WAR DIARY
or
INTELLIGENCE SUMMARY.
(Erase heading not required.)

Place	Date	Hour	Summary of Events and Information	Remarks and references to Appendices
	1-3-17		In BILLON CAMP. Companies at the disposal of Captains. Instruction in Bombing and Bayonet Fighting carried out. Part of the Battalion used the Divisional Baths. No. 2 Company returned from fatigue at the BRIQUETERIE.	
	2-3-17		In BILLON CAMP. No. 1 Company paraded at 9.0 a.m. under the Adjutant. No. 2 Company was at the disposal of the Company Commander. No. 3 Company paraded for Drill and also practised Musketry and Gas Helmet Drill. No. 4 Company was at the disposal of the Company Commander, except for one party, which paraded for Bombing.	
	3-3-17		In BILLON CAMP. Companies did Drill and Training.	
	4-3-17		In BILLON CAMP. Divine Services in the morning. Greater part of the Battalion on various fatigues.	
	5-3-17		In BILLON CAMP. Nos. 1 and 2 Companies practised Platoon Training and Tactical exercise. Nos. 3 and 4 Companies did Platoon Training and practised blobbing and extending.	
	6-3-17		In BILLON CAMP. Nos. 1 and 2 Companies practised the attack. Nos. 3 and 4 Companies did Platoon Training and practised blobbing and extended order drill.	

Army Form C. 2118.

WAR DIARY
or
INTELLIGENCE SUMMARY.
(Erase heading not required.)

Instructions regarding War Diaries and Intelligence Summaries are contained in F. S. Regs., Part II. and the Staff Manual respectively. Title pages will be prepared in manuscript.

Place	Date	Hour	Summary of Events and Information	Remarks and references to Appendices
	7-3-17		In BILLON CAMP. Nos. 2 and 3 Companies practised open fighting tactics. Nos. 1 and 4 Companies practised Platoon Training and Company Drill.	
	8-3-17		In BILLON CAMP. Battalion employed on various fatigues. Company Commanders and the Adjutant attended a lecture on Courts Martial by the D.A.A.G., Fourth Army. Lieut. R.G.C. Napier joined Battalion.	
	9-3-17		In BILLON CAMP. Companies did Drill and Training.	
	10-3-17		In BILLON CAMP. Battalion used the Divisional Baths. When clear of bathing, Companies paraded for Drill and Training.	
	11-3-17		In BILLON CAMP. Divine Services in the morning. Several fatigue parties found by the Battalion.	
	12-3-17		In BILLON CAMP. The Battalion paraded under the Adjutant at 8.45 a.m. From 10.15 a.m., No. 2 Company practised Rifle Grenade Shooting. The remainder of the Battalion practised the attack and Platoon Training. 2nd Lieut. I.F.S. Gunnis joined Battalion.	
	13-3-17		In BILLON CAMP. The Battalion was on fatigue, principally road-making.	
	14-3-17		The Battalion cleared Camp by 10.15 a.m. and marched to Camp at MAUREPAS RAVINE.	

Army Form C. 2118.

WAR DIARY
or
INTELLIGENCE SUMMARY.
(Erase heading not required.)

Instructions regarding War Diaries and Intelligence Summaries are contained in F. S. Regs., Part II. and the Staff Manual respectively. Title pages will be prepared in manuscript.

Place	Date	Hour	Summary of Events and Information	Remarks and references to Appendices
	14-3-17	(Con)	News received during the day that the Fifth Army on our left had advanced and that enemy on the French Division front have about to withdraw.	
	15-3-17		In Camp at MAUREPAS. Companies did Training. 1st Battalion Irish Guards advanced after the retiring enemy, at SAILLY SAILLISEL, with slight losses.	
	16-3-17		In Camp at MAUREPAS. Companies did Training. A cross-country was organised in the afternoon with several teams of five N.C.Os and men from each Company and an Officers' Team. No. 1 Company won the race.	
	17-3-17		In Camp at MAUREPAS. The Battalion used the foot-baths in the morning. Moved to the Line at SAILLY SAILLISEL with Battalion Headquarters in the Quarry, as in December last. Nos. 1 and 4 Companies relieved two Companies of the 1st Battalion Irish Guards and Nos. 2 and 3 Companies relieved two Companies of the 3rd Battalion Coldstream Guards on the left. The line having been further advanced during the night, 3rd Battalion Coldstream Guards is holding the outpost line with 2nd Battalion Grenadier Guards in Support. The line of BARAUME - LE TRANSLOY uphill continued.	
	18-3-17		Not a gun heard or a German seen. The outpost line has been advanced to within 1,000 yards of LE MESNIL and Cavalry patrols are being pushed through to establish touch with the enemy. Every available Battalion is employed on road-making. During the afternoon, the Battalion relieved the 3rd Battalion Coldstream Guards in the outpost line, and Battalion Headquarters moved up to the village of SAILLY.	

Army Form C. 2118.

WAR DIARY
or
INTELLIGENCE SUMMARY.
(Erase heading not required.)

Instructions regarding War Diaries and Intelligence Summaries are contained in F. S. Regs., Part II. and the Staff Manual respectively. Title pages will be prepared in manuscript.

Place	Date	Hour	Summary of Events and Information	Remarks and references to Appendices
	19-3-17		At 4.0 a.m. Battalion was ordered to send patrols forward at 8.30 a.m. This was done without opposition except some slight sniping. Outpost line was advanced during the day to the line LE MESNIL-St. MARTIN'S WOOD, with 20th Division on our left and 2nd Guards Brigade on our right. A patrol from No. 1 Company found two Russian soldiers in ETRICOURT, who had remained hidden after the German retirement.	
	20-3-17		In Outpost line as Before. Enemy still out of touch with infantry, although Cavalry report that the Germans are still holding BUS and EQUANCOURT. The Cavalry on our front usually withdraws behind out/group line at night and seldom reports anything, which our patrols have not discovered several hours previously. The Corps Cyclists arrived in the village during the evening.	
	21-3-17		A fine day. In same outpost line. Instructions received not to advance further until the construction of roads will allow guns and supplies to be brought nearer. Battalion relieved by the 2nd Battalion Coldstream Guards in the afternoon after a most instructive tour in the line. Marched to Reserve Billets in and about COMBLES. B. H.H. H.Q. and One Coy were at FREGICOURT.	
	22-3-17		Battalion marched at 2.0 p.m. to a camp of tents between GINCHY and GUILLEMONT. The whole Brigade has been taken from the line in order to make roads much to everybody's disappointment.	
	23-3-17		In Camp as above. The whole Battalion at work improving Camp - filling in shell-holes, etc.	

Army Form C. 2118.

WAR DIARY
or
INTELLIGENCE SUMMARY.

(Erase heading not required.)

Instructions regarding War Diaries and Intelligence Summaries are contained in F. S. Regs., Part II. and the Staff Manual respectively. Title pages will be prepared in manuscript.

Place	Date	Hour	Summary of Events and Information	Remarks and references to Appendices
	24-3-17		In Camp as above. Battalion employed on road-making between GINCHY and LESBOEUFS. A small party of Officers and other ranks went out during the day over the ground on which the 1st Guards Brigade attacked on 15th September, 1916. The graves of a great many men were remade and several crosses erected. A rail was placed round the grave of Captain M.K.A. Lloyd.	
	25-3-17		In Camp as above. Battalion employed on roadmaking. A beautiful day.	
	26-3-17		In Camp as above. Raining heavily all day and Battalion remained in Camp.	
	27-3-17		In Camp as above. One Company did Training and the other three Companies were employed on Road making. Rain and sleet all day.	
	28-3-17		In Camp as above. One Company did Training and the other three Companies were employed on road making.	
	29-3-17		In Camp as above. One Company did Training and the other three Companies were employed on road making.	
	30-3-17		In Camp as above. One Company did Training and the other three Companies were employed on road making. 2nd Lieut. T. Smith joined Battalion.	

Army Form C. 2118.

WAR DIARY
or
INTELLIGENCE SUMMARY.
(Erase heading not required.)

Place	Date	Hour	Summary of Events and Information	Remarks and references to Appendices
	31-3-17		In Camp as above. One Company did Training and the other three Companies were employed on Road making.	

Major,
Commanding 2nd Battalion Grenadier Guards.

WAR DIARY
or
INTELLIGENCE SUMMARY.

(Erase heading not required.)

Army Form C. 2118.

April 1917

2nd Bn. Grenadier Guards

Vol 33

Place	Date	Hour	Summary of Events and Information	Remarks and references to Appendices
	1-4-17		In Camp at GINCHY. Three Companies paraded at 8.15 a.m. for road-making. The Company in Waiting trained in the morning and collected salvage in the afternoon. Voluntary Divine Service in the evening.	
	2-4-17		In Camp as above. Three Companies paraded for road-making. The Company in Waiting trained in the morning and collected salvage in the afternoon.	
	3-4-17		In Camp as above. Three Companies paraded for road-making. The Company in Waiting trained in the morning and collected salvage in the afternoon.	
	4-4-17		In Camp as above. Three Companies paraded for Road-making. The Company in Waiting trained, etc.	
	5-4-17		In Camp as above. Three Companies paraded for road-making. The Company in Waiting trained, etc. Recreation hut built by the Pioneers of the Battalion opened in the evening.	
	6-4-17		In Camp as above. Three Companies paraded for road-making. The Company in Waiting trained, etc.	
	7-4-17		The Battalion left Camp at 8.30 a.m. and marched to a field just north of the ROCQUIGNY-LES MESNIL ROAD. The tents were struck at GINCHY before leaving and were conveyed to the place selected for new Camp under Brigade arrangements. A very wet morning, but fine in the afternoon.	

Army Form C. 2118.

WAR DIARY
or
INTELLIGENCE SUMMARY.
(Erase heading not required.)

Place	Date	Hour	Summary of Events and Information	Remarks and references to Appendices
	8-4-17		In Camp near ROCQUIGNY. Three Companies paraded at 8.35 a.m. for work on new broad gauge railway running from GINCHY via MORVAL to LES MESNIL. The Company in Waiting did training. Divine Service in the evening.	
	9-4-17		In Camp as above. Three Companies paraded for work on railway and the Company in Waiting did training.	
	10-4-17		In Camp as above. Snow during the night and a very high wind during the morning. The Battalion (four Companies) paraded at 7.40 a.m. for work on Railway.	
	11-4-17		In Camp as above. The Battalion worked on the railway.	
	12-4-17		In Camp as above. Two Companies paraded for work on the railway, and two Companies did drill and training.	
	13-4-17		In Camp as above. Two Companies paraded for work on the railway and two Companies did drill and training.	
	14-4-17		In Camp as above. Three Companies paraded for work on the railway. No. 2 Company practised the attack.	
	15-4-17		In Camp as above. Four Companies paraded for work on the railway. Raining all day.	

Army Form C. 2118.

WAR DIARY
or
INTELLIGENCE SUMMARY.
(Erase heading not required.)

Instructions regarding War Diaries and Intelligence Summaries are contained in F. S. Regs., Part II. and the Staff Manual respectively. Title pages will be prepared in manuscript.

Place	Date	Hour	Summary of Events and Information	Remarks and references to Appendices
	16-4-17		In Camp as above. Four Companies paraded for work on the railway. A bright sunny morning. The Battalion played a football match with the 1st Battalion Coldstream Guards. Battalion won by three goals to nil. Heavy rain during the night.	
	17-4-17		Heavy rain until about 8.30 a.m. the Battalion marched at 9.30 a.m. via FREGICOURT, COMBLES, MAUREPAS and MARICOURT to BRONFAY CAMP 108, arriving about 3.15 p.m.	
	18-4-17		In Camp 108, BRONFAY. Companies paraded for drill, training and kit inspection in the morning. Improved Camp during the afternoon.	
	19-4-17		In Camp as above. Companies paraded for drill, musketry and bayonet fighting and also used the Range which has been constructed by the Battalion.	
	20-4-17		In Camp as above. Battalion parade from 8.30 a.m. - 9.30 a.m. During the remainder of the day, Companies used the Range and practised Bayonet Fighting, Section Training, etc. The Band of the Regiment gave a Concert during the evening.	

Army Form C. 2118.

WAR DIARY
or
INTELLIGENCE SUMMARY.
(Erase heading not required.)

Instructions regarding War Diaries and Intelligence Summaries are contained in F.S. Regs., Part II. and the Staff Manual respectively. Title pages will be prepared in manuscript.

Place	Date	Hour	Summary of Events and Information	Remarks and references to Appendices
	21-4-17		In Camp as above. Battalion Parade from 8.30 a.m. to 9.30 a.m. During the remainder of the day, Companies used the Range and practised Bayonet Fighting, Section Training, etc. The Band of the Regiment gave a Concert during the evening.	
	22-4-17		In Camp as above. Divine Services in the morning. Inter-Battalion Football matches during the afternoon and evening. A fine sunny day.	
	23-4-17		In Camp as above. Companies paraded for Drill and Training.	
	24-4-17		In Camp as above. Companies paraded for Drill and Training.	
	25-4-17		In Camp as above. Companies paraded for Drill and Training.	
	26-4-17		In Camp as above. Companies paraded for Drill and Training. The Brigadier inspected the 1st Line Transport in the afternoon.	
	27-4-17		In Camp as above. Companies paraded for Drill and Training. Officers and all ranks of an above Platoon Sergeants attended a lecture at 3.30 p.m. on the "Attack in Open Warfare" by Lieutenant Colonel G.B.S. Follett, M.V.O., D.S.O., Coldstream Guards. The Officers of the Battalion played the Sergeants at Football in the evening. Result, a win for the Sergeants by four goals to one.	

Army Form C. 2118.

WAR DIARY
or
INTELLIGENCE SUMMARY.
(Erase heading not required.)

Instructions regarding War Diaries and Intelligence Summaries are contained in F. S. Regs., Part II. and the Staff Manual respectively. Title pages will be prepared in manuscript.

Place	Date	Hour	Summary of Events and Information	Remarks and references to Appendices
	28-4-17		In Camp as above. Companies did Drill and Training.	
	29-4-17		In Camp as above. Divine Services in the morning.	
	30-4-17		In Camp as above. Companies did Drill and Training. No. 11 Platoon, of No. 3 Company, has been chosen to take part in Brigade Competition, and this Platoon fired on the Brigade Range during the morning. The Battalion attended a lecture in the afternoon on "Bayonet Fighting." Lieut. L. St.L. Hermon-Hodge joined the Battalion.	

Lieutenant Colonel,

Commanding 2nd Battalion Grenadier Guards.

Army Form C. 2118.

WAR DIARY
or
INTELLIGENCE SUMMARY.

(Erase heading not required.)

Instructions regarding War Diaries and Intelligence Summaries are contained in F. S. Regs., Part II. and the Staff Manual respectively. Title pages will be prepared in manuscript.

May 1917 2nd Bn. Grenadier Gds Vol 34

Place	Date	Hour	Summary of Events and Information	Remarks and references to Appendices
	1-5-17		In Camp 108, BRONFAY. No. 1 Company paraded at 8.30 a.m. for Company Drill and attended a Gas Lecture. No. 2 Company practised Outpost scheme. No. 3 Company, less No. 11 Platoon, practised Advance Guard. No. 4 Company practised Advance Guard. All the above were preceded by drill. No. 11 Platoon took part in the Brigade Bayonet Fighting Competition, and secured higher marks than any other Battalion.	
	2-5-17		In Camp as above. No. 1 Company practised the attack. No. 2 Company practised Advance Guard. No. 3 Company, less No. 11 Platoon, practised a Trench to Trench Attack. No. 4 Company practised RearGuard action. No. 11 Platoon took part in the Brigade Drill Competition in the morning, before the Corps Commander, the Major General and Brigadier. Judge, S/Mjr Scarfe, 2nd Battalion Scots Guards. Result (1) 2nd Bn. Gren. Gds. (2) 3rd Bn. Cold. Gds. (3) 2nd Bn. Cold. Gds. (4) 1st Bn. Irish Gds. In afternoon, a competition in a tactical exercise was held. Judge, Lieutenant Colonel N. Orr-Ewing, D.S.O., 2nd Battalion Scots Guards. The scheme consisted of an attack on a stong point and involved the employment of Lewis gun, rifle grenades and bombs under covering fire of Stokes Mortars.	

Army Form C. 2118.

WAR DIARY
or
INTELLIGENCE SUMMARY.

(Erase heading not required.)

May 1917 2nd Bn Grenadier Gds Vol 34

Place	Date	Hour	Summary of Events and Information	Remarks and references to Appendices
	1-5-17		In Camp 108, BRONFAY. No. 1 Company paraded at 8.30 a.m. for Company Drill and attended a Gas Lecture. No. 2 Company practised Outpost scheme. No. 3 Company, less No. 11 Platoon, practised Advance Guard. No. 4 Company practised Advance Guard. All the above were preceded by drill. No. 11 Platoon took part in the Brigade Bayonet Fighting Competition, and secured higher marks than any other Battalion.	

	2-5-17		In Camp as above.
			No. 1 Company practised the attack.
			No. 2 Company practised Advance Guard.
			No. 3 Company, less No. 11 Platoon, practised a Trench to Trench Attack.
			No. 4 Company practised RearGuard action.
			No. 11 Platoon took part in the Brigade Drill Competition in the morning, before the Corps Commander, the Major General and Brigadier. Judge, S/Mjr Scarfe, 2nd Battalion Scots Guards.
			Result (1) 2nd Bn. Gren. Gds.
			        (2) 3rd Bn. Cold. Gds.
			        (3) 2nd Bn. Cold. Gds.
			        (4) 1st Bn. Irish Gds.
			In afternoon, a competition in a tactical exercise was held. Judge, Lieutenant Colonel N. Orr-Ewing, D.S.O., 2nd Battalion Scots Guards. The scheme consisted of an attack on a stong point and involved the employment of Lewis gun, rifle grenades and bombs under covering fire of Stokes Mortars.	

Army Form C. 2118.

WAR DIARY
or
INTELLIGENCE SUMMARY.
(Erase heading not required.)

Instructions regarding War Diaries and Intelligence Summaries are contained in F.S. Regs., Part II. and the Staff Manual respectively. Title pages will be prepared in manuscript.

Place	Date	Hour	Summary of Events and Information	Remarks and references to Appendices

	2-5-17 (Con)		Result. (1) 2nd Bn. Gren. Gds.
			 (2) 1st Bn. Irish Gds.
			 (3) 3rd Bn. Cold. Gds.
			 (4) 2nd Bn. Cold. Gds.
			 Result of entire competition, No. 11 Platoon won each of the four events in the competition. Total marks were :
			     2nd Bn. Gren. Gds. 128.1
			     1st Bn. Irish Gds. 118.2
			     3rd Bn. Cold. Gds. 112.8
			     2nd Bn. Cold. Gds. 105.5
			 The Drums played the winning platoon back to Camp.
			 No. 3 Company held a concert in the evening.
			 A draft of sixty three other ranks joined the Battalion.	

	3-5-17		In Camp as above. Battalion parade at 9.0 a.m. The Brigadier presented medals to No. 11 Platoon, the winners of the Brigade Competition.	
	4-5-17		In Camp as above. Battalion paraded at 9.0 a.m. for Field Day. The Band of the Regiment played in the Camp during the evening.	
	5-5-17		In Camp as above. No. 1 Company practised a flank guard scheme. No. 2 Company practised the attack. No. 3 Company practised advance guard. No. 4 Company practised advance guard and attack.	
	6-5-17		In Camp as above. Divine Services in the morning. Winter clothing and all blankets except one per man returned to Stores. Captain Sir A.L. Napier, Bart., and six other ranks joined Battalion.	

Army Form C. 2118.

WAR DIARY
or
INTELLIGENCE SUMMARY.

(Erase heading not required.)

Instructions regarding War Diaries and Intelligence Summaries are contained in F. S. Regs., Part II. and the Staff Manual respectively. Title pages will be prepared in manuscript.

Place	Date	Hour	Summary of Events and Information	Remarks and references to Appendices
	7-5-17		In Camp as above. No. 1 Company paraded for Drill and Musketry, and practised the construction of wire entanglements. This Company used the Baths at Bronfay from 1.30 p.m. to 4.30 p.m. No. 2 Company used the Baths at Bronfay from 9.0 a.m to 12.30 p.m. When not bathing, Platoons of this Company did Drill and Bayonet Fighting. No. 3 Company paraded for Drill and practised the Attack. No. 4 Company practised an Advance Guard.	
	8-5-17		In Camp as above. No. 1 Company paraded for Drill and practised the Attack. No. 2 Company praded for Drill and practised the attack. No. 3 Company used the Baths during the morning. When not bathing, Platoons of this Company did Training and practised the construction of wire entanglements. No. 4 Company paraded for Drill, Musketry and Bombing in the morning. During the afternoon, this Company used the baths.	
	9-5-17		The Battalion left Camp at 9.45 a.m. and marched via, MARICOURT, GUILLEMONT and GINCHY to a Camp vacated by the 2nd Battalion Irish Guards between GINCHY and LES BOEUFS, arriving about noon. A very warm day.	

Army Form C. 2118.

WAR DIARY
or
INTELLIGENCE SUMMARY.
(Erase heading not required.)

Instructions regarding War Diaries and Intelligence Summaries are contained in F.S. Regs., Part II. and the Staff Manual respectively. Title pages will be prepared in manuscript.

Place	Date	Hour	Summary of Events and Information	Remarks and references to Appendices
	10-5-17		In Camp between GINCHY and LES BOEUFS. Companies paraded at 8.0 a.m. for work on the roads under the 76th Company, R.E., Very warm.	
	11-5-17		In Camp as above. All Platoon Sergeants and one officer per Company paraded at 9.0 a.m. for a Tactical scheme under Major Hon. W.R. Bailey, D.S.O. Companies paraded for one hour's drill in the morning and collected salvage during the remainder of the morning. A hot day.	
	12-5-17		Battalion marched at 9.0 a.m. via LES BOEUFS, LE TRANSLOY and thence across country to a Camp vacated by the 3rd Battalion Grenadier Guards, near the village of LES MESNIL, arriving at 11.45 a.m. A very hot day.	
	13-5-17		In Camp near LES MESNILS. No. 3 Company reported for work at 6.15 a.m. and other Companies at intervals of 15 minutes under the 295th Company, R.E. on the new ROCQUIGNY Siding. Work consisted of tracking and ballasting and lasted until 1.0 p.m. A hot day- heavy rain during night.	
	14-5-17		In Camp as above. Nos. 1 and 4 Companies commenced work at 5.30 a.m. and were relieved by Nos. 2 and 3 Companies at 12.30 p.m. One officer and four Sergeants from each Company paraded at 9.0 a.m. for a tactical scheme under Major Hon. W.R. Bailey, D.S.O. A very hot and oppressive morning - heavy rain during the afternoon.	

Army Form C. 2118.

WAR DIARY
or
INTELLIGENCE SUMMARY.

(Erase heading not required.)

Instructions regarding War Diaries and Intelligence Summaries are contained in F. S. Regs., Part II. and the Staff Manual respectively. Title pages will be prepared in manuscript.

Place	Date	Hour	Summary of Events and Information	Remarks and references to Appendices
	15-5-17		In Camp as above. Companies paraded for work on the Railway. Subaltern Officers and Platoon Sergeants paraded at 9.0 a.m. for a tactical scheme under Major Hon. W.R. Bailey, D.S.O. Cooler day.	
	16-5-17		In Camp as above. Companies paraded for work on the Railway. One Platoon used the Range in the morning. A cold day with rain in the afternoon.	
	17-5-17		In Camp as above. Companies paraded for work on the Railway.	
	18-5-17		In Camp as above. Companies paraded for work on the Railway. 1st Guards Brigade Boxing Competition held in Camp during the afternoon.	
	19-5-17		In Camp as above. Companies paraded for work on the Railway.	
	20-5-17		The Battalion struck tents and marched at 8.40 a.m. via LE TRANSLOY, LES BOEUFS, GINCHY and GUILLEMONT to camp of French Huts at BRONFAY. A halt of 25 minutes was made on the road between LES BOEUFS and GINCHY to enable all ranks to view the memorial to Officers, N.C.Os and men of the Regiment, who were killed during the operations of September, 1916, which was made and erected by the 2nd Battalion. The memorial consists of an oak cross, twelve feet in height, suitably inscribed. The material was collected among the ruins of LES BOEUFS. A halt of one hour was made at	

Army Form C. 2118.

WAR DIARY
or
INTELLIGENCE SUMMARY.
(Erase heading not required.)

Place	Date	Hour	Summary of Events and Information	Remarks and references to Appendices
	20-5-17 (Con)		GUILLEMONT for dinners. Arrived in new Camp about 3.45.p.m. A very hot day.	
	21-5-17		The Battalion marched at 8.35 a.m. via BRAY to billets at SAILLY LE SEC, near CORBIE, arriving about 1.0 p.m. Heavy rain during the early part of march but fine later. Fair billets.	
	22-5-17		In Billets at SAILLY LE SEC. Kit inspection in the morning. Day otherwise spent in cleaning billets.	
	23-5-17		In Billets at SAILLY LE SEC. Nos. 1 and 4 Companies route marched. Nos. 2 and 3 Companies paraded for drill and bombing. A fine day. A draft of 17 other ranks joined.	
	24-5-17		In Billets as above. Companies did Drill, Bombing, Musketry and Route marches. A brilliant day.	
	25-6-17		In Billets as above. Nos. 1 and 4 Companies route marched. No. 3 Company practised Drill, Musketry and Bombing. A fine sunny day.	
	26-5-17		In Billets as above. Companies paraded for Drill, Bombing, Musketry and Route marches. While in these billets, a great deal of bathing has been done by all ranks in the Canal.	

Army Form C. 2118.

WAR DIARY
or
INTELLIGENCE SUMMARY.

(Erase heading not required.)

Instructions regarding War Diaries and Intelligence Summaries are contained in F. S. Regs., Part II. and the Staff Manual respectively. Title pages will be prepared in manuscript.

Place	Date	Hour	Summary of Events and Information	Remarks and references to Appendices
	27-5-17		In Billets at SAILLY LE SEC. Divine Services in the morning. A very warm and sunny day.	
	28-5-17		In Billets at SAILLY LE SEC. No. 1 Company route marched. No. 2 Company practised Musketry and Bomb throwing. No. 3 and 4 Companies practised a Tactical Scheme. All blankets handed into stores. Cooler.	
	29-5-17		In Billets at SAILLY LE SEC. Nos. 1 and 2 Companies practised Musketry and extended order drill, and paraded for a tactical exercise in the afternoon. Nos. 3 and 4 Companies route marched.	
	30-5-17		The Battalion, less No. 4 Company, marched from SAILLY LE SEC at 7.5 p.m. via TREUX and BUIRE to DERNANCOURT Station, arriving about 9.0 p.m. The Battalion entrained and left the above Station at 11.6 pm for CASSEL.	
	31-5-17		The Battalion detrained at CASSEL Station at 11.30 a.m. and marched via BAVINCHOVE to billets at RENESCURE arriving at 2.15 p.m. Very scattered billets. A warm and sunny day. No. 4 Company proceeds to join the Battalion today by train leaving DERNANCOURT at 7.55 p.m.	

Lieutenant Colonel,
Commanding 2nd Battalion Grenadier Guards.

Army Form C. 2118.

June 1917
2nd Bn. Grenadier Guards
WM 3 5

WAR DIARY
or
INTELLIGENCE SUMMARY.
(Erase heading not required.)

Instructions regarding War Diaries and Intelligence Summaries are contained in F. S. Regs., Part II. and the Staff Manual respectively. Title pages will be prepared in manuscript.

Place	Date	Hour	Summary of Events and Information	Remarks and references to Appendices
	1-6-17		In Billets at RENESCURE. No. 4 Company arrived about 3.0 p.m. Companies at the disposal of Company Commanders.	
	2-6-17		In Billets at RENESCURE. Nos. 1 and 2 Companies practised bomb throwing, Drill and fire control. No. 3 Company route marched. No. 4 Company cleaned billets and drilled.	
	3-6-17		In Billets at RENESCURE. Divine Services in the morning.	
	4-6-17		In Billets at RENESCURE. Nos. 1 and 3 Companies paraded for drill, etc. No. 2 Company paraded for wood fighting. No. 4 Company route marched.	
	5-6-17		In Billets at RENESCURE. No. 1 Company route marched. Nos. 2 and 4 Companies paraded for drill, etc. No. 3 Company paraded for wood fighting.	
	6-6-17		In Billets at RENESCURE. Nos. 1 and 3 Companies paraded for drill, etc. No. 2 Company route marched. No. 4 Company paraded for wood fighting. Officers and all ranks of and above Platoon Sergts attended a lecture by the Brigadier on Trench to Trench Attack in the evening.	

Army Form C. 2118.

WAR DIARY
or
INTELLIGENCE SUMMARY.
(Erase heading not required.)

Instructions regarding War Diaries and Intelligence Summaries are contained in F.S. Regs., Part II. and the Staff Manual respectively. Title pages will be prepared in manuscript.

Place	Date	Hour	Summary of Events and Information	Remarks and references to Appendices
	7-6-17		In Billets at RENESCURE. No. 1 Company paraded for wood fighting. Nos. 2 and 4 Companies paraded for drill, etc. No. 3 Company route marched. The Battalion played a Football match against 2nd Battalion Coldstream Guards. Battalion won by four goals to nil.	
	8-6-17		In Billets at RENESCURE. Nos. 1 and 3 Companies paraded for Drill, etc. No. 2 Company paraded for wood fighting. No. 4 Company route marched.	
	9-6-17		In Billets at RENESCURE. In the morning, 1st Battalion Grenadier Guards marched over to a field near the billets of No. 3 Company for a tug of war between the two Battalions :- Officers' Team. Staff Sergeants' Team. A team from each Company. Result, each Battalion won three events.	
	10-6-17		In Billets at RENESCURE. Divine Services in the morning. No. 1 Company held sports in the afternoon.	
	11-6-17		In Billets at RENESCURE. Companies paraded for Drill and Musketry. Divisional Horse Show and Wagon Competition held during the afternoon. Battalion won the water-cart competition.	

Army Form C. 2118.

WAR DIARY
or
INTELLIGENCE SUMMARY.
(Erase heading not required.)

Instructions regarding War Diaries and Intelligence Summaries are contained in F.S. Regs., Part II. and the Staff Manual respectively. Title pages will be prepared in manuscript.

Place	Date	Hour	Summary of Events and Information	Remarks and references to Appendices
	12-6-17		The Battalion left RENESCURE at 8.30 a.m. and marched to ZUDASQUES for two days' musketry on the range at TILQUES. A hot day and a march of about 14 kilometres. Battalion halted for dinners at TATINGHEM, where it had billeted at a year ago. The Hertfordshire Territorials, who were formerly attached to the 4th Guards Brigade, marched into the village shortly before the Battalion left it.	
	13-6-17		The Battalion fired on TILQUES RANGE from 6.0 a.m. until 4.30 p.m. Practices slow and rapid at 200 and 300 yards. A fine day.	
	14-6-17		Battalion fired on TILQUES RANGE from 6.0 a.m. and on completion of shooting, at 5.30 p.m. marched back to RENESCURE through the outskirts of ST. OMER. The following practices were fired, slow, rapid and snap-shooting at 200 yards with fixed bayonets. Total scores, No. 1 Coy. 85.2, No. 2 Coy. 84.8, No. 3, 89.9, No. 4 Coy, 84.0. Battalion average, 86.5. The Battalion has benefited much by this musketry.	
	15-6-17		In Billets at RENESCURE. Battalion bathed in the Canal during the morning. 2nd Lieut. P.A.A. Harbord joined the Battalion.	
	16-6-17		Battalion marched at 7.55 a.m. to billets two miles east of WINNIZEELE, north east of CASSEL. A distance of 15½ miles. A grilling day and a very trying march but the Battalion stood it extremely well – only six men fell out and were sent on to billets in ambulance from the last halt.	

WAR DIARY
or
INTELLIGENCE SUMMARY.

Army Form C. 2118.

Place	Date	Hour	Summary of Events and Information	Remarks and references to Appendices
	17-6-17		In Billets as above. Voluntary Divine Services in the evening.	
	18-6-17		The Battalion marched at 9.30 a.m. to a Camp ½ mile south of PROVEN, crossing the border of BELGIUM, arrived about 11.0 a.m. Majority of Battalion bivouacked. Heavy showers and thunderstorms during the day.	
	19-6-17		In bivouacs as above. The Battalion did general training. A wet day.	
	20-6-17		The Battalion marched at 7.30 a.m. to a field on the outskirts of HERZEELE to attend a presentation of Crosses of the French Legion of Honour by General Antoine, G.O.C., 1st French Army to 44 Staff Officer and 2 Regimental Officers of the 5th Army. A hot day and a trying parade, as the Battalion remained at the "Slope" throughout the presentation. After the distribution, so gratifying to the Regimental Soldier, the Battalion marched past followed by the 2nd Battalion Coldstream Guards and two French Battalions, and, after one hour's halt in a field for dinners, marched six miles back to Billets.	
	21-6-17		The Battalion had baths during the day and did training when not bathing. Showery all day.	
	22-6-17		In bivouacs as above. Battalion employed all day on fatigue.	

Army Form C. 2118.

WAR DIARY
or
INTELLIGENCE SUMMARY.
(Erase heading not required.)

Instructions regarding War Diaries and Intelligence Summaries are contained in F. S. Regs., Part II. and the Staff Manual respectively. Title pages will be prepared in manuscript.

Place	Date	Hour	Summary of Events and Information	Remarks and references to Appendices
	23-6-17		In bivouacs as above.	
	24-6-17		The Battalion marched at 9.30 a.m. to WIPPE CROSS ROADS, 1½ miles north west of ELVERDINGHE, most of the Battalion in huts, remainder under tarpaulin shelters. Two Companies on fatigue from 10.0 p.m. to 4.0 a.m. burying cable near ELVERDINGHE.	
	25-6-17		In Camp as above. Two remaining Companies on day fatigue burying Cable. A certain amount of long range shelling at night in the neighbourhood of Camp. One R.A.M.C. man attached to the Battalion for Water duties, slightly wounded but remained at Duty.	
	26-7-17		In Camp as above. Day and night fatigues continued.	
	27-6-17		In Camp as above. Fatigues continued. Considerable hostile aerial activity - two of our observation balloons brought down in flames by German aeroplanes during the day. Observers escaped by parachutes.	
	28-6-17		In Camp as above. Fatigues continued. Heavy thunderstorm during the evening. While the Battalion has been in this Camp, there has been a considerable amount of promiscuous hostile long distance shelling, chiefly on the roads at night. The Battalion has been fortunate in escaping casualties.	

Army Form C. 2118.

WAR DIARY
or
INTELLIGENCE SUMMARY.
(Erase heading not required.)

Instructions regarding War Diaries and Intelligence Summaries are contained in F.S. Regs., Part II. and the Staff Manual respectively. Title pages will be prepared in manuscript.

Hour, Date, Place	Summary of Events and Information	Remarks and references to Appendices
29-6-17	Battalion marched at 5.30 p.m. to CARDOEN CAMP, between WIPPE CROSS ROADS and ELVERDINGHE, taking over a more pleasant Camp from the 1st Battalion Scots Guards.	
30-6-17	In Camp at CARDOEN FARM. Heavy rain during the morning. In afternoon, No. 11 Platoon and part of No. 10 Platoon practised for a raid over the YSER CANAL by crossing a pond in Camp on mats made by the Royal Engineers.	

Lieutenant Colonel,
Commanding 2nd Battalion Grenadier Guards.

Army Form C.2118.

WAR DIARY
or
INTELLIGENCE SUMMARY.

(Erase heading not required.)

Instructions regarding War Diaries and Intelligence Summaries are contained in F. S. Regs., Part II. and the Staff Manual respectively. Title pages will be prepared in manuscript.

Place	Date	Hour	Summary of Events and Information	Remarks and references to Appendices
	1-7-17		In Camp at CARDOEN FARM. Divine Services in the morning. A quiet day.	
	2-7-17		The Battalion relieved 3rd Battalion Coldstream Guards in the BOESINGHE Sector, first platoon leaving Camp at 9.30 p.m. No. 3 Company on the Right, No. 4 Company on the Left, No. 1 Company in Support and No. 2 Company in Reserve. The Belgians are on our left, but in view of the coming offensive, they are, very prudently, being relieved by the French, 1st Battalion K.O.S.B. on our Right (38th Division), holding the sector occupied by the Battalion a year ago. The Battalion Frontage runs along the west bank of the YSER CANAL, and extends for a distance of 1500 yards. Relief complete by 1.35 p.m. Casualties. NIL.	
	3-7-17		In the Line as above. Most of the Battalion employed in continuous shifts in improvements of trenches by day and the carrying of material of all kinds to the front area by night. A fair amount of shelling in the early morning and afternoon. At 11.30 p.m. the Battalion undertook a raid of the German trenches. This had been ordered by the Brigade with a view to obtaining identification of the enemy and also information as to their territory. The raid was undertaken by 2nd Lieut. I.T.S. Gunnis with No. 11 Platoon, whose role it was, if possible, to capture a prisoner, and by 2nd Lieut. Lord I.B.G.T. Blackwood with a party of five other ranks from No. 10 Platoon, whose task it was to reconnoitre a definite point.	

Army Form C. 2118.

WAR DIARY
OF
INTELLIGENCE SUMMARY.
(Erase heading not required.)

Instructions regarding War Diaries and Intelligence Summaries are contained in F. S. Regs., Part II. and the Staff Manual respectively. Title pages will be prepared in manuscript.

Place	Date	Hour	Summary of Events and Information	Remarks and references to Appendices
	3-7-17 (Con.)		The obstacle to be overcome was the passage of the YSER CANAL, along the west bank of which our front line trenches ran. This was accomplished by means of 5 feet mats, made of canvas and wire netting nailed to wooden slats. Two of these were used and were unrolled by two specially detailed parties before the remainder crossed. These mats proved effective in providing a foothold over the muddy bed of the CANAL, and the party succeeded in crossing without undue delay at 11.45 p.m. and, apparently, without detection by the enemy. On the enemy side of the CANAL, however, considerable confusion arose. This was due, probably, to the fact that no German trench was found where expected from a previous study of aeroplane and other maps, but only a mass of shell-holes, wire entanglements and knife rests, which made progress and cohesion very difficult. 2nd Lieut. Lord Basil Blackwood proceeded to lead his party in the desired direction, and, after going for a considerable distance over rough and broken ground, he was passing a dugout when rifle was opened on them from another dugout, a little to their right front. Lord Blackwood's orderly was wounded in the leg, and a sapper of the Royal Engineers, who was one of the party, was killed. All the party laid down in shellholes upon being fired on. Several bombs were also thrown from the same direction as the rifle-shots. Owing to Lord Blackwood's two immediate followers having become casualties, the party, already a good deal strung out, now became further scattered, and, from this point, Lord Blackwood and the remainder lost each other. A Corporal of the Royal Engineers, who was wounded, speaks of seeing	

Army Form C. 2118.

WAR DIARY
or
INTELLIGENCE SUMMARY.
(Erase heading not required.)

Instructions regarding War Diaries and Intelligence Summaries are contained in F. S. Regs. Part II. and the Staff Manual respectively. Title pages will be prepared in manuscript.

Place	Date	Hour	Summary of Events and Information	Remarks and references to Appendices
	3/7/17 (Con).		Lord Blackwood crawl forward after the shots were fired, but he lost sight of the Officer. The two others who were left saw him fall, but never saw him again, and after crawling about for a time, they eventually returned towards the CANAL BANK. They did not, however, as was their undoubted duty, report to Captain C.F.A. Walker, M.C., the Company Commander, who, with the Commanding Officer and Second in Command, was waiting for news on the CANAL BANK. Nobody had any intimation that anything was amiss, but when Lord Blackwood failed to return and those waiting became uneasy as to the delay, nobody could be found, who was able to give any information which would enable a patrol to be sent out. What happened to the party under 2nd Lieut. I.F.S. Gunnis is more obscure. One portion of it went, as arranged, to form a "block" on the north side and the remainder went southwards in search of a prisoner. Eventually, they found a German trench, and proceeded down it until an obstruction of wire, etc., made further progress impossible; as the sides were too steep to allow of egress, 2nd Lieut. Gunnis gave the order to turn about, with the intention of retracing his steps and getting out of the trench further back. This order was, apparently, misunderstood, and some of the party became detached from the main body. 2nd Lieut. Gunnis then entered another trench with some of his Platoon and proceeded until fired at at very close range. He then led back a little way and proceeded forward again - this time outside the trench. He passed the point from which he had been first fired at, and must have lost direction, as some one opened fire on the party from the	

WAR DIARY
or
INTELLIGENCE SUMMARY.
(Erase heading not required.)

Army Form C. 2118.

Place	Date	Hour	Summary of Events and Information	Remarks and references to Appendices
	3-7-17 (Con).		reached the dead body of an Englishman, which was, probably, that of the Engineer, who had accompanied Lord Blackwood's party. 2nd Lieut. Gunnis told the two men next to him to carry the body back intending the remainder of the party to follow him. The darkness, combined with the broken state of the ground, seems to have had the same result here as in the case of Lord Blackwood's party. There was no one in close touch with these two men and when 2nd Lieut. Gunnis led on, there was no one in close support to him. While the men were picking up the body, several bombs were thrown, they took cover in shell holes, and when the bombing ceased and they got up again, 2nd Lieut. Gunnis was no longer in sight. One of those present speaks of having seen 2nd. Lieut. I.F.S. Gunnis walking to join 2nd Lieut. Lord B. Blackwood's party, but it is not possible to fix the time at which this took place. Casualties, 2nd Lieuts. I.F.S. Gunnis and Lord I.B.G.T. Blackwood, Missing and one man wounded.	
	4-7-17		In the Line as above. At about 12.40 a.m. a severe hostile artillery shoot commenced from the direction of YPRES on our right flank. At 12.50 a.m. while our party was still out, the enmy's S.O.S. Signal was sent up and a very heavy barrage of field and heavy guns was dropped on our area for about twenty minutes. A carrying party of the Scots Guards, which was at the junction of the Communication trench and our Front Line, had an Officer and fifteen other ranks killed and nine other ranks wounded. All our Companies suffered some casualties, and	

Army Form C. 2118.

WAR DIARY
or
INTELLIGENCE SUMMARY.
(Erase heading not required.)

Instructions regarding War Diaries and Intelligence Summaries are contained in F. S. Regs., Part II. and the Staff Manual respectively. Title pages will be prepared in manuscript.

Place	Date	Hour	Summary of Events and Information	Remarks and references to Appendices
	4-7-17 (Con).		we were very fortunate in not having more. This shelling may possibly explain why 2nd Lieut. Gunnis' party did not return and report immediately they found they had lost touch. No, report of any kind was made as to what had happened to the Officer until approaching daylight made a further patrol out of the question. Casualties, three men wounded and one slightly wounded, the latter remained at Duty. Intermittent shelling continued throughout the day. Several trench mortar Bombs fell on the Right Front Company. A fresh raid which had been organised to take place in the same place as before was forbidden by the Corps Commander. No further casualties.	
	5-7-17		In the Line as above. A considerable and increasing amount of shelling in the early morning. Two heavy Minenwerfers were firing from our Left Front, the bombs fell near the Support Line and range gradually lengthened until they fell close to and beyond Battalion H.Q. Compass bearings were taken and retaliation asked for with the result that not only our Front Companies and also the support Company were shelled by our own guns. Shortly afterwards, the gas alarm was given. Gas shells were fired at our Front Line and immediately behind it. The Battalion suffered no casualties through this, but a platoon of the 1st Battalion Irish Guards, which was holding a trench between our Support and Reserve Lines, had fifteen men gassed, three of whom subsequently died. Casualties, four N.C.Os. and men killed, five wounded, and two slightly wounded, the latter remained at Duty.	

Army Form C. 2118.

WAR DIARY
or
INTELLIGENCE SUMMARY.
(Erase heading not required.)

Instructions regarding War Diaries and Intelligence Summaries are contained in F. S. Regs., Part II. and the Staff Manual respectively. Title pages will be prepared in manuscript.

Place	Date	Hour	Summary of Events and Information	Remarks and references to Appendices
	6-7-17.		In the Line as above. Shelling was more pronounced than yesterday. One unlucky shell in the Support Line killed one man, wounded Lieut. L.St.L. Hermon-Hodge, and three Sergeants, one of the latter subsequently died. The Battalion on our right undertook a raid, which proved unsuccessful and the enemy put down a S.O.S. Barrage at 11.30 p.m. Several direct hits on the Signal Office and Battalion Headquarters, but no great damage was done. Casualties, three N.C.Os and men killed and five wounded.	
	7-7-17		In the Line as above. A more quiet day. The Battalion was relieved by the 2nd Battalion Coldstream Guards, and marched to billets at ROUSSEL FARM. During this tour in the trenches, a great amount of work was done by the Battalion in the improvements of trenches by day, the digging of assembly trenches and the carrying up of all kinds of material to the front area by night. During the past four days, the enemy's artillery has become more active, the shelling has increased very greatly and almost all fatigue and carrying parties have suffered casualties. Casualties, four men wounded.	
	8-7-17		In billets at ROUSSEL FARM. The Camp was shelled during the early morning. Casualties, one man killed and two wounded. Several were slightly wounded but remained at duty.	

Army Form C. 2118.

WAR DIARY
or
INTELLIGENCE SUMMARY.
(Erase heading not required.)

Instructions regarding War Diaries and Intelligence Summaries are contained in F.S. Regs., Part II. and the Staff Manual respectively. Title pages will be prepared in manuscript.

Place	Date	Hour	Summary of Events and Information	Remarks and references to Appendices
	9-7-17		In billets at ROUSSEL FARM. A Court of Enquiry consisting of Captain G.C.F. Harcourt-Vernon, D.S.O., Captain A.T.A. Ritchie, M.C. and Captain J.N. Buchanan set to enquire into all circumstances connected with the raid undertaken by the Battalion whilst in the Line.	
	10-7-17		In Billets at ROUSSEL FARM. Several men have been wounded by long range shelling during the stay in this Camp. While in this Camp, the Battalion has found daily fatigue parties for carrying ammunition to the front line by day and for pushing rations up to the front line on trucks by night. Fatigue parties amounted to 200 men daily.	
	11-7-17		The Battalion relieved the 3rd Battalion Coldstream Guards in the Support system of trenches. A quiet relief.	
	12-7-17		In the Support Line. Day passed without casualties in spite of a good deal of shelling of Nos. 1 and 2 Companies, in the "X" Line. The Belgians have now been relieved by the French who are now holding the Sector on our left. Day was occupied by continuous work and repairing trenches, which are constantly being blown in by enemy shell fire. All Officers and as many N.C.Os as possible were taken over the Battalion "forming up" ground and shown objectives and land-marks in the coming offensive.	

Army Form C. 2118.

WAR DIARY
or
INTELLIGENCE SUMMARY.
(Erase heading not required.)

Instructions regarding War Diaries and Intelligence Summaries are contained in F. S. Regs., Part II. and the Staff Manual respectively. Title pages will be prepared in manuscript.

Place	Date	Hour	Summary of Events and Information	Remarks and references to Appendices
	13-7-17		In the Support Line. Nos. 1 and 3 Companies were relieved about 10. p.m. by two Companies of the 1st Battalion Grenadier Guards, Nos. 2 and 4 Companies were relieved about midnight by two Companies of the 1st Battalion Irish Guards. On relief, the Battalion marched by Platoons to ELVERDINGHE Railhead and entrained for PROVEN.	
	14-7-17		Arrived at PROVEN by train about 4.0 a.m. and bivouacked in a field near the Railway. Breakfasts provided on arrival. The Battalion marched after dinners to the HER-ZEELE area, billeting in farms near HONDFLOND. Fairly good billets.	
	15-7-17		In billets near HONDFLOND. Divine Services in the morning. Officers and Platoon Sergeants visited the Training area, where trenches are being dug to represent the German system. Lieutenant F.A. Magnay joined the Battalion.	
	16-7-17		In Billets near HONDFLOND. No. 2 Company used the Spray Baths at HERZEELE in the morning, No. 3 Company used the baths in the afternoon. Companies practised over the Training Ground during the day. Lieutenant G.R. Westmacott and 2nd Lieut. S.H. Pearson joined the Battalion.	

Army Form C. 2118.

WAR DIARY
or
INTELLIGENCE SUMMARY.
(Erase heading not required.)

Instructions regarding War Diaries and Intelligence Summaries are contained in F. S. Regs., Part II. and the Staff Manual respectively. Title pages will be prepared in manuscript.

Place	Date	Hour	Summary of Events and Information	Remarks and references to Appendices
	17-7-17.		In Billets near HONFLOND. The Battalion practised an advance over the Practice trenches, commencing at 10.15 a.m. Advance to the second objective in artillery formation was carried out.	
	18-7-17.		In billets near HONFLOND. The Battalion practised with 2nd Battalion Coldstream Guards and thre sections of the Brigade Machine Gun Company an advance over the practice trenches.	
	19-7-17.		In Billets near HONFLOND. The Battalion practised, with 2nd Battalion Coldstream Guards, and two sections of the Machine Company, the second stage of the advance, i.e. from the BLACK LINE to the GREEN LINE. A barrage was represented by the drums of all Battalions.	
	20-7-17.		In billets near HONFLOND. The Battalion practised the second stage of the advance over the same ground as yesterday. Drums represented barrage. "Moppers up", Signallers and patrols practised their respective tasks. In the evening, the officers played the Sergeants at Football. Result, two goals all.	
	21-7-17.		The Brigade, less 3rd Battalion Coldstream Guards and 1st Battalion Irish Guards and Trench Mortars, practised an attack over the same ground with certain points held up by detachments of 3rd Battalion Coldstream Guards. Officers from the Corps Cavalry accompanied the Battalion, and Officers from 3rd Battalion Coldstream Guards and 1st Battalion Irish Guards acted as umpires.	

Army Form C. 2118.

WAR DIARY
or
INTELLIGENCE SUMMARY.
(Erase heading not required.)

Instructions regarding War Diaries and Intelligence Summaries are contained in F. S. Regs., Part II. and the Staff Manual respectively. Title pages will be prepared in manuscript.

Place	Date	Hour	Summary of Events and Information	Remarks and references to Appendices
	22-7-17		In Billets near HONFLOND. Voluntary Divine Service at 8.0 a.m. Practice attack carried out as yesterday. In the evening dinner took place in a marquee erected by the Pioneers near Battalion Headquarters, which was attended by the Brigadier, Brigade Major, Colonel R.G. Gordon-Gilmour, C.V.O., C.B., D.S.O., and other Officers from the Brigade, beside all Officers of the Battalion. The Band of the Coldstream Guards played during dinner.	
	23-7-17		In Billets near HONFLOND. Officers and N.C.Os practised wiring etc. Companies paraded for Drill, etc.	
	24-7-17		In Billets near HONFLOND. Rehearsal of attack on the GREEN DOTTED LINE. All Officers being dressed like the men, and Companies digging in on objective.	
	25-7-17		In Billets at HONFLOND. A wet day. The Brigadier addressed all Officers and Sergeants.	
	26-27/7/17		In Billets at HONFLOND. Companies occupied in drill, wiring and inspection of Lewis Guns and all equipment.	
	28-7-17		Battalion moved at 8.0 a.m. in lorries to ROUSSEL FARM, leaving Lieut. G.R. Westmacott and 2nd Lieut. S.H. Pearson and 80 other ranks in a Reinforcement Camp. Rumours that Germans had retired from the BOESINGHE	

Army Form C. 2118.

WAR DIARY
or
INTELLIGENCE SUMMARY.

(Erase heading not required.)

Place	Date	Hour	Summary of Events and Information	Remarks and references to Appendices
	28-7-17	(Con)	SECTOR were very prevalent, but proved to be only partially true, the fact being that they found part of their Front Line untenable, and this had been occupied by our troops.	
	29-7-17		Divine Service in the morning. Battalion moved to bivouacs in the FOREST AREA in the afternoon. Information received that today is "Y" day.	
	30-7-17		Battalion bivouacked as above. Morning spent in the distribution of bombs, tools, S.A.A., etc., Afternoon spent in resting until 10.30 p.m. after which time see attached narrative.	
	31-7-17		See attached narrative by Lieutenant Colonel C.R.C. de Crespigny, D.S.O.	

Lieutenant Colonel,

Commanding 2nd Battalion Grenadier Guards.

NARRATIVE OF OPERATIONS

by

Lieutenant Colonel C.R.C. de Crespigny, D.S.O.,

Commanding 2nd Battalion Grenadier Guards.

Period. From 30th July, 1917 to 2nd August, 1917.

On the night of 30th July, at about 10.30 p.m. the Battalion moved from bivouacs in the FOREST AREA, 2½ miles west of ELVERDINGHE, to a field near ROUSSEL FARM, about a mile nearer the Front Line.

Platoon guides and cookers had been sent forward under an Officer, and on arrival, tea and rum were issued to the men, who afterwards bivouacked by platoons in the open. The weather was fine, and there was no shelling near the Battalion during the night.

ZERO was fixed for 3.50 a.m. Officers for the first time were dressed like the men. Battalion breakfasted at 3.0 a.m. and at 4.0 a.m. moved off by platoon blobs at 100 yards interval, the following Officers being with the Battalion :-

Headquarters.

Lieutenant Colonel C.R.C. de Crespigny, D.S.O.,
Acting Second in Command, Captain C.F.A. Walker, M.C.
Adjutant, Lieutenant A.H. Penn.
Medical Officer, Captain J.A. Andrews, M.C., R.A.M.C.

No. 1 Company.	No. 2 Company.
Captain J.N. Buchanan.	Captain A.T.A. Ritchie, M.C.,
2nd Lieut. R.G. Briscoe.	Lieut. A.S.L. St. J. Mildmay.
2nd Lieut. P.A.A. Harbord.	Lieut. F.H.G. Layland-Barratt, M.C.
	Lieut. R.G.C. Napier.

No. 3 Company.	No. 4 Company.
Captain Sir A.L. Napier, Bart.	Lieut. J.H. Jacob.
Lieut. K.O.G. Harvard.	Lieut. R.E.H. Oliver.
2nd Lieut. H. Minto Wilson.	2nd Lieut. F.H.J. Drummond.

All other Officers and a proportion of Other Ranks were left with the 1st Line Transport.

The task assigned to the Battalion, together with the 2nd Battalion Coldstream Guards, was the capture of the furthest objective allotted to the Division, a distance of about 2½ miles from the Front Line.

The 2nd Battalion Coldstream Guards was on the left of the Battalion, and the 17th Battalion Royal Welsh Fusiliers (38th Division) on the right, 3rd Battalion Coldstream Guards and 1st Battalion Irish Guards in Divisional Reserve. The capture of the three itermediate lines was allotted to Battalions of the 2nd and 3rd Guards Brigades on the right and left respectively. On leaving the "forming up" area, the Battalion divided, Nos. 1 and 3 Companies, (left front and rear) and Battalion Headquarters moving by HUNTER STREET, Nos. 2 and 4 Companies by RAILWAY STREET, parallel tracks, the Battalion meeting at a point about 1,000 yards west of the YSER CANAL, along the west bank of which ran the Front Line.

From this point, which was reached at exactly the scheduled time, 5.20 a.m. the Battalion advanced in Artillery Formation. During the early stages of the advance the shelling was very slight and it was not until the Canal was reached that the Battalion began to suffer casualties.

A considerable amount of heavy shelling was met with on both sides of the Canal, and several platoons and Headquarters lost men, but apart from this, the advance to the GREEN LINE was without particular incident. The Battalion advanced with perfect steadiness, intervals and distance being kept as though on a field day.

The Canal was crossed by temporary bridges at about 6.0 a.m.

(2)

and from here onwards the Battalion gained on the time allotted for the advance, so that all platoons were able to halt occasionally in shell-holes at the discretion of Company Officers in order to avoid any zones which appeared to be received particular attention from enemy shelling.

The enemy were continually shortening his range, and there is no doubt that by moving away from the shelling as necessity demanded, many casualties were avoided.

At about 2,000 yards from the old Front Line, the leading Companies, No. 1 (Left) and No. 2 (Right) came under machine gun and rifle fire and deployed, their example being followed by Nos. 3 and 4 Companies when they reached the same point, and the advance was continued in two lines to a point about 500 yards south west of the GREEN LINE, about 3,000 yards from the old Front Line, where the Battalion halted according to plan until 8.20 a.m.

During this period, the 2nd Guards Brigade was timed to advance to and capture the GREEN LINE, and 25 minutes later the Battalion advanced according to orders, through the 2nd Guards Brigade and up to the barrage, which was supposed to stay 200 yards east of the GREEN LINE for some minutes and then advance to cover the attack of the 1st Guards Brigade.

The GREEN LINE was not a line of trenches, but only a line on the map about 100 yards in front of a road which provided a convenient land-mark, and when the leading Companies reached this line, the Right Company (No. 2) found the 3rd Battalion Grenadier Guards digging in as expected, but Captain J.N. Buchanan, Commanding No. 1 Company on the left, could see no trace of the 1st Battalion Coldstream Guards, who should have been consolidating on the left of the 3rd Battalion Grenadier Guards. As his Company was slightly in advance of their time, Captain Buchanan commenced to dig in, the position reached being on the crest of the hill and exposed to considerable machine gun fire. A message was at this moment received from Captain A.T.A. Ritchie, M.C., Commanding the Right Front Company, to say that his Company was held up by machine gun fire and that there was no sign of the Battalion on his right.

The whole line was at this period under considerable machine gun and rifle fire from farms and strong points and at this juncture, both Captain A.T.A. Ritchie, M.C., and Lieut. R.G.C. Napier, of No. 2 Company, were hit by machine gun bullets, the command of the Company passing to Lieut. A.S.L. St. J. Mildmay.

Captain Buchanan decided that he ought not to stop whilst it was possible to push on, so continued his advance, sending to No. 3 Company to ask them to garrison the GREEN LINE for the present.

Owing to the delay caused on the left by absence of the 1st Battalion Coldstream Guards, (who, as afterwards transpired had gone too far to the right and became mixed up with the 3rd Battalion Grenadier Guards) and on the right by the failure of the 17th Battalion Royal Welsh Fusiliers, the advance was not continued until 15 minutes or so after the barrage was timed to move away. By this time, however, the barrage was extremely uncertain, dropping sometimes across the STEENBEEK, 800 yards off, and sometimes to close as to cause the Company to halt, so that the delay was not the disaster which it might have been. Captain Buchanan's Company succeeded in advancing to SIGNAL and RUISSEAU FARMS where twenty or thirty German prisoners, including several Officers, were captured, and, finally, with the assistance of a platoon from No. 3 Company, most ably led by Lieut. K.O'G. Harvard, he crossed the STEENBEEK and dug in 60 yards beyond the east bank.

The manner in which this Company pushed on under the leadership of Captain J.N. Buchanan and 2nd Lieuts R.G. Briscoe and P.A.A. Harbord was quite admirable.

Meanwhile, the position on the right of the Battalion was more difficult. When it was found that the 17th Battalion Royal Welsh Fusiliers had failed to advance up to the GREEN LINE, a platoon of No. 4 Company under Lieut. R.E.H. Oliver at once formed a defensive flank to the right.

By this time, No. 2 Company, by throwing out flank parties with snipers and by Lewis Gun fire had succeeded in silencing some of the opposing machine guns, and was again able to advance, but, owing to the failure on his right, Lieut. Mildmay was forced to use half of his Company to defend his flank, and was thus unable to maintain touch with No. 2 Company, which had pushed forward on his left.

Lieut. J.H. Jacob, who commanded No. 4 Company with great resource throughout the operation, sent one platoon to assist the advance of No. 2 Company, and, after consultation with Captain Buchanan, despatched a third platoon under 2nd Lieut. F.H.J. Drummond to prolong the right of No. 3 Company, who had by now advanced in support of No. 1 Company.

2nd Lieut. Drummond was here wounded by a shell, which killed a man on either side of him, but in spite of this and a later wound in the neck from a bullet, he remained at duty until the Battalion was relieved and displayed most conspicuous ability in grasping and dealing with every situation which arose.

By this time a handful of the Royal Welsh Fusiliers had appeared on the right rear, and, mindful of the importance of pushing forward, Lieut. Mildmay continued his advance up to within 80 yards of the STEENBEEK.

Heavy machine gun fire from LANGEMARCK VILLAGE made progress over the stream impracticable, and as his Company was occupying a position with a good field of fire, Lieut. Mildmay ordered the Company to dig in where it was.

During the whole of the period from the GREEN LINE, the Battalion was under steady shell fire from the enemy which caused many casualties. Under cover of darkness, the line was straightened and strengthened and touch established between all units.

During the night, a steady drizzle commenced, which continued practically without intermission until the relief of the Battalion by the 1st Battalion Irish Guards two days later on the night of 2nd August.

Owing to the exposed position of our line and the impossibility, owing to the wet, of digging deep trenches, the enemy was able to inflict several casualties by sniping, amongst them Lieut. K.O'G. Harvard, who received a wound whilst supervising his platoon from which he died on reaching the Regimental Aid Post.

We suffered greatly through the proximity of the 38th Division who, day and night, persisted without any counter-attack in sending up S.O.S. Signals, which brought down our barrage, some of which was on our own line and also retaliation from the enemy.

The conditions for the men were very bad, shell holes and trenches were waterlogged, and little better than those occupied during the past winter.

The Battalion was relieved on the night of 2nd/3rd August by the 1st Battalion Irish Guards, and marched to BLUET FARM, where hot tea was provided in a tent, and, afterwards, at about 6.0 a.m. marched to ELVERDINGHE to entrain for a Camp near PROVEN.

Owing to a shell having blown up the line, no train was available, and the Battalion went into bivouacs near CARDOEN FARM until lorries were provided to take the Battalion into Camp between PROVEN and HERZEELE, which was reached at 12.30 p.m. on 3rd August.

Casualties, Lieut. K.O'G. Harvard, Killed.
Lieut. R.G.C. Napier, Wounded and died from wounds.
Captain A.T.A. Ritchie, M.C., Wounded.
Lieut. J.H. Jacob, Wounded.
Lieut. A.S.L. St. J. Mildmay and 2nd Lieut. F.H.J. Drummond were slightly wounded, but remained at duty. Other ranks, Killed 44, Wounded, 191, Missing 15, slightly wounded, but remained at duty, 11, a total of 261 other ranks.

Lieutenant Colonel,

Commanding 2nd Battalion Grenadier Guards.

6th August, 1917.

WAR DIARY
or
INTELLIGENCE SUMMARY.

(Erase heading not required.)

Army Form C. 2118.

2nd Bn Gren Guards

August 1917

Place	Date	Hour	Summary of Events and Information	Remarks and references to Appendices
	1-8-17 and 2-8-17		As per narrative of 7th August, forwarded with Diary for month ending 31st July, by Lieutenant Colonel C.R.C. de Crespigny, D.S.O.	
	3-8-17		Battalion arrived at PLUMSTEAD CAMP, between HERZEELE and PROVEN, at 12.30 p.m. Remainder of day spent in rest and the drying of clothes, but the weather was not favourable for the latter.	
	4-8-17.		In Camp as above. Day spent in the drying of clothes and the cleaning of rifles and equipment. A fine sunny day.	

	5th to 20th August.		In Camp as above. Battalion employed in Drill, Musketry, etc. On 11th August, a draft of 133 N.C.Os and men joined the Battalion. The following Officers joined the Battalion on the dates given :-
			    Captain C.N. Newton, M.C., 18-8-17.
			    2/Lieut. H.White, 7-8-17.
			    2/Lieut. R.H.R. Palmer, 11-8-17.
			    2/Lieut. H.B.G. Morgan, 18-8-17.
			The following Officers, Non-Commissioned Officers and men have received decorations as under :-
			
			MILITARY CROSS.
			    Captain J.N. Buchanan.
			    2/Lieut. R.G. Briscoe.
			    2/Lieut. P.A.A. Harbord.
			    2/Lieut. F.H.J. Drummond.
			    Lieut. A.S.L. St. J. Mildmay.
			    Lieut. G.G.M. Vereker.	

Army Form C. 2118.

WAR DIARY
or
INTELLIGENCE SUMMARY.
(Erase heading not required.)

DISTINGUISHED CONDUCT MEDAL.

```
14269, Sgt   Sharpe      G.
17892, L/S   Tullett     H.
14034, L/C   Topps       F.
24989, L/C   Birtles     F.
15374, Pte   Tyrrell     A.
14358,  "    Corrigan    T.
24174,  "    Young       C.
```

MILITARY MEDAL.

```
11629, Sgt   Holliday    R.
25819, L/C   Moulding    J.
13789, L/C   Ward        H.
17882, L/C   Warrender   W.
12704, L/C   Wall        A.
15564, Pte   Wilding     H.
21214,  "    Bailey      G.
24053,  "    Chivers     A.E.
25622,  "    Tickner     E.J.
23981,  "    Brierley    P.
27101,  "    Galley      P.H.
24679,  "    Arrowsmith  J.
24657,  "    Page        F.
```

Awarded "CROIX DE GUERRE."

Captain and Adjutant A.H. Penn.

Place	Date	Hour	Summary of Events and Information	Remarks and references to Appendices
	21-8-17		In Camp between HERZEELE and PROVEN. A draft of 137 other ranks joined the Battalion. Battalion marched at 4.30 p.m. to PROVEN and entrained for ELVERDINGHE. The Battalion went in to bivouacs at BLUET FARM, between ELVERDINGHE and BOESINGHE, arriving	

Army Form C. 2118.

WAR DIARY
or
INTELLIGENCE SUMMARY.

(Erase heading not required.)

Instructions regarding War Diaries and Intelligence Summaries are contained in F. S. Regs., Part II. and the Staff Manual respectively. Title pages will be prepared in manuscript.

Place	Date	Hour	Summary of Events and Information	Remarks and references to Appendices
	22-8-17		In bivouacs at BLUET FARM. Three Companies worked on the roads on PILCKEM RIDGE. One Company paraded for Drill.	
	23-8-17		In bivouacs as above. Three Companies worked on the roads on PILCKEM RIDGE. One Company paraded for Drill.	
	24-8-17		In Bivouacs as above. Three Companies paraded for work as above. One Company paraded for Drill. The Battalion marched at 2.15 p.m. to ELVERDINGHE and entrained for BANDINGHEM and returned to the Camp between PROVEN and HERZEELE, arriving at 5.0 p.m.	
	25-8-17		In Camp as above. The Battalion paraded for Drill and training.	
	26-8-17		In Camp as above. Divine Services in the morning. The following Officers, Captain J.N. Buchanan, M.C., Lieuts. G.R. Westmacott, F.A.M. Browning, J.C. Cornforth, J. Tabor, and 2nd Lieuts. R.G. Briscoe, M.C., P.A.A. Harbord, M.C., R.H. Palmer, S.H. Pearson, and H. White and Captain J.A. Andrews, M.C., R.A.M.C., played a team of Officers of the 2nd Battalion Coldstream Guards at Football. Result, Coldstreamers defeated by three goals to one.	
	27-8-17		In Camp as above. The Battalion paraded at 9.40 a.m. under the Commanding Officer for the presentation of medal ribbons to Officers, N.C.Os and men by the Brigadier for decorations gained during the operations of 31st ult. A wet and stormy evening.	

Army Form C. 2118.

WAR DIARY
or
INTELLIGENCE SUMMARY.
(Erase heading not required)

Instructions regarding War Diaries and Intelligence Summaries are contained in F. S. Regs., Part II. and the Staff Manual respectively. Title pages will be prepared in manuscript.

Place	Date	Hour	Summary of Events and Information	Remarks and references to Appendices
	28-8-17		In Camp as above. A wet morning. Battalion marched at 1.30 p.m. to PROVEN and entrained for ELVERDINGHE. Marched to a camp of bivouacs (HARROW CAMP) near BLUET FARM. Weather cleared a little during the day.	
	29-8-17		In bivouacs near BLUET FARM. Companies paraded for Drill and Training. A quiet Day.	
	30-8-17		In bivouacs as above. No. 4 Company on fatigue carrying material to the front line in the early morning. The other Companies paraded for Drill and Training. A great deal of promiscuous shelling by the enemy during the day. One shell pitched on the Cookers of the 3rd Battalion Coldstream Guards in ETON CAMP, adjoining that occupied by this Battalion, killing three men and wounding more or less seriously fourteen others, two travelling cookers were blown to pieces. One man of this Battalion was wounded in the evening by a shell which killed one French Soldier and two horses. The Battalion was exceedingly fortunate in suffering so slightly.	
	31-8-17		The Battalion moved back about ½ mile out of the shelled area. Commenced moving at 8.0 a.m. taking bivouacs and tents. New Camp pitched by 10.0 a.m. Wild shelling by the enemy continued but no shells fell in the Camp.	

Lieutenant Colonel,
Commanding 2nd Battalion Grenadier Guards.

WAR DIARY
or
INTELLIGENCE SUMMARY.
(Erase heading not required.)

Army Form C. 2118.

September 1917
2nd Bn Grenadier Guards

Place	Date	Hour	Summary of Events and Information	Remarks and references to Appendices
	1-9-1917 to 4-9-17.		The Battalion was in Camp near ELVERDINGHE. Enemy aircraft dropped many bombs in this neighbourhood during the past few days, and also shelled the vicinity of Camp occasionally, but only one man was wounded.	
	5-9-1917 to 8-9-1917		On 5th inst. The Battalion relieved the 1st Battalion Grenadier Guards, in the section of the line immediately to the left of the Steden Railway. The line was held by a series of posts running across the TRIEBEEK. A lucky relief - only a few casualties being incurred notwithstanding considerable hostile shell fire. The line is a very unpleasant one to occupy, as the nature of the ground makes movement by day practically impossible and the ground is extremely marshy. Enemy shelling is extremely heavy by day and night. Nos. 1, 3 and 4 Companies in the Front line, and No. 2 Company in Support. Captain C.F.A. Walker, M.C., commanded the Battalion whilst the Commanding Officer was in temporary command of the Brigade. During the tour in the line, the Battalion sustained the following casualties, chiefly from shell fire. Killed, 6 N.C.Os and men, Wounded, 32 N.C.Os and men. 2nd Lieut H.B.G. Morgan and three other ranks were slightly wounded but remained at Duty. The Battalion was relieved on the night of 9th/10th by the 1st Battalion Irish Guards, who were heavily shelled during the relief whilst on the Langemarck-Widjundrift Road and sustained between 20 and 30 Casualties, before reaching the line. Considering the circumstances, the Battalion had on	

Army Form C. 2118.

WAR DIARY
or
INTELLIGENCE SUMMARY.

(Erase heading not required.)

Instructions regarding War Diaries and Intelligence Summaries are contained in F. S. Regs., Part II. and the Staff Manual respectively. Title pages will be prepared in manuscript.

Place	Date	Hour	Summary of Events and Information	Remarks and references to Appendices
	10-11-17 to 13-11-17		extremely good relief, and arrived at ROOTY CAMP, between ELVERDINGHE and POPERINGHE at 8.0 a.m. on 10th. In Bivouacs (Tents) Camp. An extremely unpleasant four days. During the stay the Battalion was shelled, bombed and gassed with the greatest freedom. Several large fatigue parties were found for carrying material, etc., towards the Front line. Whilst in this Camp, we sustained the following casualties. Killed, 1 man. Shell fire. " 1 N.C.O. (Gas.) Wounded, 3 (Shell fire) Gassed, 11 N.C.Os and men admitted to Hospital. During the novice of the Battalions departure, six 5.9 inch shells fell into the Camp, without inflicting any casualties. Three shell holes were carefully handed over to the 3rd Battalion Grenadier Guards on relief. During the past four days, 3rd Battalion Coldstream Guards occupying the left sector of the Brigade Frontage, were twice raided and, in the early morning of 13th, the 2nd Battalion Irish Guards, who relieved the Coldstream Guards, were attacked in force by the enemy under cover of a heavy creeping barrage, and sustained a large number of casualties. The Battalion marched to De Wippe Camp, relieving the 1st Battalion Welsh Guards.	
	14-0-17		In Camp at De Wippe. The Battalion paraded for Training. Weather very wet and misty. Lieut. H.D. Strafford joined.	

Army Form C. 2118.

WAR DIARY
or
INTELLIGENCE SUMMARY.
(Erase heading not required.)

Instructions regarding War Diaries and Intelligence Summaries are contained in F.S. Regs., Part II. and the Staff Manual respectively. Title pages will be prepared in manuscript.

Place	Date	Hour	Summary of Events and Information	Remarks and references to Appendices
	15-9-17		In Camp as above. Companies paraded for Drill and Training. The Band of the Scots Guards played in Camp during the afternoon.	
	16-9-17		In Camp as above. Divine Service during the morning. The Band of the Scots Guards played in Camp during the afternoon.	
	17-9-17		In Camp as above. Companies paraded for Drill and Training.	
	18-9-17		130 other ranks per Company marched to a Camp near MICKEM HILL, relieving the 2nd Battalion Hampshire Regiment, for work on roads, etc. in the forward area. The remainder of the Battalion remained at De Wippe until 20th when they will march to Plumsteed Camp in the P.O.W. lines. ... with a view to imperial operations, all ranks who had been detailed in consequence, three Companies marched back to De Wippe.	
	19-9-17		In Camp at De Wippe. Companies paraded for Drill and Training.	
	20-9-17		Three Companies returned to De Wippe and were employed on fatigues until dusk.	
	21-9-17		2nd Lieut. G.H. Hawking and a draft of 151 other ranks joined the details at Plumsteed Camp.	

Army Form C. 2118.

WAR DIARY
or
INTELLIGENCE SUMMARY.
(Erase heading not required.)

Instructions regarding War Diaries and Intelligence Summaries are contained in F. S. Regs., Part II. and the Staff Manual respectively. Title pages will be prepared in manuscript.

Place	Date	Hour	Summary of Events and Information	Remarks and references to Appendices
	22-9-17		Four Companies on fatigues, which were not of a very exacting nature, and only one casualty was sustained. The Battalion was relieved by the 2nd Battalion Coldstream Guards, marched to RUYSSIGNORE and entrained for BANDIGHEM for Plumstead Camp. Brigadier General G.D. Jeffreys, C.M.G., left the Brigade and proceeded to take command of the 19th Division, the command of the Brigade passing to the Commanding Officer, Lieutenant Colonel C.R.C. de Crespigny D.S.O., Brigadier General Jeffreys made a farewell speech to the details of the Battalion, many of whom had served under him as the Commanding Officer of the Battalion.	
	23-9-17		In Plumstead Camp. Divine Services in the morning. Major G.E.C. Rasch, D.S.O., assumed command of the Battalion.	
	24-9-17		In Camp as above. Battalion paraded for Drill and Training.	
	25-9-17		In Camp as above. The Battalion paraded for Drill and Training.	
	26-9-17		In Camp as above. The Battalion paraded for Drill and Training.	

Army Form C. 2118.

WAR DIARY
or
INTELLIGENCE SUMMARY.
(Erase heading not required.)

Instructions regarding War Diaries and Intelligence Summaries are contained in F. S. Regs., Part II. and the Staff Manual respectively. Title pages will be prepared in manuscript.

Place	Date	Hour	Summary of Events and Information	Remarks and references to Appendices
	27-9-17		In Camp as above. The Battalion paraded for Drill and Training.	
	28-9-17		In Camp as above. The Battalion paraded for Drill and Training.	
	29-9-17		In Camp as above. The Battalion paraded for Drill and Training.	
	30-9-17		In Camp as above. Divine Services in the morning.	
			[signature] Major, Commanding 2nd Battalion Grenadier Guards.	

Army Form C. 2118.

WAR DIARY
or
INTELLIGENCE SUMMARY.

(Erase heading not required.)

2ND BN GRENADIER GUARDS   Vol 39

October 1917

Date	Hour	Summary of Events and Information	Remarks and references to Appendices
1-10-17		In Camp at PLUMSTEAD, near WATOU. Companies paraded for Drill and Training. All Officers attended a lecture by Major General Montgomery in the evening.	
2-10-17		In Camp as above. The Battalion practised an attack.	
3-10-17		In Camp as above. The Battalion practised an attack.	
4-10-17		In Camp as above. The Battalion practised the attack.	
5-10-17		In Camp as above. The Battalion practised the attack.	
6-10-17		In Camp as above. The Battalion practised the attack.	
7-10/10/17 inclusive.		As per attached narrative by Lieut. Colonel G.E.C. Rasch, D.S.O.,	
11 & 12/10/17		In Camp at Charterhouse, Near ELVERDINGHE.	
13-17/10/17		On afternoon of 13th, the Battalion marched to relieve the Front Line on north side of STADEN-LANGEMARCK Railway. The front line had been slightly advanced by the 3rd Guards Brigade since the attack by the Battalion 9th and ran on relief about 500 yards from the southern edge of HOUTHULST FOREST. There had been much rain in the past few days, and the whole area between the front line and the YSER CANAL, was a sea of mud.	

Army Form C. 2118.

WAR DIARY
or
INTELLIGENCE SUMMARY.
(Erase heading not required.)

Instructions regarding War Diaries and Intelligence Summaries are contained in F. S. Regs., Part II. and the Staff Manual respectively. Title pages will be prepared in manuscript.

Place	Date	Hour	Summary of Events and Information	Remarks and references to Appendices
	17 & 18/10/17		The Battalion marched to BOESINGHE STATION, had hot tea, etc, from the Divisional Soup Kitchen, and entrained at 1.30 a.m. for BANDAGHEM STATION, near PROVEN, reaching there between 2.0 a.m. and 3.0 a.m. on 17th inst. and going into tents and bivouacs. Casualties, six killed, fourteen wounds, one missing. One man was slightly wounded but remained at Duty. Battalion spent the day in cleaning equipment, etc. Lieut.O. Martin-Smith and Lieut. S.T.S. Clarke joined the Battalion.	
	19-10-17		Battalion paraded at 5.0 a.m. and marched to PROVEN, entraining for WATTEN. Reached WATTEN at 9.30 a.m. and marched to TOURNEHEM, reaching there about noon. A delightful village in lovely country - rolling downs and beech woods. Billets for men rather cramped and need improvement.	
	20-10-17		In Billets at TOURNEHEM. Day spent in cleaning billets, etc.	
	21-10-17		In Billets as above. Church parade in the Village Square in the morning. In the afternoon, H.R.H. The Duke of Connaught, Colonel of the Regiment, visited and inspected the Battalion, which was drawn up in the Square to receive him. His Royal Highness subsequently sent the message which is attached hereto.	

Army Form C. 2118.

WAR DIARY
or
INTELLIGENCE SUMMARY.

(Erase heading not required.)

Instructions regarding War Diaries and Intelligence Summaries are contained in F. S. Regs., Part II. and the Staff Manual respectively. Title pages will be prepared in manuscript.

Place	Date	Hour	Summary of Events and Information	Remarks and references to Appendices
	22-10-17		In billets as above. Day spent in training – Bombing, Musketry, Lewis Gunnery, etc., also baths.	
	23-10-17		In Billets as above. A wet day. Companies at the disposal of Os. C. Companies. Attached message received from His Majesty The King.	
	24-10-17		In Billets as above. The 1st Guards Brigade paraded to practice for a review and march past by Field Marshal Sir Douglas Haig, Commander in Chief. The Band of the Scots Guards played in the Square during the afternoon.	
	25-10-17		The Commander in Chief inspected the Division near NORTHBECOURT, at 11.30 a.m. Battalions were drawn up and marched past in close column of half Companies. A high wind made words of command almost inaudible, and thus spoilt the arm drill, but the Division marched past well.	
	26-10-17		In Billets as above. The Battalion paraded for musketry, Lewis gunnery etc.	

Army Form C. 2118.

WAR DIARY
or
INTELLIGENCE SUMMARY.

(Erase heading not required.)

Instructions regarding War Diaries and Intelligence Summaries are contained in F. S. Regs., Part II. and the Staff Manual respectively. Title pages will be prepared in manuscript.

Place	Date	Hour	Summary of Events and Information	Remarks and references to Appendices
	27-10-17		In Billets as above. Battalion paraded for Bayonet Fighting, Lewis Gunnery, etc.;	
	28-10-17		In billets as above. Battalion paraded for Divine Services in the morning. A Brigade Gymkana was held in the afternoon, the Battalion competing in a Five Mile Race and obtained the second place. A number of Officers in the Division also competed in Horse Races, the Battalion being represented in this Event.	
	29-10-17		In Billets as above. Battalion paraded for Bayonet Fighting, Bombing. Lewis Gunnery and Drill. The following Officers attended a Course of Anti-Gas Instruction: EPERLECQUES under the Division -al Gas Officer:- Lieut. O. Martin-Smith, Lieut. S.T. S.Clarke, 2nd. Lieut. G.H.Hanning, 2nd. Lieut. R.H.R. Palmer. Officers clear of duty attended a Lecture by G.S.O.1. Guards Division, in the afternoon at NORTLEULINGHEM.	
	30-10-17		In Billets as above. Battalion paraded for Bayonet Fighting, Lewis-Gunnery and Drill, Route Marching and a Tactical Scheme was also exercised.	
	31-10-17		In Billets as above. Battalion paraded as yesterday. The undermentioned N.C.O's and Men have been	

A0935. Wt. W12639/M1292 750,000. 1/17. D;D. & L., Ltd. Forms/C2118/12.

Army Form C. 2118.

WAR DIARY
or
INTELLIGENCE SUMMARY.
(Erase heading not required.)

Place	Date	Hour	Summary of Events and Information	Remarks and references to Appendices
	31-10-17		(Continued) awarded the MILITARY MEDAL for the Recent Operations	

No. 14892. Sgt. Walton. B.
13414. L/Sgt. Pearson. T.
9334. " Pitt. W.
16533. Sgt. Sears. F.
12043. L/C. Leach. E.
25610. " Acland. G.
17252. Pte. Stenning. A.
13893. L/C. Hartshorn. C.
14294. Pte. Newman. H.
15203. Sgt. Hill. R.
16321. L/Sgt. Thompson. A.
13725. " Mawby. H.
19317. L/C. Dean. R.
13769. " Tomlinson. J.
11702. Pte. O'Neill. M.
12744. " Fitch. S.
23992. " Middleditch. W.
11183. " Drinkwater. P.

Authority D.R.O. 752, dated 29-10-17 and D.R.O. 753, dated 30-10-17.

Battalion played a Football Match in the afternoon against 10th. Battalion Lancashire - Fusiliers.

1st. November. 1917.

Lieutenant Colonel.
Commanding 2nd Battalion Grenadier Guards.

NARRATIVE OF OPERATIONS

by

Lieutenant Colonel G.E.C. Rasch, D.S.O.,

Commanding 2nd Battalion Grenadier Guards.

Period :- 7th to 10th October, 1917.

Map Reference :- BROENBEEK.

On 7th October, 1917, the Battalion, with the exception of certain details who marched to the Guards Division Reinforcement Camp, HERZEELE, proceeded by train at 9.0 a.m. to CHARTERHOUSE CAMP, between the YSER CANAL and ELVERDINGHE.

The accommodation in this Camp, (which we shared with the 2nd Battalion Coldstream Guards) was very moderate, and a steady drizzle which commenced as the Battalion arrived helped to make the men very uncomfortable.

The afternoon was spent in distributing fighting stores to Nos. 1 and 2 Companies, and at 6.0 p.m. the above two Companies, with a strength of 32 all ranks per platoon, marched off to take over their battle positions, then occupied by the 4th Battalion Grenadier Guards. The following Officers took part in the Battalion operations :-

Headquarters.

Commanding, Lieut. Colonel G.E.C. Rasch, D.S.O.,
Acting Second in Command, Captain G.C.F. Harcourt-Vernon, D.S.O.,
Acting Adjutant, Lieutenant F.A.M. Browning.
Medical Officer, Captain J.A. Andrews, M.C., R.A.M.C.,

No. 1 Company.	No. 2 Company.
Lieut. J.C. Cornforth.	Captain Sir A.L. Napier, Bart.,
2nd Lieut. S.H. Pearson.	Lieut. Hon. F.H. Manners.
2nd Lieut. H.D. Stratford.	2nd Lieut. H.B.G. Morgan.

The night was cold and windy and the darkness intense. The relief was a very long and troublesome one, owing to the sodden and shattered state of the ground, but was accomplished without many casualties.

On the following afternoon, Nos. 3 and 4 Companies left CHARTERHOUSE CAMP to take up their positions behind Nos. 2 and 1 Companies respectively. The following officers accompanied Nos. 3 and 4 Companies :-

No. 3 Company.	No. 4 Company.
Captain C.N. Newton, M.C.,	Lieut. G.R. Westmacott.
Lieut. A.W. Acland.	Lieut. R.A.W. Bicknell.
2nd Lieut. H. White.	Lieut. J. Tabor.

The day had been fine until about 4.0 p.m. when a steady rain commenced which increased to a soaking downpour and continued until the early morning preceding ZERO hour, making the position occupied by the troops, which were at at the best only shell holes, miserable in the extreme.

Rum and rations were sent up to the Front Companies on the night before ZERO, also hot tea in specially improvised containers, consisting of petrol tins in packs, tightly surrounded with dry hay.

The condition of the BROENBEEK, which ran parallel to our Front Line, at a distance of 250 yards, was a matter for great anxiety. Patrols during the past week had reported it to be impassable at various places, and it was feared that the recent rain had done much to render it a grave obstacle. Both Companies sent patrols to reconnoitre it during the nights preceding the attack without very reassuring result, although Lieut. Hon. F.H. Manners found one or two points at which he was able to

Mats and light bridges were carried to the Front Companies by night to be taken forward by the leading waves of the attack, but, as subsequent facts proved, it was found possible to dispense with them to a large extent.

The French were to attack on the left of the Guards Division, and the 29th Division on the right. 2nd Guards Brigade was on the left of the Division, 1st Guards Brigade on the right. The Battalion was on the right of the 1st Guards Brigade with the 2nd Battalion Coldstream Guards on the left and the 4th Battalion Worcestershire Regiment on the Right.

To Nos. 2 and 1 Companies (from left to right) was allotted the capture of the first objective, about 1,000 yards in depth. After a pause of 45 minutes, Nos. 3 and 4 Companies were to pass through these Companies and to capture and consolidate the second objective, 800 yards further on; after another pause, the 1st Battalion Irish Guards were to pass through the Battalion to a third objective.

The line of advance of the Battalion was parallel to and about 300 yards to the north of the STADEN-LANGEMARCK Railway, and the third objective was just at the southern fringe of HOULTHULST FOREST.

There was no preliminary bombardment, but at ZERO, fixed at 5.20 a.m. an intense barrage from 18 pounder guns and Stokes Mortars dropped on and beyond the line of the BROENBEEK. Under cover of this the leading Companies closed up as near as possible.

It was considered of the first importance that the barrage should not be lost by delay in crossing the stream, and some casualties were caused to men who pressed too close to it in the half light, which made its exact line very difficult to determine.

The stream proved to be far more easily crossed than was anticipated. Some crossed by means of fallen trees, others by planks and duckboards fromerly used by the Germans, and others waded, though shell holes in the bed of the stream made this method very uncertain.

Fortunately, the Division opposite had only been relieved a few hours previous to the attack. They were taken by surprise and made a poor resistance. Their line was held by a series of posts converted from shell-holes.

The advance continued practically unchecked, and, thanks to able leadership by Officers and Non-Commisioned Officers the Battalion was able to keep its direction, which was oblique to the line of "jumping off" ground.

Minor adjustments were necessary from time to time with the Battalion on the right, who lost direction occasionally and drifted too far towards the Battalion, but the first objective was gained and consolidated without heavy opposition or loss, and, at the proper time, No.s 3 and 4 Companies passed through to the capture and consolidation of the second objective, which was successfully effected.

Nothing could have exceeded the steadiness of the advance, which was all the more remarkable in view of the miserable conditions prevailing before ZERO.

Very soon after the capture of the objectives, enemy aircraft became very active, flying at very low altitude over the line, and all Companies were subjected to very heavy shelling until relief. This shell fire caused nearly all the casualties, which amounted to:-

Officers.   Lieutenant J. Tabor,..........................Wounded.
            2nd Lieutenant H.D. Stratford...............Wounded.
            Captain Sir A.L. Napier, Bart.,............Slight wound,
                                                       but remained
                                                       at Duty.

Other ranks.   Killed...33
               Wounded..123
               Missing...11
               Slightly wounded, who remained at Duty. 21

               T O T A L................................188 other ranks

On the night of 9th October, Nos. 1 and 2 Companies were given orders for relief and returned to LARREY CAMP, near ELVERDINGHE, a comfortable camp with Nissen huts.

The Companies came in admirably and found clean clothing, tea, rum and braziers awaiting them.

Nos. 3 and 4 Companies and Battalion Headquarters were relieved by the 1st Battalion Grenadier Guards on the following night and rejoined the remainder of the Battalion at LARREY CAMP.

Rasch
Lieutenant Colonel,
Commanding 2nd Battalion Grenadier Guards.

13th October, 1917.

Army Form C. 2118.

WAR DIARY
or
INTELLIGENCE SUMMARY.
(Erase heading not required.)

Instructions regarding War Diaries and Intelligence Summaries are contained in F. S. Regs., Part II. and the Staff Manual respectively. Title pages will be prepared in manuscript.

Place	Date	Hour	Summary of Events and Information	Remarks and references to Appendices
			The Battalion halted in Wood 15, north of the Canal, for teas, and, at dusk, continued the relief. This proved to be very confusing, as the Battalion was relieving parts of three Battalions of the 3rd Guards Brigade. The going for the last thousand yards was very bad indeed, the mud being almost as bad as that encountered last winter.	
			An Officer and a man of the 1st Battalion were "bogged" so severely in the mud, close to Battalion Headquarters that it was half an hour before they could be extricated, and many men were too exhausted to find their way to the Canal.	
			Once the relief was complete, the conditions were much better. The line was held by a series of posts, three Companies in front and one in support.	
			All movement by day was restricted to a minimum, and the Battalion reaped a benefit which was not shared by the Battalion of the West Yorkshire Regiment on the right, who exposed themselves freely and were heavily shelled in consequence. No. 1 Company had an unlucky shell, causing two Sergeants to become casualties, also eight other ranks, but apart from this, the casualties were not so heavy as had been anticipated.	
			The three days in the line were fine and the duckboards were pushed on by about 500 yards, so that conditions had much improved by the time that the relief took place. The Battalion was relieved by the 17th Battalion Lancashire Fusiliers on the night of 16th October. The relief was quiet and extremely successful, being complete by 7.30 p.m	

All Units.   G.D. No. 1199/3/A.

The Major General has received the following letter, which should be communicated to all ranks :-

"His Majesty has read with admiration and satisfaction the story of the splendid achievements of the Guards Division, and the King heartily congratulates you and the Division on all that has been accomplished in spite of the most unfavourable conditions of weather and mud.

As Colonel in Chief of the Guards His Majesty is proud to think that there has been imposed upon the Division no task that has not been successfully fulfilled.

The King has no doubt that after a well-earned rest, re-built and re-equipped, the Division will distinguish itself in the future as it has distinquished itself in the past, and His Majesty sends you all his best wishes."

(Signed) Francis Alston,
Lieutenant Colonel,
A.A. & Q.M.G., GUARDS DIVISION.

H.Q., Guards Division.
20/10/17.

SPECIAL ORDER OF THE DAY
BY
MAJOR GENERAL G.P.T. FEILDING, C.B., C.M.G., D.S.O.
COMMANDING GUARDS DIVISION.

Headquarters, Guards Division.
22nd October, 1917.

Field Marshal H.R.H. The Duke of CONNAUGHT, K.G., Senior Colonel of the Brigade of Guards, desires to express his pleasure at having been able to visit the Guards Division yesterday. He is much pleased that the Brigade of Guards should continue to maintain in such an excellent manner, the high traditions which they have always held, and congratulates all ranks on their splendid achievements during the last six months.

H.R.H. feels certain that the Division will always keep up the same standard and will for ever be a pattern of what a Division should be.

He wishes them the very best of luck in the future.

G. Feilding

Major-General,
Commanding GUARDS DIVISION.

WAR DIARY
or
INTELLIGENCE SUMMARY.

(Erase heading not required.)

Army Form C. 2118.

WAR DIARY OF 2ND BATTALION GRENADIER GUARDS FOR THE MONTH OF NOVEMBER, 1917.

Date	Summary of Events and Information
1-11-17.	In Billets at TOURNEHEM. Battalion practised Platoon Training, Lewis Gunnery, Bombing, etc., In the afternoon the Battalion played against the 4th Machine Gun Guards in 1st Tie of Divisional Competition.
2-11-17.	In Billets as above. Battalion practised a Tactical scheme under the Commanding Officer. The Divisional Gas N.C.O. completed the inspection of Gas Equipment. Baths were allotted to the Battalion during the day.
3-11-17.	In Billets as above. Battalion did Drill and Section Training also Lewis Gunnery.
4-11-17.	In Billets as above. Battalion attended Divine Services in the morning. The Autumn Meeting of the 2nd Guards Brigade was held in the afternoon, in which several Officers of the battalion competed.
5-11-17.	In Billets as above. Battalion paraded for Drill, Training, Lewis Gunnery, and a Practice Tactical Scheme. Voluntary shooting on the Range in the afternoon was also carried out.
6-11-17.	In Billets as above. Battalion paraded at 9.0 a.m. and marched to attend the presentation of French Decorations to the Guards Division, by General Antoine, G.O.C., 1st French Army, arriving at the Review Ground (J34 Central) at 10.30 a.m. in a drizzling rain. Owing to the rain the presentation did not take place and the Battalion marched back to billets

Army Form C. 2118.

WAR DIARY
or
INTELLIGENCE SUMMARY.
(Erase heading not required.)

Instructions regarding War Diaries and Intelligence Summaries are contained in F. S. Regs., Part II. and the Staff Manual respectively. Title pages will be prepared in manuscript.

Place	Date	Hour	Summary of Events and Information	Remarks and references to Appendices
	7-11-17.		In billets as above. Battalion paraded for Route marching, Drill, Lewis Gunnery and a Tactical Scheme under the Commanding Officer. The undermentioned were awarded the Distinguished Conduct Medal, for the recent operations. No. 18191. L/S. Davis. H. No 1 company. " 15478. Pte. Moots. J. " 2 "	
	8-11-17.		In billets as above. Battalion paraded for Route Marching and musketry.	
	9-11-17.		In billets as above. Battalion paraded for Firing and Training. Bayonet Fighting and Bombing was also practised. The Battalion were allotted Baths during the day.	
	10-11-17.		In Billets as above. Battalion paraded for Drill in the morning, under the Adjutant. A Tactical Scheme under the Commanding Officer was also practised.	
	11-11-17.		Battalion paraded at 8.15 a.m. and marched to HERBELLE, via MENTQUE, NORTBECOURT, MORINGHEM, QUELMES, and ESQUERDES, a distance of about 15 and a half miles. A downpour of rain delayed our start, and followed us more or less persistently throughout the day, but we were fortunate in finding covered accomodation during the halt for dinners at QUELMES. It was nearly dark when we reached Billets, which were not very comfortable, though the men were dry by the time they got in.	
	12-11-17.		The Battalion resumed march about 9.0 a.m. and marched to LAIRES, which was reached in time for dinners. Owing to the barns being full of crops, the accomodation at this time of the year is rather scanty, but the Battalion was fairly comfortable.	
	13 to 17-11-17.		The 1st Guards Brigade resumed March on a lovely morning and marched to LA THIEULLOYE, where we remained till the 17th. Captain. J.N. Buchanan.	

Army Form C. 2118.

WAR DIARY
or
INTELLIGENCE SUMMARY.
(Erase heading not required.)

Instructions regarding War Diaries and Intelligence Summaries are contained in F.S. Regs., Part II. and the Staff Manual respectively. Title pages will be prepared in manuscript.

Place	Date	Hour	Summary of Events and Information	Remarks and references to Appendices
	13 to 17-11-17 Continued.		Assistant Staff Captain on the 14th, the command of No 1 Company passing to Lieutenant.J.C.Cornforth.M.C. On the 15th there was a Conference of Commanding Officers and Brigadiers at Divisional Headquarters and Battalions were informed that the Division was about to continue its march South, and take over from the French near ST QUENTIN. It was further explained that owing to a great number of lorries having been used by the French to convey guns and troops to ITALY, no lorries would be available for the move, and that consequently all greatcoats and Officers' Kits in excess of 50lbs per Officer would be stored in ST POL. This was done on the following day. During its three days stay in this area the Battalion practised two Schemes, embracing Advance Guards, developing into outposts. 2nd.Lieutenant.H.M.Chapman and 49 other ranks joined Battalion on the 15th. Division Whilst in this area, the Guards Reinforcement Battalion was reformed. This is a plan which has been adopted during the past summer whenever the Division has been taking part in active operations, and has become necessary owing to the great numbers of all ranks who are now "left out" during an attack. Companies nowadays neither attack nor go into the line with a greater average strength then 32 other ranks per platoon, and 3 Officers per Company, and the Reinforcement Battalion is formed to accomodate the surplus of all Battalions. Although admirable in theory, the working is generally chaotic, a hurriedly improvised staff of Officers working under the Q side of the Guards Division, is hardly an ideal administrative machine, and the difficulties of Battalions is usually greatly increased by the Division	

A7092. Wt.W2839/M1291 750,000. 1/17. D.D & L. Ltd. Forms/C2118/4.

Army Form C. 2118.

WAR DIARY
or
INTELLIGENCE SUMMARY.

(Erase heading not required.)

Instructions regarding War Diaries and Intelligence Summaries are contained in F. S. Regs., Part II. and the Staff Manual respectively. Title pages will be prepared in manuscript.

Place	Date	Hour	Summary of Events and Information	Remarks and references to Appendices
	13-11-17 to 17-11-17 (Cont'd)		insisting on sending to the Reinforcement Battalion all ranks coming off leave and Courses. The result is, that, Battalions never know whom they can expect to be available for duty either in Officers, N.C.O's or Men. This time however the above obstacle was removed and men off leave returned direct to their unit.	
	17-11-17.		The Battalion left LA THIEULLOYE at 9.0 a.m. and marched to MANIN, a distance of about 11 miles. The Battalion was very much benefitted by its 4 days march. Fair Billets left rather dirty by last occupants.	
	18-11-17.		The Brigade marched from MANIN to BLAIRVILLE about 14 miles, going into a very good camp of Nissen huts. Dinners at mid-day halt, camp reached at about 3.0 p.m. In the morning the Commanding Officer explained the outline of the operations of the 3rd Army, which was to commence towards CAMBRAI. Its chief features were its ambitious scope, and its novel character, in dispensing with a prolonged bombardment, depending for its success almost wholly by surprise, and the employment of about 370 Tanks. The Guards Division was not intended to take part in the first stages of the operation, but to take over the defences of BOURLON WOOD and village after the capture of that locality, and later to join in the thrust Northwards. The best omen for the success of this operation is the secrecy with which it has been surrounded. Though many people suspected that the Battalion was not going to relieve the French as had been given out, nobody guessed our real task.	
	19 to 20-11-17.		Battalion marched at 5.0 p.m. in the dark to a tented camp at GOMIECOURT about 8 miles. Battalion in great heart, all singing and marching splendidly. Here we spent 2 tedious days in a thin drizzle waiting anxiously for news of the advance, all of which seemed very satisfactory.	

Army Form C. 2118.

WAR DIARY
or
INTELLIGENCE SUMMARY.

(Erase heading not required.)

Instructions regarding War Diaries and Intelligence
Summaries are contained in F.S. Regs., Part II.
and the Staff Manual respectively. Title pages
will be prepared in manuscript.

Place	Date	Hour	Summary of Events and Information	Remarks and references to Appendices
	21-11-17.		About 7.0 p.m. orders were received to march at once to HERMELLINCOURT, and thence to embus for the BARASTRE area. The Battalion marched off in 20 minutes from receiving orders and after a messy march mostly in single file past an interminable line of buses, and other troops, embussed in rear of the 2nd Battalion Coldstream Guards and proceeded at a leisurely crawl to BARASTRE, where we found an excellent hutted camp which we reached about 1.30 a.m. though the distance to be travelled was not more than about 15 miles.	
	22 to 23-11-17.		A day full of orders. Countermanded orders, new orders, and lack of orders. Finally the Battalion marched off in the dark at 5.0 a.m. on the 23rd to a field between BEAUMETZ and DOIGNIES, where a camp was quickly formed by pitching a number of bivouac sheets. At about 4.0 p.m. a warning order was received to the effect that the Battalion would probably go into the line the same night, and at 7.20 p.m. orders were received for the head of the Brigade to march off at 7.30 p.m. No hint was given as to whom we were to relieve, or where, all details who were intended to stay with 1st line were ordered to parade with their companies, and the 1st line Transport followed the Battalion, until a Staff Officer indulged in the whim of diverting it, unknown to the Battalion, to an undisclosed destination, with the gratifying result that we were left without Lewis Guns to take into the line. After a long walk the Brigade Major was encountered, and divulged a thin clue as to where we were going. The Commanding officer thereupon rode forward to Brigade Head-quarters, and the Battalion, which was then halted, very tired, near the HINDENBURG line followed wearily towards GRAINCOURT, after sorting out the 1st line Transport and Details, bidding them and 3 Officers to find their way as best they could to RIBECOURT, which by then, had been announced as their destination.	

Army Form C. 2118.

WAR DIARY
or
INTELLIGENCE SUMMARY.

(Erase heading not required)

Instructions regarding War Diaries and Intelligence Summaries are contained in F. S. Regs., Part II. and the Staff Manual respectively. Title pages will be prepared in manuscript.

Place	Date	Hour	Summary of Events and Information	Remarks and references to Appendices
22 to 23-11-17. Continued.			It was then nearly darkight. A guide was found at GRAINCOURT, who led the Battalion unhesitatingly to Brigade Headquarters, where it was discovered for the first time that the Battalion was relieving the 9th Battalion Royal Scots, (152nd Brigade) in front of CANTAING village. From this point the relief proceeded without incident. The relieved Battalion lent us their Lewis Guns and at about 5.0 a.m. the relief was complete, after a most instructive day, and plenty of it. Reveille having been at 3.45 a.m. and the Battalion having been on the move continuously for 25 hours.	
	24-11-17.		Battalion in line in front of CANTAING village. No 4 Company on left in touch with 1st Battalion Irish Guards, No 2 Company in centre, No 1 Company on right in touch with 8th Battalion Beds Regiment. An interesting line full of German equipment and stores of every kind all indicating the complete nature of the enemy's surprise, and the hurry of his retirement. The line consists of a series of posts, the enemy are a considerable distance off, shelling is intermittent and sniping practically absent. The surrounding country is dotted with derelict tanks, which have in the past 3 days played a most conspicuous part in the success of the operations. A fairly quiet day. Lieutenant.N.G.A.Alexander was wounded in the left hand, in throwing from the post he was occupying a German bomb, which had been thrown among some of his men, by an enemy patrol.	
	25-11-17.			
	26-11-17.		Fine day and uneventful. Much fighting in the neighbourhood of BOURLON, on the left of the Brigade. Battalion relieved by one Battalion of 1st Battalion Scots Guards, and the 2nd. Battalion D.L.I. (18th. Brigade).	

Army Form C. 2118.

WAR DIARY
or
INTELLIGENCE SUMMARY.
(Erase heading not required.)

Instructions regarding War Diaries and Intelligence Summaries are contained in F. S. Regs., Part II. and the Staff Manual respectively. Title pages will be prepared in manuscript.

Place.	Date	Hour	Summary of Events and Information	Remarks and references to Appendices
	26-11-17 (Contd)		Late relief by the latter complete at midnight. Battalion marched to RIBECOURT in a snowstorm, and found their only accomodation was the old German line which was not quite so comfortable as the front line which they had just left.	
	27-11-17.		Both greatcoats and blankets being in store, the Battalion spent a most miserable night. Rain stopped during the morning, and the day was spent in trying to make some sort of provision for the comfortable accomodation of the Battalion.	
	28-11-17.		Battalion relieved by 2. Battalion of the South Staffordshire Regiment, and marched to METZ.	
	29-11-17.		In Billets at METZ.	
	30-11-17.		Day spent in improving Billets, which were anything but comfortable, and left in an extremely dirty state by previous occupants. Battalion also cleaned Lewis Guns, Equipment, etc., during the day. See attached narrative.	

(signature)

G. Rocke
Lieutenant Colonel.
Commanding 2nd Battalion Grenadier Guards.

2nd Battalion Grenadier Guards.

Narrative of Operations for period November 30 - December 2 1917

Map Reference:- VALENCIENNES $\frac{1}{20,000}$

November 30th 1917.

In Billets at METZ-EN-COUTURE. At about 7:0 a.m. some enemy shells were burst over the village and heavy shelling was heard from the forward area. Shortly afterwards all roads from the front line became choked with gunners, infantry, transport of all kinds and wounded, all of them in great confusion and most of them spreading alarmist rumours of the enemy having broken through the front line.

Soon after 9:0 a.m. a wire from the Division brought news that the 111 Corps was being heavily attacked at GONNELIEU (about 4 miles away and ordered the Brigade to be ready to move at short notice.

At 10:30 a.m. orders were received for the Brigade to advance towards GOUZEAUCOURT, to clear METZ at 12:25 p.m. Commanding Officers to report mounted to Brigadier forthwith. Details were separated to stay with 1st Line Transport, waterbottles filled, blankets and packs stacked, and the Battalion marched off in fighting order with the following Officers:-

Headquarters.
Commanding Officer. Lieut: Col: G. E. C. Rasch. D.S.O.
Second in Command.   Captain G. C. F. Harcourt-Vernon. D.S.O.
Adjutant.   Captain A. H. Penn.
Medical Officer.   Captain J. A. Andrews. M.C.

No 1 Company.
Lieutenant J. C. Cornforth. M.C.   Company Commander.
2nd Lieut: P. A. A. Harbord. M.C.
2nd Lieut: S. H. Pearson.

No 2 Company.
Lieutenant F. A. M. Browning.   Company Commander.
Lieut: F. H. G. Layland-Barratt. M.C.
2nd Lieut: F. H. Drummond. M.C.

No 3 Company.
Lieutenant A. W. Acland. M.C.   Company Commander.
Lieutenant F. A. Magnay.
Lieutenant R. Y. T. Kendall.

No 4 Company.
Lieutenant G. R. Westmacott.   Company Commander.
Lieutenant W. H. S. Derfft.
Lieutenant F. P. Loftus.

Major Hon: W. R. Bailey D.S.O., Lieutenants S. T. S. Clarke and Ponsonby remained with details; all other Officers were on leave or Courses.

Half a mile from METZ the Commanding Officer met the Battalion with Officers Commanding Companies, who had preceded the Battalion, and informed the Battalion that the enemy had broken the line and was believed to have penetrated through GOUZEAUCOURT, that the Brigade would advance immediately until it met the enemy and would then attack them, 1st Battalion Irish Guards on North of GOUZEAUCOURT-METZ road, the two Battalions of the Coldstream Guards on the South side, the 3rd Battalion in centre, next the Irish Guards, the 2nd Battalion on right, the 2nd Battalion Grenadier Guards in Brigade Support.

The whole front area was by this time covered with all arms streaming back, and the A. P. M., at METZ was busily engaged herding stragglers.

Throughout the advance by the 1st Brigade, not the slightest trace was seen of any defending infantry.

On reaching GOUZEAUCOURT WOOD, a low scrubby plantation on the reverse side of a slope, the Battalion blobbed on the South side of the road. A few casualties were caused by shell fire, but the slope of the ground saved the Battalion from casualties from bullets fired at the other three Battalions, who were meanwhile advancing and suffering considerably from rifle and machine gun fire.

By nightfall however, they had cleared GOUZEAUCOURT and the intervening ground and established a line on the Eastern fringe of t the former.

Two Companies of the Battalion moved up as soon as it was dark to occupy some trenches nearer to the village, the Battalion otherwise remained in GOUZEAUCOURT WOOD throughout the night.

At about 1.30 a.m. the Battalion received orders to attack at 6.30 a.m. with 3rd Battalion Coldstream Guards on left, in conjunction with 3rd Guards Brigade on left of 1st Brigade, and Cavalry on right.

The objective of the Battalion was the Eastern edge of GAUCHE WOOD, an oblong wood about 700 yards long by 300 yards broad at its eastern edge.

The wood is on high ground with its nearest edge about 1200 yards from the jumping off ground. It commands the whole of the intervening area.

Orders were issued for Nos 3 and 1 Companies to lead the attack; Nos 2 and 4 Companies in Support.

The Commanding Officer went forward with the Officers Commanding Companies to reconnoitre forming up ground, and the Battalion marched off at 4;30 a.m. after breakfast, picking up tools on the way. All Companies were in their places by 6.0 a.m. There was no barrage, but 20 Tanks were allotted to the Brigade and the Infantry was ordered to follow them at 400 yards distance. It was probably owing to short notice, or the absence of any opportunities for recon-naisance that these tanks were unable to fulfil their role, and after waiting for them for 10 minutes, the attack was launched without them.

From the start the Battalion came under a very heavy machine gun fire, and the casualties, particularly in Officers, became severe. The Cavalry, who should have attacked simultaneously on the right, were an hour late in coming up, and although they lent the most valuable assistance, when they did arrive- particularly the 18th Lancers (Native) and the 7th Dragoon Guards, their absence during the early stages of the attack left our right flank - (the South side of GAUCHE WOOD) dangerously in the air.

Several tanks had however, followed the Battalion and all of them were either knocked out or ditched, but by taking their Lewis Guns from them and moving these to the exposed flank, the position was considerably strengthened.

The Battalion advanced at a great pace and reached the WOOD by about 7.0 a.m. The fringe was very thickly manned with machine guns, and whilst rushing one of these 2nd Lieutenant. P.A.A.Harbord. M.C., received wounds from which he died later in the day.

On reaching the WOOD, Lieutenant.G.R.Westmacott, swung part of his Company round to face the right flank and was able to repel two counter attacks almost at once, accounting for about 70 of the enemy.

The sniping in the WOOD from the outskirts of VILLERS-GUISLAIN, about 500 yards away, was very heavy, and 2nd Lieutenant S.H Pearson was shot through the head leading his Platoon. By the time the objective was reached, Lieutenants Cornforth.M.C., and Acland.M.C., (Commanding Nos 1 and 3 Companies respectively) Magnay, Dent Kendall, Layland-Barratt.M.C., and Drummond.M.C., were all wounded. This left only Lieutenants Westmacott, Browning and Loftus available and to the two former is largely due the complete success of the Battalion's attack.

Between them they reorganised and controlled the entire line, gaining touch with their flanks, forming a support line and sparing themselves neither exertion nor exposure.

In the afternoon a Company of the 2nd Battalion Coldstream Guards was sent up to strengthen the line and take up extra S.A.A. with Captain.G.C.F.Harcourt-Vernon.D.S.O.,

Shelling and sniping continued throughout the day, and the Battalion was fortunate in the circumstances in losing only :-

```
KILLED...................25 N.C.O's and Men.
MISSING..................11 N.C.O's and Men.
WOUNDED..................115 N.C.O's and Men
```

TOTAL................151 N.C.O's and MEN.

Among these unfortunately, were many excellent N.C.O's whom it will be hard to replace.

The Battalion captured 3 Field Guns, shooting the teams as they tried to limber up, and a great number of Machine Guns.

We were relieved at night by one company of the 3rd Battalion Grenadier Guards, the Poona and Deccan Horse and marched back to bivouacs in GOUZEAUCOURT WOOD, reaching there in the early morning of the 2nd inst.

The following messages received on the 5th. December, 1917, speak for themselves :-

(1) <u>The Commander-in-Chief telegraphed as below.</u>

"I desire to congratulate the Guards Division most warmly on their fine counter attacks at GOUZEAUCOURT and GONNELIEU. The promptness of decision and rapidity of action displayed by them was successful in dealing with a difficult situation."

(2) <u>From Corps Commander, H.Q., lll Corps.</u>

" The Corps Commander wishes to express to all ranks of the Guards Division, his high appreciation of the prompt manner in which they turned out on the 30th November, counterattacked through a disorganised rabble and retook GOUZEAUCOURT. The very fine attack which they subsequently carried out against QUENTIN RIDGE and GAUCHE WOOD, resulting in the capture of these important positions, was worthy of the highest traditions of the Guards."

Lieutenant Colonel.
<u>Commanding 2nd Battalion Grenadier Guards,</u>

2nd Battalion Grenadier Guards.

Narrative of Operations for Period November 30 - December, 2, 1917.

Map Reference :- VALENCIENNES. 1/20,000

November 30th, 1917.

In Billets at METZ-EN-COUTURE. At about 7.0 a.m, some enemy shells were burst over the Village and heavy shelling was heard from forward area. Shortly afterwards all roads from the front line became choked with gunners, infantry, transport of all kinds and wounded, all of them in great confusion and most of them spreading alarmist rumours of the enemy having broken through our front line.

Soon after 9.0 a.m. a wire from the Division brought news that the III Corps was being heavily attacked at GONNELIEU (about 4 miles away) and ordered the Brigade to be ready to move at short notice.

At 10.30 a.m. orders were received for the Brigade to advance towards GOUZEAUCOURT, to clear METZ at 12.25 p.m. Commanding Officers to report mounted to Brigadier forthwith. Details were separated to stay with 1st Line Transport, waterbottles filled, blankets and packs stacked, and the Battalion marched off in Fighting Order with the following Officers :-

Headquarters.

Commanding Officer..................Lieut.Col.G.E.C.Rasch.D.S.O.,
Second in Command.................Capt.G.C.F.Harcourt-Vernon.D.S.O.,
Adjutant...........................Captain.A.H.Penn.
Medical Officer....................Captain.J.A.Andrews.M.C.,R.A.M.C.,

No 1 Company.

Lieutenant J.C.Cornforth.M.C.,.........Company Commander.
2nd.Lieut.P.A.A.Harbord.M.C.,
2nd.Lieut.S.H.Pearson.

No 2 Company.

Lieutenant.F.A.M.Browning............Company Commander.
Lieutenant.F.H.G.Layland-Barratt.M.C.,
2nd.Lieut.F.H.J.Drummond.M.C.,

No 3 Company.

Lieutenant A.W.Acland.M.C.,...........Company Commander.
Lieutenant.F.A.Magnay.
Lieutenant.R.Y.T.Kendall.

No 4 Company.

Lieutenant.G.R.Westmacott............Company Commander.
Lieutenant.W.H.S.Dent.
Lieutenant.F.P.Loftus.

Major.Hon.W.R.Bailey.D.S.O., Lieutenants S.T.S.Clarke and Ponsonby remained with Details; all other Officers were on Leave or Courses.

Half a mile from METZ the Commanding Officer met the Battalion with Officers Commanding Companies who had preceded the Battalion, and informed the Battalion that the enemy had broken the line and was believed to have penetrated through GOUZEAUCOURT, that the Brigade would advance immediately until it had met the enemy and would then attack them, 1st Battalion Irish Guards on North of GOUZEAUCOURT-METZ Road, the 2 Battalions of the Coldstream Guards on the South Side, the 3rd Battalion in centre, next the Irish Guards, the 2nd Battalion on Right, the 2nd Battalion Grenadier Guards in Brigade Support.

The whole front area was by this time covered with all arms streaming back, and the A.P.M., at METZ was busily engaged herding stragglers.

Throughout the advance by the 1st Brigade, not the slightest trace was seen of any defending Infantry.

On reaching GOUZEAUCOURT WOOD, a low scrubby plantation on the reverse side of a slope, the Battalion blobbed on the South Side of the Road. A few casualties were caused by shell fire, but the slope of the ground saved the Battalion from casualties from bullets fired at the other 3 Battalions, who were meanwhile advancing and suffering considerably from rifle and machine gun fire.

By nightfall however, they had cleared GOUZEAUCOURT and the intervening ground and established a line on the Eastern Fringe of the former.

2 Companies of the Battalion moved up as soon as it was dark to occupy some trenches nearer to the Village, the Battalion otherwise remained in GOUZEAUCOURT WOOD throughout the night.

At about 1.30 a.m. the Battalion received orders to attack at 6.30 a.m. with 3rd Battalion Coldstream Guards on left, in conjunction with 3rd Guards Brigade on left of 1st Brigade, and Cavalry on right.

The objective of the Battalion was the Eastern Edge of GAUCHE WOOD, an oblong wood of about 700 yards long by 300 yards broad at its Eastern Edge.

The WOOD is on high ground with its nearest edge about 1200 yards from the "Jumping off ground". It commands the whole of the intervening area.

Orders were issued for Nos 3 and 1 Companies to lead the attack Nos 2 and 4 Companies in Support.

The Commanding Officer went forward with the Officers Commanding Companies to reconnoitre forming up ground, and the Battalion marched off at 4.30 a.m. after breakfast, picking up tools on the way. All Companies were in their places by 6.0 a.m. There was no barrage, but 20 Tanks were allotted to this Brigade and the Infantry was ordered to follow them at 400 yards distance. It was probably owing to short notice, or the absence of any opportunities for reconnaisance that these Tanks were unable to fulfil their role, and after waiting for them for 10 minutes, the attack was launched without them.

From the start the Battal-ion came under a very heavy machine gun fire, and the casualties, particularly in Officers, became severe. The Cavalry, who should have attacked simultaneously on the right, were an hour late in coming up, and although they lent the most valuable assistance, when they did arrive - particularly the 18th Lancers (Native) and the 7th Dragoon Guards, their absence during the early stages of the attack left our right flank - (the South Side of GAUCHE WOOD) dangerously in the air. Several Tanks had however, followed the Battalion and all of them were either knocked out or ditched, but by taking their Lewis Guns from them and moving these to the exposed flank, the position was considerably strengthened.

The Battalion advanced at a great pace and reached the WOOD by about 7.0 a.m. The Fringe was very thickly manned with machine guns, and whilst rushing one of these 2nd Lieutenant P.A.A.Harbord. M.C., received wounds from which he died later in the day.

On reaching the WOOD, Lieutenant G.R.Westmacott, swung part of his Company round to face the right flank and was able to repel 2 counter attacks almost at once, accounting for about 70 of the enemy.

The sniping the WOOD from the outskirts of VILLERS-GUISLAIN about 500 yards away, was very heavy, and 2nd Lieutenant S.H.Pearson, was shot through the head leading his Platoon. By the time the objective was reached, Lieutenants Cornforth.M.C., and Acland.M.C., (Commanding Nos 1 and 3 Companies respectively) Magnay, Kendall, Layland-Barratt.M.C., and Drummond.M.C., were all wounded. This left only Lieutenants Westmacott, Browning and Loftus available, and to the two former is largely due the complete success of the Battalion's attack.

Between them they reorganised and controlled the entire line, gaining touch with their flanks, forming a Support Line and sparing themselves neither exertion nor exposure.

In the afternoon a Company of the 2nd Battalion Coldstream Guards was sent up to strengthen the line and take up extra S.A.A., with Captain.G.C.F.Harcourt-Vernon.D.S.O.,

Shelling and sniping continued throughout the day, and the

Battalion was fortunate in the circumstances in losing only :-

```
KILLED.....................25 N.C.Os and Men.
MISSING....................11 N.C.Os and Men.
WOUNDED....................115 N.C.Os and Men.
TOTAL......................151 N.C.Os and Men.
```

Among these unfortunately, were many excellent N.C.Os whom it will be hard to replace.

The Battalion captured 3 Field Guns, shooting the Teams as they tried to limber up, and a great number of Machine Guns.

We were relieved at night by 1 Company of the 3rd Battalion Grenadier Guards, the Poona and Deccan Horse and marched back to bivouacs in GOUZEAUCOURT WOOD, reaching there in the early morning of the 2nd. inst.

The following messages received on the 5th. December.1917. speak for themselves :-

(1) <u>The Commander-in-Chief telegraphed as below.</u>

"I desire to congratulate the Guards Division most warmly on their fine counter-attacks at GOUZEAUCOURT and GONNELIEU. The promptness and of decision and rapidity of action displayed by them was successful in d dealing with a difficult situation."

(2) <u>From Corps Commander. H.Q., III Corps.</u>

" The Corps Commander wishes to express to all ranks of the Guards Division, his high appreciation of the prompt manner in which they turned out on the 30th November, counter-attacked through a disorganised rabble and retook GOUZEAUCOURT. The very fine attack which they subsequently carried out against QUENTIN RIDGE and GAUCHE WOOD, resulting in the capture of these important positions, was worthy of the highest traditions of the Guards."

G. Rasch

Lieutenant Colonel,
<u>Commanding 2nd Battalion Grenadier Guards.</u>

Army Form C. 2118.

WAR DIARY
or
INTELLIGENCE SUMMARY.

(Erase heading not required.)

Instructions regarding War Diaries and Intelligence Summaries are contained in F. S. Regs., Part II. and the Staff Manual respectively. Title pages will be prepared in manuscript.

WAR DIARY OF 2nd BATTALION GRENADIER GUARDS FOR THE MONTH OF DECEMBER, 1917.

Place	Date	Hour	Summary of Events and Information	Remarks and references to Appendices
	1-12-17. 2/4-12-17.		As per attached narrative. The Battalion remained in bivouacs in GOUZEAUCOURT WOOD until relieved on the night of the 4th by the 8th Battalion Argyll & Sutherland Highlanders (9th Division) and then marched to billets in METZ.	
	5-12-17.		Marched at 8.0 a.m. to ETRICOURT to entrain for BEAUMETZ. After a long delay, owing to the line having been bombed on the previous night, the Battalion left at about 3.0 p.m. and travelling along the line laid by the Guards Division after the German retirement in April, 1917, passed through MORVAL, LESBOEUFS, GINCHY, and GUILLEMONT, where the Battalion fought during the operations on the SOMME, finally reaching BEAUMETZ about 7.0 p.m. and marched to billets at BERNEVILLE.	
	6-12-17. 7-12-17.		In Billets at BERNEVILLE.) Training and reorganisation, ditto.) including Refresher Classes for N.C.Os of all grades.	
	8-12-17.		In Billets at BERNEVILLE. Training as yesterday. MASS celebrated in Village Church for Roman Catholics of the Battalion.	
	9-12-17.		Divine Services in the morning. Battalion required to find Garrison Fire Picquet, 1 N.C.O., and 10 men.	
	10-12-17.		In billets at BERNEVILLE. Battalion paraded for Training, and were allotted the Baths during the day. The Rev. T. Head delivered a lecture on "First Battle of YPRES" in Church Army Hut.	
	11-12-17.		In Billets at BERNEVILLE. Training and Drill continued as yesterday. A Brig ade Bayonet Fighting Course assembled which was attended by several N.C.Os of the Battalion.	

Army Form C. 2118.

WAR DIARY
or
INTELLIGENCE SUMMARY.

(Erase heading not required.)

Instructions regarding War Diaries and Intelligence Summaries are contained in F. S. Regs., Part II. and the Staff Manual respectively. Title pages will be prepared in manuscript.

Place	Date	Hour	Summary of Events and Information	Remarks and references to Appendices
	12-12-17.		Battalion paraded for Company Training and LEWIS GUNNERY. Brigade Gas N.C.O., inspected the Gas Equipment of the Battalion during the day.	
	13-12-17.		Training continued as yesterday. Band of the IRISH GUARDS played selections in the Square from 3.0 to 4.0 p.m.	
	14-12-17.		Battalion practised Firing on the Range and also Drill & Training under Company Commanders.	
	15-12-17.		Battalion paraded for Drill and Training, and instruction in Wiring was given by party from 75th. Company R.E.,	
	16-12-17.		Battalion paraded for Divine Services. 2nd Lieutenant.F.J Langley joined the Battalion from the Guards Divn. Reinforcement Battalion.	
	17-12-17.		Battalion did Drill & Platoon Training. Instruction in Wiring was continued.	
	18-12-17.		Drill & Training as yesterday. A Brigade Bayonet Fighting Course commenced and was attended by the following Officers :- Lieutenant M.H.Ponsonby. Lieutenant F.P.Loftus. 2nd.Lieut. G.H.Henning. 2nd.Lieut. F.J.Langley.	
	19-12-17. 20-12-17.		Battalion paraded for Drill & Route Marching. Practice & Instructional Parades were also carried out.	
	21-12-17.		Drill & Route Marching as yesterday. Lewis Gunnery was also practised. Garrison Fire Picquet and Town Duties were found by the Battalion.	
	22-12-17.		Battalion did Sectional Drill; Practice & Instructional Parades were also carried out. Lieutenant G.B.Wilson, 2nd. Lieutenants R.T.Sharpe, C.C.T.Giles, and S.C.K.George joined the Battalion.	
	23-12-17.		Battalion paraded for Divine Services in the morning.	

Army Form C. 2118.

WAR DIARY
or
INTELLIGENCE SUMMARY.
(Erase heading not required.)

Place	Date	Hour	Summary of Events and Information	Remarks and references to Appendices
	24-12-17.		Drill, Route Marching & Section Training was carried out, also Lewis Gunnery & Practice Bombing.	
	25-12-17. (XMAS DAY).		Battalion Paraded for Divine Services in the morning. Battalion had XMAS DINNERS at 1.0 p.m. Nos 1, 2 and 3 Companies in the Theatre, No 4 Company in Billets. The Commanding Officer and Officers Commanding Companies were present during Dinner, when the usual cheers were given, and the health of the Commanding Officer and Officers Commanding Companies were toasted by the oldest soldier in each Company. A Concert was held in the Theatre in the afternoon, and was atteded by nearly the whole Battalion. Weather very cold and intermittent snowstorms in the afternoo.	
	26-12-17.		Battalin paraded for Route March, Drill & Section Training. Snipers under Instruction, and Lewis Gunners also paraded in the morning.	
	27-12-17.		Battalin Practised Firing on the Range; Platoon Training was also carried out. Garrison Fire Picquet was found by the Battalion, also the usual Town Duties. Weather continues to be very cold, the ground being covered with snow.	
	28-12-17.		Battalio paraded for Route March, Platoon & Section Training, and Lewis Gunnery. Practice & Instructional Parades were also carried out.	
	29-12-17.		Drill & raining as yesterday. Very hard Frost, with snow greatly in evidence.	
	30-12-17.		Battalio paraded for Divine Services in the morning.	

Army Form C. 2118.

2nd Grenadier Guard
2 C.C.
January, 1918

WAR DIARY
or
INTELLIGENCE SUMMARY.

(Erase heading not required.)

of 2nd Battalion Grenadier Guards for the month ending January 1918.

Place	Date	Hour	Summary of Events and Information	Remarks and references to Appendices
Jan: 1st: 1918.	to 8th:		On January 1st the Battalion marched from BERNEVILLE to ARRAS, going into billets in LEVIS BARRACKS. Quite good billets though dark, and more entertainments for the troops than in billets lately occupied. The ensuing week was spent in training of all kinds - musketry, wiring, drill, trench routine, bombing, etc., for men, and special instruction for N. C. Os. 2nd Lieutenants J. S. Carter and the Hon: S. A. S. Montagu and 50 other ranks joined the Battalion on the 8th inst.	
(Map FAMPOUX 1/40,000).	Jan: 9th: to 24th: 1918.		The Battalion went into the line for a tour of 16 days, in front line and support for 4 days alternately. The Battalion frontage for the first 4 days (front line) is astride the River SCARPE, one Company (No 4) on the	

WAR DIARY
or
INTELLIGENCE SUMMARY.

(Erase heading not required.)

Army Form C. 2118.

Place	Date	Hour	Summary of Events and Information	Remarks and references to Appendices
	31-12-17.		Battalion paraded for Drill & Sectional Training: Bombing was also practised, and Snipers under Instruction also paraded in the morning. Battalion played against 4th Battalion Grenadier Guards at Football in the Divisional Tie at DAINVILLE. Weather much milder, thaw having set in during the day.	

31-12-1917.

Lieutenant Colonel,
Commanding 2nd Battalion Grenadier Guards.

Army Form C. 2118.

WAR DIARY
or
INTELLIGENCE SUMMARY.
(Erase heading not required.)

Instructions regarding War Diaries and Intelligence Summaries are contained in F. S. Regs., Part II. and the Staff Manual respectively. Title pages will be prepared in manuscript.

Place	Date	Hour	Summary of Events and Information	Remarks and references to Appendices
			WAR DIARY (continued)	
	Jan: 9th: to 24th. 1918.		North Side, in the village of ROEUX (this Company coming under the Command of the Officer Commanding the left Battalion of the Brigade) the remaining three Companies on the South Side of the River, two in front line and support (Nos: 2 & 3) and one (No 4) in reserve. The line is convenient in many ways - there is a light Railway and a Canal which enable troops and rations to be brought within about a mile of the line, and there are also cookhouses where hot meals for the troops may be cooked, and from where they can be conveyed to the line in hot-food containers by men specially detailed for this purpose. Shelling is very slight, and there is a continuous line of Communication throughout the Battalion area, a thing which has not been experienced - save in the breastworks at BOESINGHE, for 18 months.	

Army Form C. 2118.

WAR DIARY
or
INTELLIGENCE SUMMARY.

(Erase heading not required.)

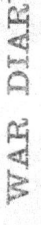

Place	Date	Hour	Summary of Events and Information	Remarks and references to Appendices
	Jan: 9th to 24th 1918.		WAR DIARY (continued). On the other hand, the trenches, which have been in occupation since the fighting in the early summer of last year, have been very much neglected. Many of them are entirely un-revetted, and although in fine weather the chalk will stand of itself, rain is sure to play havoc and bring them all toppling in. The wire is very thin everywhere. The Battalion relieved 1st Battalion Scots Guards without particular incident - the weather was very cold and snow still lies. The first night was spent in reconnoitring the wire; on the second night (the 10th) a thaw began and during this and the following day all men who could be spared from wiring, were employed in repair and upkeep of the fast disappearing trenches. A frost on the 12th temporarily suspended the calamities of which two days thaw had	

Army Form C. 2118.

WAR DIARY
or
INTELLIGENCE SUMMARY.

(Erase heading not required.)

Place	Date	Hour	Summary of Events and Information	Remarks and references to Appendices
	Jan: 9th to 1918.	24th	WAR DIARY (continued). give us a foretaste, and our relief by the 1st Battalion Irish Guards was carried out without particular difficulty. Casualties during tour in front line:- 1 Sergeant and three other ranks wounded. The Battalion, on going into support was disposed with Nos: 1 & 4 Companies North of the River, in the western outskirts of ROEUX, Battalion H. Q., and the remainder of the Battalion in and near the Railway Cutting in H. 23 and LANCER LANE in H. 29. Rain continued throughout this and the next few days. Colonel Lord Ardee (Irish Guards) assumed temporary command of the Brigade vice Lieutenant Colonel G. B. S. Follett (on leave) who had been commanding for a month in the absence of Brigadier General C. R. C. de Crespigny D.S.O.	

WAR DIARY
or
INTELLIGENCE SUMMARY.

Army Form C. 2118.

Place	Date	Hour	Summary of Events and Information	Remarks and references to Appendices
	Jan: 9th to 24th: 1918.		WAR DIARY (continued).	

to reclaim parts of the derelict trenches.

On the 17th the Commanding Officer went on a month's leave, Major Hon: W. R. Bailey. D.S.O., taking over the Command, and Captain G. C. F. Harcourt-Vernon. D.S.O., 2nd in command.

Throughout this period the enemy hostility on the Battalion frontage was very slight, being confined to an occasional spasmodic bombardment by Trench Mortars, usually at dusk and dawn.

The left Battalion of the Brigade were unfortunate in suffering several casualties on the 18th from Gas Shells projected from Mortars.

The Corps Commander - Lieutenant General Sir C. Fergus-son (Grenadier Guards) visited the Battalion on the 19th.

Army Form C. 2118.

WAR DIARY
or
INTELLIGENCE SUMMARY.

(Erase heading not required.)

Place	Date	Hour	Summary of Events and Information	Remarks and references to Appendices
	Jan.9th. to 24th.1918.		WAR DIARY (Continued).	
			On the 21st the Battalion relieved the Irish Guards in Support - 1 Company(No 4 Coy) in LANCER LANE, No 2 Company in CRUMP TRENCH, the other 2 Companies in the ROEUX CAVES.	
	Jan 25/31. 1918.		The chief incident of note during our tour in Support was a very heavy bombardment by Gas Shells on the 25th. inst; the night of relief by 4th Battalion Grenadier Gds. This was directed chiefly on the Railway on which Two Companies were awaiting the relief train and on the road below it, and lasted continuously from 9.0.p.m. for about an hour and a quarter. Several Shells fell among the Companies(Nos 2 & 4) which were waiting to entrain, but owing to good Gas Discipline, casualties were slight, the chief injuries being caused to men who were splashed with the liquid from the exploding shells.
Owing to the shelling, the train which was to take the Battalion back to ARRAS was very late in arrival, and the Battalion did not get into Barracks until past 1.0 a.m. During the next 2 days several men had to be evacuated from the effects of gas, and a party of 37 which was detached from the Battalion for work with the New Zealand Tunnelling Company, suffered over 20 Casualties from the same cause.
The Battalion spent the remaining 6 days of the month in LEVIS BARRACKS in ARRAS. We had to find one night fatigue of 400 men but most of the time was spent in Training of all kinds.	

[signature] Major,
Commanding 2nd Battalion Grenadier Guards.

Army Form C. 2118.

WAR DIARY
or
INTELLIGENCE SUMMARY.
(Erase heading not required.)

Place	Date	Hour	Summary of Events and Information	Remarks and references to Appendices
	Jan: 9th: to 24th: 1918.		WAR DIARY (continued). During our tour of duty in the Support line rain fell almost unceasingly. Trenches everywhere became impassable, and the Germans were in all directions observed to be in a plight similar to our own, having to carry out all their movements overground. The Battalion had almost as much work to do in Support as in the front line. On the 17th the Battalion returned to the front line Sector. No 1 Company North of the River, Nos 4 & 3 Companies front and support, No 2 Company reserve. The relief was carried out overground, owing to the waterlogged state of the trenches. All of these and especially communication trenches were in a dreadful state. During this and the 3 next days the Battalion worked very hard day and night, wiring, patrolling and trying	

Army Form C. 2118.

WAR DIARY
or
INTELLIGENCE SUMMARY.

(Erase heading not required.)

WAR DIARY

of 2nd Battalion Grenadier Guards for the month ending

JANUARY.1918.

During the past year the Battalion has seen several changes.

It has served under three Brigadiers,- Brig.Gen.C.E. Pereira,D.S.O., (Coldstream Guards) who commanded the Brigade during the SOMME offensive of 1916, and left in January,1917, to command the 2nd Division; Brigadier Gen. G.D.Jeffreys,C.M.G., who succeeded him, and commanded until promoted to the 19th. Division in September,1917; and finally Brig. Gen.C.R.C.de Crespigny,D.S.O., who took his place after having served with the Battalion almost continuously since March.1915, for 18 months as Commanding Officer. The Command of the Battalion in September, 1917 passed to Major.G.E.C.Rasch.D.S.O., who came from Second in Command of 3rd Battalion. Other departures were those of Captain.M.Beckwith-Smith,D.SO.,M.C., (Coldstream Guards), who had for a long time been Brigade Major and a great ally of the Battalions, and Regimental Sergeant Major.H.Wood,D.C.M., who exchanged duty with Regimental Sergeant Major J.L.Capper, from the 5th.(Res.) Battalion in December.

Of the Officers who were with the Battalion in January.1917, 8 remain at the beginning of the New Year:- Major.Hon.W.R.Bailey.D.S.O.,Second in Command, Captain. A.H.Penn, Adjutant, Hon.Captain.W.E.Acraman,M.C., Quarter -master, Captain.F.A.M.Browning.D.S.O., Captain.J.A. Andrews,M.C.,R.A.M.C., Lieutenants G.G.M.Vereker,M.C., (Transport Officer) Hon.F.H.Manners,M.C., R.A.W.Bicknell, M.C.,

WAR DIARY
or
INTELLIGENCE SUMMARY.

(Erase heading not required.)

Army Form C. 2118.

Place	Date	Hour	Summary of Events and Information	Remarks and references to Appendices
			WAR DIARY. (Continued). 63 Officers have passed through the Battalion in the 12 months, of whom 6 have been killed, 15 Wounded, the remainder promoted, transferred to other employments, sick, &c., Battle Casualties in O.R. numbered 650. The principal changes in Administration were the formation of the Reinforcement & Works Battalions, and the largely increased insistence on the importance of the Platoon as an independent unit for Training purposes. The winter of 1916-7 was the most severe known for many years. An intensely keen frost which started in January lasted without a break for 4 months and snow fell almost into May. The health of the Battalion was nevertheless extraordinarily good, the Sick Returns being throughout the year far below those of any other Battalion in the Division. During the early months of the year the Battalion was in the SOMME area, and in March followed up the German Retirement from SAILLY-SAILLISEL where it was at that time occupying the line. After holding an outpost line in the neighbourhood of BUS-LE-MESNIL-ETRICOURT, the Battalion was withdrawn with the remainder of the Division, and was employed in making roads and railways over the country abandoned by the enemy, making a great name for the amount of work completed in the time allotted. During this period the Battalion had considerable opportunities for training, and in April won, with No 11. Platoon, Commanded by 2/Lieutenant I.F.Gunnis, a Platoon Competition instituted by the Brigadier and open to the	

Army Form C. 2118.

WAR DIARY
or
INTELLIGENCE SUMMARY.

(Erase heading not required.)

Place	Date	Hour	Summary of Events and Information	Remarks and references to Appendices

		on	WAR DIARY. (Continued).
			
			Whole Brigade, being first in every item.—Musketry, Drill, Bayonet-Fighting, and a Tactical Exercise.
			
			    In May the Division left the SOMME, and entrained for FLANDERS, where it held and improved the line at BOESINGHE until the opening of the Summer Offensive on July. 31st, when it attacked, with the French on the left, from BOESINGHE, towards the STEENBEEK.
			    The Battalion captured with the 2nd Battalion Coldstream Guards the furthest objective allotted to the Division, being fortunate in suffering only 5 Officer Casualties, but losing 250 O.R.,
			    After a rest, the Battalion held the line again, and October 9th took part in a further attack from the BROENBEEK River towards HOUTHULST FOREST, successfully capturing all objectives with a loss of 2 Officers Wounded, 1 Officer Slightly Wounded and 35 O.R. Killed, 11 Missing & 144 Wounded.
			    Almost immediately afterwards the Division was withdrawn to a back area between ST. OMER, and BOULOGNE for reorganisation and rest.
			    Nothing of note occurred here save Reviews of the Division by the Field Marshal, Commander-in-Chief, and General Antoine, G.O.C., 1st French Army, and a visit to the Battalion by H.R.H., the Duke of Connaught, Colonel of the Regiment.
			    On November, 11th, the Battalion commenced a 5 day march towards the CAMBRAI front.
			    The operations never reached the stage at which the Division was intended to undertake a definite role, and the 1st Brigade did little save hold the line between GANTAING and BOURLON WOOD, though the 2nd and part of the 3rd	

Army Form C. 2118.

WAR DIARY
or
INTELLIGENCE SUMMARY.

(Erase heading not required.)

WAR DIARY (Continued).

Brigade suffered very heavy casualties in an attack on FONTAINE on the 27th. inst.
After this the Battalion was withdrawn to the METZ area, but on the 30th. was hurriedly called out to counter-attack the Germans at GOUZEAUCOURT and restore a dificult situation caused by the disorderly retirement of certain troops of the 3rd Army, who should have been holding the line, but failed to withstand an attack by the enemy in the neighbourhood of GONNELIEU and VILLERS GUISLAIN.
This operation and a further attack on GAUCHE WOOD on December 1st, though it cost 9 Officers and over 150 O.R., earned the thanks and congratulations of the Army Commander, and the Commander-in-Chief, and completed a year of undiminished achievement.

WAR DIARY
INTELLIGENCE SUMMARY.
(Erase heading not required.)

Army Form C. 2118.

February 1918   2nd Bn Grenadier Guards

Vol 43

FEBRUARY, 1918.

In the early part of this month a redistribution of the Battalions in the Division was made, and three Battalions (one from each Brigade) left the Division to form a new Brigade in the 31st. Division.

The three Battalions chosen were the 4th. Battalion Grenadier Guards, the 3rd. Battalion Coldstream Guards, and the 2nd. Battalion Irish Guards. These three left ARRAS in the first week of February to form once more a 4th. Guards Brigade, under the Command of Brigadier General Lord Ardee.

As a result of this arrangement, the Divisional frontage was re-allotted, each Brigade having one Battalion in front line, one in support, and the third in reserve, usually in ARRAS.

The 1st. Brigade took over the Centre Sector, with the 3rd. Guards Brigade on right, and the 2nd. Guards Brigade on left.

Three Companies of the right Battalion, occupied the

WAR DIARY
or
INTELLIGENCE SUMMARY.

(Erase heading not required.)

Army Form C. 2118.

Place	Date	Hour	Summary of Events and Information	Remarks and references to Appendices
Map: FAMPOUX, 1/10000	FEB: 2nd.		February (cont.)	

front line, (each Company finding its own support), the right Company being astride the ARRAS-DOUAI Railway, with support in neighbourhood of ROEUX CHEMICAL WORKS, the other two front Companies occupying the remaining 500 yards of frontage, each with a strong point in support, and the 4th. Company in CADIZ RESERVE TRENCH, about 1500 yards behind the front line.

The supporting Battalion was principally accommodated in trenches immediately north of the western fringe of FAMPOUX Village.

On the 2nd. February the Battalion took over the support position from parts of the 2nd. Brigade, with Battalion H.Q. and No. 2 and 4 Companies in PUDDING TRENCH (H.16), No. 3 on south of river in a large dug-out on the ARRAS-FAMPOUX road, and No. 1 in COLT RESERVE, (H.18), near forward Battalion Headquarters.

During this four days' tour the Battalion was chiefly occupied in fatigues, digging out forward trenches and carrying wire, duck-boards, etc., for improving and constructing trenches.

WAR DIARY
or
INTELLIGENCE SUMMARY.

(Erase heading not required.)

Army Form C. 2118.

Place	Date	Hour	Summary of Events and Information	Remarks and references to Appendices
	Feb. 6th		February (cont.) 1 N.C.O. and 1 other rank were wounded by the accidental explosion of a bomb whilst cleaning a trench. On the 6th. inst. the Battalion moved into the front line, relieving the 2nd. Battalion Coldstream Guards. Much work was done throughout the Sector in making communication throughout more easy, and wire everywhere more thick. A system of distributing the troops in depth was developed by the repair and construction of strong points sited in commanding positions, and intended to hold up any advance which should succeed in breaking the front line. - Casualties:- 1 N.C.O. and 4 men wounded.	
	Feb. 10th		On the 10th. the Battalion was relieved by the 1st. Battalion Irish Guards, and trained back to ARRAS, going into billets at the PRISON - a mournful and not over-clean residence. Whilst here the Pioneers erected an excellent Russian Steam Bath at the Transport Lines, which was much used whilst	

Army Form C. 2118.

WAR DIARY
or
INTELLIGENCE SUMMARY.
(Erase heading not required.)

Place	Date	Hour	Summary of Events and Information	Remarks and references to Appendices
	February (Cont.)		troops were in billets and where arrangements were made for the washing of their clothes whilst they were in the line.	
			From the PRISON the Battalion practised training of all kinds, principally drill.	
	Feb. 14th.		On the 14th. 2/Lieut. M.P.de Lisle and a draft of 50 other ranks arrived from the Reinforcement Battalion.	
			On the 14th. inst. the Battalion returned to the Support Line, and during this and the succeeding four days in the front system, continued the work of improving and strengthening the line.	
			The weather throughout was remarkably fine, and save for one Platoon of No. 4 Company, who had some Gas Shells near them, which ultimately caused the evacuation of nearly all the Platoon, casualties were very few, amounting in all to:-	
			1 Killed, 5 Wounded, 29 Wounded (Gas).	
			The rumours at this time of a coming German offensive were daily increasing, great activity being displayed on all sides.	

WAR DIARY
or
INTELLIGENCE SUMMARY.

(Erase heading not required.)

Army Form C. 2118.

Place	Date	Hour	Summary of Events and Information	Remarks and references to Appendices
	FEB: 22ND		**February** (cont.) 　　Staff Officers could frequently be observed, and new trenches in unexpected places sprang up almost every night. 　　On the 22nd. the Battalion went into Reserve, marching, on relief by the Irish Guards, to GORDON CAMP, a most excellent hutted camp near ATHIES, where the Battalion spent four very pleasant days, returning to the Support line on the 26th. 　　　　　　　　　　　　　　　　/Ross/　Lt.Col. 　　　　　　　　　　　　　　Commanding 2nd.Battalion, Grenadier Guards.	

WAR DIARY
or
INTELLIGENCE SUMMARY.
(Erase heading not required.)

Place.	Date	Hour	Summary of Events and Information	Remarks and references to Appendices
	1918 MARCH		**MARCH 1918.**	
	1-12		Except for the successful Raid on March 4th, Narrative of which is attached, trench routine in the area north of the SCARPE RIVER continued as usual without particular incident during the period under review. Precautions however against an attack were increased more and more. More trenches in back areas were dug, and wire everywhere was increased. An attack was expected on the 13th inst: and on the previous day the Reserve Battalion of all Brigades moved from ARRAS to camps midway between that town and the trench area. In the 1st Brigade the two Companies of the Battalion, which was then in Reserve, occupying PUDDING TRENCH moved forward to HAVANA and JUTLAND TRENCHES (new trenches behind CADIZ TRENCH) and two Companies of the Irish Guards - the Battalion in Reserve took their places, the remainder of the Battalion moving up to STIRLING CAMP just behind the railway at H.13.d. During the night our artillery fired continual bursts of harassing fire, and at 5 o'clock all troops stood to arms whilst our guns put down a heavy shoot on the German lines and back areas. Retaliation was not heavy and subsequent aeroplane reconnaissance confirmed the belief of all troops in the front system that no attack in this locality was imminent. (?) 1 Sergeant was killed and 3 other ranks wounded in the enemy's retaliation.	
	13			
	14		On the night of the 14th the Battalion relieved the 2nd Battalion Coldstream Guards in the front line. The next 4 days passed without particular incident except for some gas shelling which caused a few casualties in No 1 Company. The enemy's artillery was however noticeably more active and many trenches were blown in.	
	18		On the 18th the Battalion was relieved by the Irish Guards; Nos 2 & 3 Companies proceeding to PUDDING TRENCH, and the remainder of the Battalion marched to STIRLING CAMP.	
	20		On the 20th the 1st Guards Brigade was relieved by the 11th Infantry Brigade, 4th Division. Headquarters, Nos 1 & 4 Companies were	

WAR DIARY
or
INTELLIGENCE SUMMARY.
(Erase heading not required.)

Army Form C. 2118.

Instructions regarding War Diaries and Intelligence Summaries are contained in F.S. Regs., Part II. and the Staff Manual respectively. Title pages will be prepared in manuscript.

Place	Date	Hour	Summary of Events and Information	Remarks and references to Appendices
	MARCH			
	21		relieved at STIRLING CAMP in the early afternoon and marched to SCHRAMM BARRACKS, ARRAS. The other two companies followed when relieved the same night; comfortable billets, and improvement on other quarters usually previously occupied in ARRAS.	
Map:- LENS 11. 6.51.B. S.W. 1/10000	22		On the 21st. heavy gunfire was heard in the early morning and several shells fell in ARRAS. Three of the men of the transport were wounded and there were many casualties in other parts of the town. Rumours throughout the day indicated a heavy attack to the South of MONCHY, but except that the 5th Corps on our right had been forced to leave its front and support system of trenches very little news was obtainable. 2/Lieut. F.V.Pelly and 50 other ranks from the Household Battalion joined today. Orders received this morning that the Battalion were to be prepared to move at an instant's notice; all blankets were rolled and stacked under a guard and all transport was packed. The 2nd Brigade during this afternoon moved South, but the Battalion was told that the 1st Brigade was unlikely to move today. Blankets and kits have been taken out of store and preparations made for a quiet night. 11.0.p.m. Orders received that Brigade moves at midnight to BOIRY ST. MARTIN, about 7 miles South of ARRAS, to dig and possibly to occupy a new line of defence. During the day the town has been further shelled and this morning the front of Battalion H.Q. was blown in and a sentry was killed. Parade 11.55.p.m. By this time the town had been largely cleared of the inhabitants and shells are falling in the town and round it. March behind and Batt. Coldstream Guards and 1st Irish Guards to rendezvous near BOIRY where we get orders to stay in Reserve for the night. Rumours during the day have been as plentiful as reliable information has been scarce, but all accounts seem to agree that the Germans have launched an attack on a 50 miles frontage with a great measure of success, particularly on both flanks, towards BAPAUME in the North and LA FERE (South of ST. QUENTIN) in the South. Billet in deserted hutted camp and get to bed about 6.30 a.m.	

WAR DIARY or INTELLIGENCE SUMMARY

Army Form C. 2118

(Erase heading not required.)

Place	Date	Hour	Summary of Events and Information	Remarks and references to Appendices
	MARCH 23		A quiet day, full of rumours :- "MONCHY evacuated - Enemy have taken 18000 prisoners and 300 guns, - PERONNE fallen, - ARRAS-BAPAUME Road cut", etc. etc. Many People seem to have taken temporary leave of their senses and not only have innumerable camps full of every kind of stores been incontinently abandoned, but in this village alone a large Expeditionary Force Canteen has been set on fire with all its contents, and a water reservoir supplying the surrounding district has been blown up though neither are in the slightest immediate danger of capture. With a view to relief of 2nd brigade, the Army line held by them running from HAMELINCOURT to BOYELLES has been reconnoitred during the day. It is known that owing to the evacuation by the enemy of HENIN HILL, MONCHY has had to be evacuated and with it all the trenches further northward astride the SCARPE, which the Battalion has been holding for the last two months.	
	24		Fairly quiet day in camp. The Battalion is informed that the Brigade will relieve the 2nd Brigade in the 3rd system running Northwest of ST. LEGER tomorrow night. Arrangements have been made to relieve the 1st Battalion Scots Guards and the trenches have been reconnoitred. 4th Division are reported to have had a great shoot from the trenches we have been making during the last three months and to have killed great numbers of the enemy without loss of ground. Late at night telegram announces the Germans have cut the ARRAS-BAPAUME ROAD at ERVILLERS and are marching on GOMIECOURT and that all transport will proceed at 2.0.a.m. back to RANSART or BAILLEULMONT, so as to clear roads for a further retirement which appears still to be going on along this part of front. All students at Divisional and Corps Schools are being returned and their staffs are digging like beavers to make a G.H.Q. line. It is reported that all RAC's are being organized to dig a further line with AMC's and Town Majors' lines in close support, but confirmation of this is necessary - All preparations made to relieve 1st Batt. Scots Guards in Army line running North from St. LEGER towards HENIN. At 4.30.p.m. however, this relief was cancelled and shortly afterwards orders were received from Brigade that the enemy had taken GOMIECOURT about 6 miles to our right front, and were advancing towards COURCELLES, 4 miles due South. Battalion	
	25			

Army Form C. 2118.

WAR DIARY
or
INTELLIGENCE SUMMARY.

(Erase heading not required.)

Instructions regarding War Diaries and Intelligence Summaries are contained in F. S. Regs., Part II. and the Staff Manual respectively. Title pages will be prepared in manuscript.

Place	Date	Hour	Summary of Events and Information	Remarks and references to Appendices
	MARCH		was ordered to take up outpost line on high ground S.W. of BOIRY, looking towards MOYENVILLE. Commanding Officer went off at once with Company Commanders to settle dispositions and boundaries, the Battalion following. No. 1 Company placed on left with 2, 3 & 4 on its right, each Company finding its own supports – two platoons of No. 1 Company in Battalion Reserve. Line of resistance just forward of slope – some Companies digging new posts, others occupying parts of an old German line. Patrols established the presence of various units of 31st Division still holding line in front of us. – night passed without incident. The following Officers accompanied the Battalion :-	
			HEADQUARTERS.	
			Commanding Officer. Lieut: Colonel/ G.E.C.Rasch, D.S.O.	
			Acting 2nd in Comm. Captain G.C.F.Harcourt-Vernon, D.S.O.	
			Adjutant. Captain A.H.Penn.	
			Medical Officer. Captain W.H.Lister, L.S.O., M.C.	
			No. 1 COMPANY. **No. 2 COMPANY.**	
			Capt. A.M.Browning D.S.O. Capt. O.Martin-Smith.	
			2/Lieut. H.B.O.Morgan 2/Lieut. S.G.K.George	
			2/Lieut. J.S.Carter 2/Lieut. A.W.P.de Lisle.	
			No. 3 COMPANY. **No. 4 COMPANY.**	
			Lieut. S.T.S.Clarke, M.C. Captain G.B.Wilson.	
			2/Lieut. F.J.Lansley Lieut. J.A.Jacob	
			2/Lieut. Hon.S.A.S.Montagu Lieut. D.Harvey.	
	26		At "stand to" masses of troops are seen moving Southwards across our front about a mile away. These prove to be various units of 31st.Division who have received orders to withdraw too late for them to do so under cover of dark. During the morning the 4th Guards Brigade appear on our right flank and dig in, in continuation of our outpost line, with orders to cover the withdrawal of the remainder of their Division. The 3rd & 2nd Guards Brigades have had to conform to the retirement on the right by withdrawing during the night from the Army Line to a line in prolongation of the left of our outpost line, the 2nd Battalion Coldstream Guards & 1st	

WAR DIARY
or
INTELLIGENCE SUMMARY.

Army Form C. 2118.

Place	Date	Hour	Summary of Events and Information	Remarks and references to Appendices
	MARCH 26		Battalion Irish Guards who were in support to the other two Brigades sidestepping to their right until they joined the left of the Battalion, so that at daybreak all four Guards Brigades were in line together, the 3rd Brigade on the left, with a line running between BOISLEUX ST. MARC & BOISLEUX AU MONT, then the 2nd & 1st Brigades and finally the 4th Brigade with its right refused to the North of AYETTE. During the morning several Battalions of the 31st Division retired right through the left flank of the Battalion; most of them seemed vague as to their destination and purpose and none appeared to have any definite orders. Later in the day, some of them reappeared from behind us, having been apparently been sent forward again. They did not seem to know what they were intended to do & the majority of them faded away again before dark leaving some stray Companies behind who attached themselves to us. Meanwhile the enemy were following close behind the retirement and at about 7.p.m. the Officer Commanding No. 4 Company (left centre company) reported that about 100 could be seen advancing on the crest 1000 yards in front. They were preceded by machine gunners who opened fire on our posts causing a few casualties. Further advance was prevented by our Lewis Gun and rifle fire and no action developed. We pushed out patrols as soon as it was dark and began wiring of our front. At 11.30 p.m. orders were received for the 1st Brigade to relieve the 2nd Brigade, relief to be complete by 4.30 a.m. The Battalion relieved the 1st Battalion Coldstream Guards in the front line, astride the ARRAS - ALBERT railway, Nos. 4 & No 3 on the west, Nos. 2 & 1 Companies on the east. The 2nd and Battalion Coldstream Guards took over from the 3rd Battalion Grenadier Guards in support continuing the outpost line just vacated by the Battalion. The Battalion's new position is an unenviable one. It includes 3 sunken roads and a railway and is sited on the forward slope of a hill which runs (south) down to the valley of the COJEUL. It is overlooked from the outskirts of MOYENNEVILLE on the right and from a high ground all along the front, where a number of deserted huts at distances from 500-800 yards give ideal cover for snipers and machine guns. During the night the right flank of the Battalion (No. 2 Company) was refused towards the Support Battalion, who pushed forward some posts to fill up the gap which	

WAR DIARY
or
INTELLIGENCE SUMMARY.

(Erase heading not required.)

Army Form C. 2118.

Place	Date	Hour	Summary of Events and Information	Remarks and references to Appendices
	MARCH 27		had been created on the right of the Front Battalion by the absence of the 31st Division. Enemy infantry appeared soon after daylight evidently intending to continue their advance. They have developed a new plan of advance during these operations, by which they push forward by ones and twos and thus gradually build up a line for an assault or a further advance by driblets. They adopted this method now, feeling for a weak place in the line. It is a difficult method to counter in many ways, for no sufficient target for artillery is offered and it inevitably results in a great expenditure of S.A.A. very often with little result. All Companies had a good deal of shooting with good effect, especially in the case of No. 1 Company who were able to enfilade enemy as they advanced in driblets towards No. 2 Company. We also brought down an enemy aeroplane with rifle fire. The whole Battalion front was pretty heavily shelled, and No. 4 Company on the right suffered very severely from artillery and machine gun fire. Lieut. D.Harvey M.M. was killed and Captain G.B.Wilson M.C. and trench mortar fire. 2/Lieut. A.W.P. da Risis wounded. No determined attack developed against the Battalion and the chief force of the enemy thrust drifted during the morning further to the South, the 3rd Battalion,(who had relieved us the night before,) being heavily attacked. They suffered fairly heavily but repulsed all attacks and inflicted very severe casualties on the enemy infantry. Activity had quietened down by late afternoon. 2/Lieut. Hon. S.A.S. Montagu attached No. 4 Company from No. 3 Company. Casualties killed 2 O.R. wounded 31 OR.	
	28		Report from right Company just before daybreak stated that patrols had found enemy lined up in open 100 yards from our trench. Our artillery dispersed them with casualties and no strong attack followed on our front during the day though small parties covered by machine gun fire, made continual efforts to penetrate our line. Nos. 1 & 2 Companies heavily shelled during morning. The enemy have direct observation to whole of line and their shooting is very accurate. wounded. Lieut.J.H.Jacob and 42 O.R., missing 1 Casualties killed 23 2/Lieut. H.B.G. Webb attached from No. 1 Company to command No. 4 Company.	

Army Form C. 2118.

WAR DIARY
or
INTELLIGENCE SUMMARY.
(Erase heading not required.)

Instructions regarding War Diaries and Intelligence Summaries are contained in F. S. Regs., Part II. and the Staff Manual respectively. Title pages will be prepared in manuscript.

Place	Date	Hour	Summary of Events and Information	Remarks and references to Appendices
	MARCH 2/l			
	30		A quieter day. Lieutenants A.W.Ackland.M.C. Hon.F.H.Manners.M.C. Hon.H. F.F.Lubbock, 2/Lieutenants R.T.Sharpe and P.V.Pelly came up to the line and Captain O.Martin-Smith. 2/Lieutenants J.S.Carter and Hon.S.A.S. Montagu went down to 1st Line Transport for a rest. Major Hon.W.R.Bailey, D.S.O. relieved the Commanding Officer. Casualties 5 killed, about 3 wounded. Very heavy shelling from 9 a.m. " 11.15 a.m. on whole Divisional front resulting in two attacks on 1st Battalion Grenadier Guards on our left, one astride the railway in S.18. made by two Battalions, another Southwest from BOIRY BECQUERELLE, both of which were defeated with very severe loss; enemy also made two fainthearted attacks on the Battalion frontage, one up railway, broke down altogether; in the other on the west of the railway, about a dozen of the enemy succeeded in gaining a footing in a post of No. 3 Company from which most of the occupants had been blown by shell fire. They were at once ejected and the post re-established. Lieut. Hon.F.H.Manners & 2/Lieut. W.J.Langley wounded. Killed 10, wounded 35 O.R. missing 1. Lieut. R.H.R.Palmer relieved Lieut. S.T.S.Clarke, M.C. During the last three days about 40 other ranks have been relieved nightly by a similiar number from the Reinforcement Battalion.	
	3/l		Quiet day. Battalion relieved at night by parts of Irish Guards and 2nd Coldstream Guards and go into Brigade Reserve, Nos. 2 & 4 Companies in huts near BOIRY ST. MARTIN remainder of Battalion in the same camp between HENDECOURT & BLAIRVILLE which we occupied on our way to the CAMBRIA fighting in November. Some shelling of both camps but no casualties. Men all very tired and badly need a rest.	

G. Reech.
Lieut: Colonel.
Commanding 2nd Battalion Grenadier Guards.

SECOND BATTALION, GRENADIER GUARDS.
NARRATIVE OF RAID-MARCH 5TH.

Map refers:- see Graveland Hill Trench Map or Palves 1/10000.

On the 26th. February when the Battalion came into the support line, the commanding officer was informed that the Battalion would be required to do a raid during its coming tour in the Front line.

Raids lately have become regrettably fashionable owing to the anxiety of the Higher Command to obtain a constant supply of prisoners who may give them information of the German offensive which is expected.

The place selected for the raid was opposite the extreme left of the Battalion frontage and was chosen because from aeroplane photographs and ground observation the enemy wire seemed thinner here than elsewhere, also because rising ground on the left appeared to give partial protection from Machine Gun fire. The plan first projected was a silent raid to be carried out by part of a platoon of No. 2 Company under the command of Lieut. R.A.S.Palmer; No. 2 Company having occupied the sector chosen for the raid during the last three tours in the line. This party consisting of 24 all ranks proceeded to Gordon Camp where the 1st.Battalion Irish Guards were then billetted, and practised on dummy trenches. A few days later however the plan was changed and a raid on a larger scale, with an Artillery and Trench Mortar barrage, was ordered by the Division. In view of the very great difficulty of a considerable number of men getting through thick enemy wire unobserved and the great success achieved a short time before by the 1st.Battalion Coldstream Guards, who raided behind a barrage there is no doubt that this alteration was a great improvement. Eight volunteers from each of the remaining Companies were called for to complete the number required and these also went to Gordon Camp under Lieut. S.T.S. Clarke ; Captain F.A.M.Browning,D.S.O. went with the party to supervise and assist in its training. Whilst the raiders were training a great deal of valuable reconnaissance and preparation was carried out from the front line by Captain G.Martin-Smith, O.C. No. 2 Company. Wire cutting was also carried out by 6 inch Newton Trench Mortars. The number of the raiders was later further reduced so that the final numbers amounted to Lieut.Clarke and 26 other ranks.

The visibility during the few days before the raid was unfortunately very unfavourable and a great deal of the wire cutting had to be done on the day before the raid in spite of the danger of arousing the enemy's suspicions. This wire cutting was carried out at different places all along the Divisional frontage in order to deceive the enemy of the exact position of the coming raid. By the evening preceding the raid the wire at the point of entry was very much knocked about though it was not possible to detect a clear path through it.

The general plan was for the raiding party to form up on a tape in No Man's Land about 120 yards from the enemy trench, (the total distance between the trenches being about 240 yards.) An 18 pounder barrage was to fall on the front line at Zero for one minute when it was to lift and remain on the enemy support line 150 yards in rear; at the same time two separate barrages were to be dropped on either flank and suspected saps, machine guns and communication trenches were to have a standing barrage of 6" Newton Trench Mortars, 4.5 and 6" Howitzers put on them. Gas and smoke was also to be employed if the wind was favourable, and Machine Guns and Stokes Mortars were to operate throughout the Divisional frontage.

The raiders were divided into three parties, the right and left parties each consisting of a Sergeant and eight other ranks, who were to enter simultaneously and wheel outwards along the front trench. The O.C.Raid, with a N.C.O., two stretcher-bearers and five other ranks was to remain at point of entry whence he could best control the raid and cover the withdrawal. The raid was in any case to last not more than 20 minutes and the withdrawal was to be ordered immediately a prisoner had been captured. At Zero minus 20 most of the front line posts were withdrawn into dugouts and arrangements were made for a great quantities of coloured lights to be put up at Zero along the whole Divisional front in order to

NARRATIVE OF RAID MARCH 8th. [SHATTERED]

confuse the enemy.

The night of the raid proved fine and bright. The raiders were brought up from Gordon Camp by bus and after an issue of rum at Advanced Battalion Headquarters (in Curly Trench,) formed up as arranged at Zero minus 4. The barrage was excellent and the wire was sufficiently cut to enable the raiders to get through it without great difficulty. On entering the trench everything went exactly as practised. The enemy were taken completely by surprise, although as the subsequent examination of the prisoners proved, they had been warned of the possibility of a raid. Several small shelters containing Germans were bombed and two men and a machine gun were quickly captured. This gun was mounted on the parapet covering the gap in the enemy wire, the team was bayoneted and the gun carried back by Pte. Marshall, No. 17687, No. 1 Company. The O.C. raid at once ordered the withdrawal which was carried out without confusion and the whole party was back in the front line trench with the two prisoners and machine gun at about Zero plus 12. The enemy dropped a heavy retaliation of machine guns, Trench Mortars and Artillery at Zero plus 3 but no casualties occurred before the raiders reached the dugout which was awaiting them.

The enemy retaliation died down completely as soon as our shelling had stopped and when all was quiet the raiders returned to Gordon Camp by omnibus.

The prisoners were identified as belonging to the 10th. Bavarian Imperial Regiment. One was a machine gunner and the other an orderly. Another prisoner who was captured and who gave great difficulty in the withdrawal was shot.

The point of exit chosen was at I.8.c.1½.7½. and the point of entry I.8.c.b½. 9.

Lieut; Colonel.
Commanding 2nd Battalion Grenadier Guards.

Guards Division.
1st Guards Brigade.

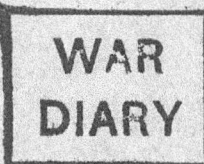

2nd BATTALION

THE GRENADIER GUARDS

APRIL 1918

Army Form C. 2118.

April 1918
2nd Bn. Grenadier Guards

WAR DIARY
or
INTELLIGENCE SUMMARY.
(Erase heading not required.)

Place	Date	Hour	Summary of Events and Information	Remarks and references to Appendices
MAP. LENS 11. 51 B. S. W. 1/10,000.	**APRIL 1918.**			
	1		Battalion relieved at night by parts of Irish Guards and 2nd Coldstream Guards, and go into Brigade Reserve, Nos 2 & 4 Companies in huts near BOIRY ST MARTIN, remainder of Battalion in the same camp between HENDECOURT & BLAIRVILLE, which we occupied on our way to the CAMBRAI fighting in November. Some shelling of both camps but no casualties - men all very tired and badly need a rest.	
	2 & 3		In billets as above. 2/Lieutenant R.C.M.Bevan arrived with a draft of 27 O.R. On the 3rd the 32nd Division (who relieved the 31st) capture AYETTE which will considerably ease the situation on our right flank.	
	4		On the night of the 3rd Battalion relieves Irish Guards in left sector of Brigade, Nos 3 & 1 Companies in front, Nos 2 & 4 in Support. Right Company occupies position formerly held by our left Company, with right on sunken road east of railway at about S.23. d. Rain at night; trenches very wet. No 1 Company (on right) were shelled for half an hour during morning; an	

Army Form C. 2118.

WAR DIARY
or
INTELLIGENCE SUMMARY.
(Erase heading not required.)

Place	Date	Hour	Summary of Events and Information	Remarks and references to Appendices
	April 4		unlucky shell pitched in trench and killed Lieutenant Hon: H. F. P. LUBBOCK and 2 other ranks and wounded 5 others.	
	5		A quiet day, no casualties. Support Companies relieved Front Companies.	
	6		A quiet day, no casualties.	
	7		A quiet day. Heavy rain during afternoon. The Battalion was relieved by the 2nd Battalion Coldstream Guards and went into camp between HENDECOURT & BLAIRVILLE. This camp had been shelled in the afternoon before the Battalion arrived, and there had been a direct hit on one of the huts. 2/Lieutenant H. H. G. MORGAN went to hospital.	
	8		In billets as above; camp was not shelled. Weather very wet and it was very difficult for the men to get their clothes dry. Lieutenant F.H.J.DRUMMOND and 2/Lieutenant G.F.LAWRENCE joined the Battalion with 88 O.Rs. from the Re-inforcement Battalion.	
	9		The Battalion relieved the 1st Battalion Irish Guards in the right sector of the Brigade, Nos. 2 & 4 Companies in the Front line, No. 3 in Support and No. 1 Company in Reserve. A very quiet relief.	

WAR DIARY
or
INTELLIGENCE SUMMARY.

Army Form C. 2118.

Place	Date	Hour	Summary of Events and Information	Remarks and references to Appendices
	April 10		A quiet day. No casualties.	
	11		A quiet day. Fine weather. A few shells and Trench Mortars were fired into our front line; no casualties. No 2 Company relieved No 4 Company in the front line and No 1 relieved No 2 Company. No 2 Company went into Support and No 4 Company into Reserve. Owing to an expected attack patrols were sent out all along the front before daybreak, but nothing unusual was heard.	
	12		A quiet day. Enemy was active with Trench Mortars on our front line and 2 were killed and 4 wounded.	
	13		The 1st Guards Brigade was relieved by the 5th Infantry Brigade, 2nd Division. The Battalion was relieved by the 2nd Battalion Highland Light Infantry, and on relief marched to BLAIRVILLE, and then embussed to SAULTY, arriving at 4:0 a.m. Nos 1 & 4 Companies camped in tents and bivouacs, Nos 2 & 3 in billets. Owing to the hospitality of the Tank Brigade, Battalion H. Q. Mess and Nos 1 & 4 Companies Mess were in the Chateau.	
	14		Reveille at 2:0 p.m.; afternoon was spent in cleaning up.	

Lieutenant W. H. S. DENT, 2/Lieutenants J. A. PATON & C. A. FITCH

Army Form C. 2118.

WAR DIARY
or
INTELLIGENCE SUMMARY.
(Erase heading not required.)

Instructions regarding War Diaries and Intelligence Summaries are contained in F.S. Regs., Part II. and the Staff Manual respectively. Title pages will be prepared in manuscript.

Place	Date	Hour	Summary of Events and Information	Remarks and references to Appendices
	April 14		with a draft of 128 O.Rs arrived from the Reinforcement Battalion.	
	15		The Battalion paraded for cleaning equipment etc.	
	16		The Battalion paraded for Battalion and Platoon Training. O. Rs recently joined from the Household Battalion and young Corporals paraded under the Adjutant. A Class of Instruction was started for young Officers in Drill, Bombing and Bayonet Fighting, and a Class of Lewis Gunnery started under the Battalion Lewis Gun Officer for all Lewis Gun Section Commanders. One of the chief lessons learnt from the recent German Offensive was the importance of the tactical handling of light machine guns, great stress being laid upon the importance of getting the best men of the Lewis Gun Sections and training them to act on their own initiative. Captain G. R. WESTMACOTT. D.S.O., left the Battalion to become liaison Officer attached to the French Army. The Brigade Gas N. C. O., inspected the gas equipment of the Battalion.	
	17		Training carried out as on the 16th.	
	18		Training as usual. Major W. R. BAILEY. D.S.O., lectured all Officers and N. C. Os on the tactical importance of Lewis Guns. Hon:	
	19		Paraded for arm drill and training as usual. The Lewis Gun Class carried out a tactical scheme under Company arrangements.	

Army Form C. 2118.

WAR DIARY
OF
INTELLIGENCE SUMMARY.
(Erase heading not required.)

Instructions regarding War Diaries and Intelligence Summaries are contained in F. S. Regs., Part II. and the Staff Manual respectively. Title pages will be prepared in manuscript.

Place	Date	Hour	Summary of Events and Information	Remarks and references to Appendices
	APRIL 20th to 23rd.		Training of all kinds continued at SAULTY. The Battalion has benefitted very much from its rest. Companies are well up to strength, and the recent drafts good. The weather has been fair, and a good deal of football has been played. 2/Lieut. C.Gwyer arrived with a draft of 5 O.R.	
	24		Battalion embussed at 2:0 p.m. and proceeded to BIENVILLERS AU BOIS to relieve the 15th Battalion H. L. I., 14th Infantry Brigade, 32nd Division, in reserve west of DOUCHY LES AYETTE. Teas and cigarettes were provided at debussing point by the courtesy of the above Division, and the Divisional Band played the Battalions past. Two Companies were billeted in the old German line just west of MONCHY AU BOIS. The other two Companies were in trenches between DOUCHY LES AYETTE and MONCHY AU BOIS. Owing to the great shortage of men with the Reserve Battalion, Platoons are going into the line with only 25 O. R., all other ranks surplus to this number remaining at 1st line Transport, POMMIER, where various classes of instruction are proceeding under selected Officers.	
	25 & 26		Two quiet days spent in improving accommodation. On the night of the 26th the Battalion relieved the 1st Battalion Irish Guards	

WAR DIARY
or
INTELLIGENCE SUMMARY.

Army Form C. 2118.

Place	Date APRIL	Hour	Summary of Events and Information	Remarks and references to Appendices
	26		in the left sector of the Brigade frontage. The 2nd Brigade is on the left, 3rd Brigade on the right. Nos 4 and 2 Companies in front line (from left to right), No 3 in Support, No 1 in Reserve. The Battalion covers a frontage of about 900 yards on the eastern outskirts of AYETTE, the Support runs between DOUCHY LES AYETTE and AYETTE, and the Reserve Company occupying a trench running north and south about 1,000 yards west of DOUCHY LES AYETTE, with its right resting on the dry bed of the COJEUL STREAM.	
	27 to 29.		The line in this part is extraordinarily quiet, and a great contrast to our last, the enemy having apparently thinned out his troops in this district in order to increase his forces available for the thrust further north. Quiet days. Very little enemy activity; owing to the village of AYETTE being out of observation by the enemy, movement by day is possible throughout the most of the Battalion Sector, and hot meals can be cooked for most of the men. On the night of the 29th 2nd Lieutenant C. A. FITCH was wounded in the head and right arm by a bomb thrown from a German post whilst he was on patrol in front of his Company. 2nd Lieutenant C. GWYER came up to take his place.	

WAR DIARY
or
INTELLIGENCE SUMMARY.

Army Form C. 2118.

Place	Date	Hour	Summary of Events and Information	Remarks and references to Appendices
	APRIL 29		The same night there was an inter-company relief, No 1 Company relieving No 4 Company on the left front, and No 3 Company relieving No 2 Company on the right front. Casualties, 2 O.R. Wounded.	
	30		The work undertaken consisted principally in improving the trenches, joining isolated posts, cleaning the area, which is very dirty, and salvaging through-out the great quantity of material which is lying everywhere. Casualties, 5 O.R. Wounded.	

(sd) G. RASCH,   Lieut: Colonel.
Commanding 2nd Battalion Grenadier Guards.

WAR DIARY
or
INTELLIGENCE SUMMARY.
(Erase heading not required.)

Army Form C. 2118.

May, 1918.

Place	Date	Hour	Summary of Events and Information	Remarks and references to Appendices
	MAY 1		In the front line at AYETTE.	
			MAY 1918. The Battalion was relieved by the 2nd Batt: Coldstream Guards and marched to MONCHY AU BOIS and remained there in Brigade Reserve until the 4th., when we relieved the 1st Battalion Irish Guards in the right sector. During this tour an American Company Commander and three N. C. Os were attached to the Battalion under instruction for three days.	
	MAY 4		A quiet relief, No 4 Company on the right, No 2 Company on the left, No 3 Company in support and No 1 Company in reserve. The line had been slightly advanced by the Irish Guards since the last relief, and the work undertaken consisted chiefly in wiring the new position.	
	MAY 5		On the 5th a Sergeant in charge, covering a wiring party was killed by a Sniper.	
	MAY 7		On the 7th the support Company relieved the left front Company, and the reserve Company the right front. The wiring of the new line was continued by night, and accommodation for the troops improved by day. The system of visual signalling was completed.	
	MAY 8		On the 8th the reserve Company suffered from some heavy shelling which was directed on a neighbouring battery. One man killed, six wounded.	

Army Form C. 2118.

WAR DIARY
or
INTELLIGENCE SUMMARY.
(Erase heading not required.)

Instructions regarding War Diaries and Intelligence Summaries are contained in F. S. Regs., Part II. and the Staff Manual respectively. Title pages will be prepared in manuscript.

Place	Date	Hour	Summary of Events and Information	Remarks and references to Appendices
	MAY 10		On the 10th relieved by the 2nd Battalion Coldstream Guards and returned to MONCHY AU BOIS, where the details of the Battalion, left out of the line, are billeted. A great deal of instruction has been going on at POMMIER, Musketry, Lewis Gunnery, Bombing, Bayonet Fighting and Technical Classes have been formed, and special lectures by various Officers from different branches of the Division, have been arranged from time to time. The numbers left out of the line usually amount to two to three Officers per Company, and two to three hundred men.	
	MAY 11		On the 11th Lieutenant J. C. CORNFORTH, M.C. and nine O. R. joined the Battn: This Officer was posted to Command No 3 Company.	
	MAY 13		The Battalion relieved the 1st Battalion Irish Guards in the left sector. A quiet relief. No 1 Company on the left, No 3 Company on the right, No 2 in support, No 4 in reserve.	
	MAY 16		On the 16th the reserve Company relieved the left Company, and the support Company relieved the right Company. The work undertaken consisted of joining up the posts and deepening the communications. All the posts were joined up during this tour in the line, and a considerable amount of salvage was collected.	

Army Form C. 2118.

WAR DIARY
or
INTELLIGENCE SUMMARY.
(Erase heading not required.)

Instructions regarding War Diaries and Intelligence Summaries are contained in F. S. Regs., Part II. and the Staff Manual respectively. Title pages will be prepared in manuscript.

Place	Date	Hour	Summary of Events and Information	Remarks and references to Appendices
	MAY 19		The Battalion was relieved by the 2nd Battalion Coldstream Guards, and returned to MONCHY AU BOIS.	
	MAY 20		At POMMIER the usual instructional classes were in progress for the details. Lieutenant/t C. A. GORDON joined the Battalion and was posted to No 2 Company. 2/Lieutenant H. A. Finch joined the Battalion and was posted to No 4 Company.	
	MAY 22		The Battalion relieved the 1st Battalion Irish Guards in the right sector. No 2 Company on the left, No 4 Company on the right, No 1 in support and No 3 in reserve. A quiet relief.	
	MAY 23		The 2nd Battalion Coldstream Guards on the left raided German Posts successfully in the early morning, securing a prisoner without loss to themselves, save four wounded by our own barrages. Increased shelling during the night, and a heavy shoot on front line during "stand to". Both front Companies started making mined dug-outs in the sunken road which forms the front line. Casualties Lieutenant A. W. Acland. M.C. and two other ranks wounded. Lieutenant F. H. J. Drummond. M.C., came up to take the place of Lieutenant A. W. Acland. M.C.	
	MAY 24		A wet and dull day, less artillery activity than usual owing to bad observation.	

Army Form C. 2118.

WAR DIARY
or
INTELLIGENCE SUMMARY.
(Erase heading not required.)

Instructions regarding War Diaries and Intelligence Summaries are contained in F. S. Regs., Part II. and the Staff Manual respectively. Title pages will be prepared in manuscript.

Place	Date	Hour	Summary of Events and Information	Remarks and references to Appendices
	MAY 26		The reserve Company was shelled fairly heavily at intervals during the afternoon. Inter-Company relief. No 1 Company relieving No 2 Company in left front. No 3 Company relieving No 4 Company in right front. Nos 2 and 4 Companies going into support and reserve respectively. Casualties:- 2 killed. 2 wounded. Front area barraged for about 20 minutes at 12:30 p.m., 2:45 p.m. and 3:20 p.m. One post suffered a direct hit which killed or wounded every occupant. Our guns still shooting short - one shell killed a Corporal, others only just escaped doing further damage. Everybody much exasperated. Casualties:- 2 killed. 6 wounded.	
	MAY 27		A fairly lively morning, but the rest of the day quieter. Casualties:- 1 killed. Another heavy shoot during "stand to". Several direct hits: 9 killed and 8 wounded. Enemy aircraft very active, patrolling front line continually by day, in spite of rifle and Lewis Gun fire. Battalion Headquarters heavily shelled by 5.9's and 4.2's from 12:30 p.m. to 1:45 p.m., and again for half an hour in the afternoon. DOUCHY LES AYETTE also received much attention.	

Army Form C. 2118.

WAR DIARY
or
INTELLIGENCE SUMMARY.
(Erase heading not required.)

Instructions regarding War Diaries and Intelligence Summaries are contained in F. S. Regs., Part II. and the Staff Manual respectively. Title pages will be prepared in manuscript.

Place	Date	Hour	Summary of Events and Information	Remarks and references to Appendices
	May 29		During the night and early morning the Welsh Guards, and (on our right) and 1st Battalion Irish Guards, (on our left) both did a raid to secure identification of a new Division in front of us. Irish Guards obtained five prisoners without a casualty, but the Welsh Guards failed to achieve their purpose. Battalion relieved by the 2nd Battalion Coldstream Guards after a fairly quiet day, and went back to MONCHY camp, where they remained till the 31st. This line, so quiet when we first came into it, has, as a result of our increased activity, become far less peaceful, and during this tour we have lost 19 killed and 18 wounded.	

A. Rusk. Lieut: Colonel.
Commanding 2nd Battalion Grenadier Guards.

WAR DIARY or INTELLIGENCE SUMMARY

Army Form C. 2118.

June 1918. 2nd Batt. Coldstream Guards

VOL 47

WAR DIARY, JUNE 1918.

Place	Date	Hour	Summary of Events and Information	Remarks and references to Appendices
	JUNE 1		On the night of the 31st we relieved 1st Battalion Irish Guards in the left sector of the Brigade. The route to the front line was heavily shelled from 9:0 to 10:0 p.m., consequently the relief was delayed, but no casualties were sustained. No 1 Company on the left, No 3 Company on the right, No 2 Company in support and No 4 Company in reserve.	
	JUNE 2		DOUCHY LES AYETTE and AYETTE received much attention during the day. During the night, the enemy projected gas against the front on our left. This gas travelled across our front, and Respirators had to be worn for about three hours. The support Company was shelled at intervals during the day, and/the left front Company was heavily shelled during the afternoon. Casualty :- One other rank wounded.	
	JUNE 3		Hostile artillery was still more active, and paid great attention to the support Company line and AYETTE. Inter-company relief. No 4 Company relieving No 1 Company in the left front, and No 2 Company relieving No 3 Company in the right front. Nos 3 and 1 Companies going into support and reserve respectively. Capt. R. McOliver joined the Battalion.	

Army Form C. 2118.

WAR DIARY
or
INTELLIGENCE SUMMARY.
(Erase heading not required.)

Instructions regarding War Diaries and Intelligence Summaries are contained in F. S. Regs., Part II. and the Staff Manual respectively. Title pages will be prepared in manuscript.

Place	Date	Hour	Summary of Events and Information	Remarks and references to Appendices
	JUNE 4/5		Hostile artillery still active on the front and support lines, but only two other ranks were wounded.	
	JUNE 6		A quiet day. The 1st Guards Brigade was relieved by the 6th Infantry Brigade, the Battalion being relieved by the 17th Battalion, Royal Fusiliers. Harassing fire had been put down on the tracks, consequently the relief was much delayed. No 4 Company were unlucky going out, and had three killed and ten wounded. The total casualties during the relief were three killed and fourteen wounded. The Battalion marched to entraining point at MONCHY AU BOIS, and proceeded to SAULTY. The whole Battalion did not arrive at SAULTY until 4:30 a.m. on	
	JUNE 7		the 7th. Billets were not vacated until the evening, and the troops spent the day in the open in the CHATEAU grounds. Getting into their billets about 6:0 p.m. that evening. No 4 Company billeted in tents in the CHATEAU grounds, and the rest of the Battalion in billets in the village. The	
	JUNE 8		day was spent in cleaning billets, clothing and equipment. The Battalion was allotted the Baths in the village.	
	JUNE 9/23		In billets as above. Platoon Training of all kinds was practised during this period. Drill, bombing, musketry, and bayonet fighting with Platoon	

Army Form C. 2118.

WAR DIARY
or
INTELLIGENCE SUMMARY.
(Erase heading not required.)

Instructions regarding War Diaries and Intelligence Summaries are contained in F.S. Regs., Part II. and the Staff Manual respectively. Title pages will be prepared in manuscript.

Place	Date	Hour	Summary of Events and Information	Remarks and references to Appendices
			Tactical Schemes and classes for Lewis Gunners and other specialists, although the latter were reduced to a minimum in order to give Platoon Officers a chance to really Command their Platoons. One Company Route Marched each day.	
			A Platoon Competition was also organised, a Platoon from each Company entering. The following were the events :-	
			Bomb throwing.	
			Rifle bombing.	
			Competition for Message Carrying by Platoon Runners.	
			Stretcher Bearer Competition.	
			Bayonet fighting.	
			Lewis Gunnery.	
			Musketry.	
			Tactical Scheme.	
			Drill.	
			The Tactical Scheme was judged by two other Commanding Officers from the Brigade, and the Drill by three Regimental Sergeant Majors. The result was as follows :- {No 7 Pln. Comnr: Lt.R.H.R.Palmer. No 4 Comnr: 2/Lt.R.CM.Bevan. " 16 " " " " Sgt.N.G.Taylor. " 10 " " R.T.Sharpe.	

Plat:	Bomb'g.	R. Gren:	R'nrs.	Str:Brs:	B:Ftg:	L. G.	Tac:Sch:	Shoot:	Drill.	TOTAL.
No. 7.	2.5	4	2	3.25	7.5	9.5	24	23.04	40.16	115.95.
16.	3.5	4	2	4.75	6.8	2.5	25	24.13	37.6	110.28.
4.	4.	3	4	2.75	8.7	8.5	5	23.07	38.05	97.07.
10.	2	2.5	3	4	6.6	3.5	10	22.79	37.3	91.69.

Army Form C. 2118.

WAR DIARY
or
INTELLIGENCE SUMMARY.

(Erase heading not required.)

Instructions regarding War Diaries and Intelligence Summaries are contained in F. S. Regs., Part II. and the Staff Manual respectively. Title pages will be prepared in manuscript.

Place	Date	Hour	Summary of Events and Information	Remarks and references to Appendices
	JUNE 19		During this time a further draft of 16 N. C. Os were sent to England to train recruits. On the 19th. Major Kerr: W. R. Bailey, D.S.O. who has been with the Battalion since September 1914, left to proceed to the 1st Battalion, the Commanding Officer of which (Lord Gort) was about to proceed to the Command of a Brigade	
	JUNE 22		On the 22nd. the Gunrds Divisional Horse Show took place. The Battalion achieved great distinction, winning a cup given by the Major General for the Battalion which gained most points. The prizes won were :- 1st for Heavy Draught Horse. 1st for pair of horses in Water Cart. 2nd for Water Cart. 2nd for pair of horses in Cooker. 2nd Light Draught Horse. 3rd Pack Animal. "Ben"&"Molly" won for the third times in the Divisional Horse Show.	
	JUNE 23		On the 23rd. Lieutenant N. M. Jesper, Lieutenant L. St: L. Herman-Hodge and 2nd Lieutenant F. J. Langley, rejoined the Battalion. The Commanding Officer went to Command the Brigade whilst the Brigadier General was on leave, and Captain G. C. P. Harcourt-Vernon. D.S.O., acted as Commanding Officer.	
	JUNE 24		On the 24th. Company Training started. Training commenced with ½ an hour	

Army Form C. 2118.

WAR DIARY
or
INTELLIGENCE SUMMARY.
(Erase heading not required)

Place	Date	Hour	Summary of Events and Information	Remarks and references to Appendices
	JUNE 27		Battalion Parade under the Adjutant on half the days of the week, during which young officers and a class for N. C. Os also paraded, and on the other half of the week Companies paraded for half hour Company drill. Advance Guards, Outposts and Tactical Schemes of all kinds were practised, and one Company per day fired on the range. On the 27th. Captain R. A. W. Bicknell, M.C., who had been with the Battalion since the end of September 1916, proceeded to England for six months tour of duty. The Command of No. 4 Company passed to Lieutenant F. H. J. Drummond, M.C., with 2nd Lieutenant J. S. Carter as second in Command.	
	JUNE 28		On the 28th. at 8:15 a.m., just as Training was commencing, the Battalion received orders to march to rendezvous "B" with transport, in accordance with a Divisional Scheme issued when the Battalion came into rest. The Battalion dressed in fighting order and marched off forthwith, returning to dinner, after the above having been a practice for the whole Brigade.	
	JUNE 29		On the 29th. the Battalion took part in a Brigade Scheme under Divisional arrangements, consisting first in an Outpost Scheme, developing into an Advance Guard with a Flank Guard, and an attack. Cookers accompanied the Battalion, which returned early in the afternoon.	

Army Form C. 2118.

WAR DIARY
or
INTELLIGENCE SUMMARY.
(Erase heading not required.)

Place	Date	Hour	Summary of Events and Information	Remarks and references to Appendices
	JUNE 30		A Guard of Honour of 100 O. R. under Captain F. A. M. Browning. D.S.O., 2nd Lieutenant H. White and 2nd Lieutenant G. F. Lawrence, proceeded by bus to the 3rd Army Headquarters at HESDIN, to form a Guard of Honour for H.R.H. the Colonel of the Regiment, on the occasion of the presentation of some decorations to French Officers. On the 30th. the prize winners at the Divisional Horse Show paraded at Divisional Headquarters for H.R.H. the Duke of Connaught.	

R. Rasch
Lieut: Colonel.
Commanding 2nd Battalion Grenadier Guards.

WAR DIARY
or
INTELLIGENCE SUMMARY.
(Erase heading not required.)

Army Form C. 2118.

Place	Date	Hour	Summary of Events and Information	Remarks and references to Appendices
SAULTY.	JULY/4		**WAR DIARY, JULY 1918.**	

SAULTY. — Training of all kinds continued. On the 3rd, Battalion Concert was held in the Open-Air Theatre in the CHATEAU grounds. July 2nd: Battalion carried out a concentration march, all Companies marching to a rendezvous by different routes, with reference to timing their start so as to arrive simultaneously. On arrival, various attack and approach march formations were practised.

The following was received from 3rd Army Headquarters.

Guard of Honour supplied last month to HRH The Colonel of the Regiment. This Guard made a remarkable impression; its turn-out was so good that many of the onlookers refused to believe that the men forming the Guard ever went into the Line and maintained either that they came out from England for the express purpose of finding the Guard or that they were struck off to accompany H/ H.R.H. during his visit.

"G. O. C.,

VI CORPS.

The Army Commander wishes me to express his satisfaction with the Guard of Honour of the 2nd Grenadier Guards which was furnished at Army Headquarters to-day, on the occasion of the visit of Field Marshal H.R.H. The Duke of Connaught, to present decorations to French Officers.

The turn-out and bearing of the Guard, their marching and handling of arms were all beyond criticism. The Army Commander would be glad if you would convey his appreciation both to the General Officer Commanding the Guards Division and the Officer Commanding, 2nd Battalion Grenadier Guards.

Third Army A/A/1318Q

WAR DIARY
or
INTELLIGENCE SUMMARY.

(Erase heading not required.)

Army Form C. 2118.

Place	Date	Hour	Summary of Events and Information	Remarks and references to Appendices
			The Army Commander also wishes me to express his appreciation of the Band of the Grenadier Guards, which added so much to the success of the Ceremony.	
			(signed) A. F. Sillem. Major General.	
			D. A. & Q. M. G., Third Army."	
	30-6-18.			
			During the last week of the Battalion's stay in SAULTY, a series of valuable demonstrations and lectures were given at Divisional Headquarters by picked officers and N. C. Os from the Canadian Corps, who particularly excel in this practice. These were attended by various Officers and N. C. Os from the Battalion, and all Companies started practising patrolling on the lines taught.	
AYETTE Combined Sheet 1/20000	JULY 5		The Battalion (less Details, who marched under Captain G. C. F. HARCOURT. VERNON, D.S.O. to BAILLEULMONT with Transport) proceeded by train from SAULTY to RANSART, where tea was provided by the courtesy of the 32nd Division, and guides from the 5/6th ROYAL SCOTS (14th Infantry Brigade, 32nd Division) were met and the Battalion led to take over the Reserve Battalion's position in a trench 500 yards east of RANSART. The Division is occupying a Sector with its right joining the 2nd Division between AYETTE and MOYENNEVILLE, and its left joining the Canadian Corps on the south-eastern outskirts of BOISLEUX St MARC. The 1st Brigade occupies the Centre Sector, 3rd Brigade on the left and the 2nd Brigade on the right. Each Brigade has one Battalion in front,	

Army Form C. 2118.

WAR DIARY
or
INTELLIGENCE SUMMARY.
(Erase heading not required.)

Place	Date	Hour	Summary of Events and Information	Remarks and references to Appendices
	JULY 6		one in Support and one in Reserve.	
	JULY 7/14		The accommodation was beautifully clean but rather inadequate, the relieved Battalion having only been in the position for a few days. Day was devoted to improving existing accommodation and during the remaining four days in reserve the Battalion carried out training by Companies in the outskirts of RANSART. Scouting and patrolling by day, by men wearing darkened glasses which produce a night effect, was carried on by Companies under the Battalion Intelligence Officer, 2/Lieutenant S. G. K. George, and competitions were carried out both for shooting and for the best construction of a new shelter. In the first competition 1 N.C.O. and 6 men from Batt: H.Q. shot against any other section in the Battalion. All Companies entered two sections and three events were shot off - slow, rapid, and an improvised event in which the competitors approached the firing point from the rear and, under the direction of their section commander, had to knock out as many partially concealed objects as possible in two minutes. Results: 1st H.Q., 2nd No. 4 Company, 3rd No. 2 Company. The shelter competition - judged by Lieut: Colonel R. R. C. Baggalley, M.C. (commanding 1st Irish Guards), and the Brigade Major - produced great keenness and excellent results. 1st No. 2 Platoon, 2nd. No. 6 Platoon, 3rd No. 16 Platoon. Marks were awarded	

WAR DIARY
or
INTELLIGENCE SUMMARY.
(Erase heading not required.)

Army Form C. 2118.

Place	Date	Hour	Summary of Events and Information	Remarks and references to Appendices
	JULY 11/7		for construction, weather-proof condition, neatness and general appearance. These six days in reserve passed in fine weather and only one casualty was sustained. On the 11th the Battalion moved forward into support, relieving 1st Batt: Irish Guards in trenches around the south-western outskirts of HENDECOURT. One Company (No. 1) proceeded to BOIRY ST: MARTIN for attachment to the front line battalion. Companies were mostly occupied in making dug-outs in their battle positions, and in carrying out various fatigues for the R.E. A place was found for a cricket ground in a sheltered valley near Batt: H.Q. and two matches were played with composition balls and pioneer-made bats on the last two evenings of the Battalion's occupation. Fine weather; no casualties.	
	JULY 17/25		On the 17th the Battalion relieved the 1st Battalion Irish Guards in the front line, occupying approximately the same line as held by the Battalion at the end of March. Battalion Headquarters are in the east end of BOIRY ST: MARTIN, with two companies (No. 4 Company and one company attached from the Support Battalion) in reserve. No. 3 Company occupy the Support Line along the old German trench in S.16.c and S.21.b, where Battalion H.Q. were in the March fighting; the remaining two companies being distributed in depth, two platoons in front and two in support.	

Army Form C. 2118.

WAR DIARY
or
INTELLIGENCE SUMMARY.
(Erase heading not required.)

Instructions regarding War Diaries and Intelligence
Summaries are contained in F. S. Regs., Part II.
and the Staff Manual respectively. Title pages
will be prepared in manuscript.

Place	Date	Hour	Summary of Events and Information	Remarks and references to Appendices
			The right Company (No. 1) holds astride the ARRAS-ALBERT Railway in S.28.b and S.23.c. No. 2 Company continuing this line N.E. through S.23.b. The line which was formerly held by isolated posts is now a continuous trench, but owing to the now universally adopted plan of holding in depth, the line is only occupied by posts at intervals and the trench, in consequence, is in a very poor state of repair. Enemy activity is not remarkable; he, like us, appears to be holding his front line by posts. Shelling has much died down since we were last here and the sector on the whole is a quiet one. On the 20th No. 4 Company relieved No. 1, and No. 3 relieved No. 2 Company. Weather throughout was good. Casualties were not heavy, although there was usually a certain amount of shelling on the front line during "Stand-to", and various localities further back at intervals during the night. Active patrolling was carried out nightly, but a full moon made success extremely difficult, and a projected attempt to capture a prisoner on the night of the 22nd had to be abandoned owing to a raid by the next Division. The Battalion was relieved on the 23rd by the 2nd Battalion ♯♯♯♯♯ Coldstream Guards: a good relief without casualties. The Battalion marched back to the Reserve Line near RANSART. Casualties during tour in front line: 2 killed and 8 wounded.	

Army Form C. 2118.

WAR DIARY
or
INTELLIGENCE SUMMARY.
(Erase heading not required.)

Instructions regarding War Diaries and Intelligence Summaries are contained in F. S. Regs., Part II. and the Staff Manual respectively. Title pages will be prepared in manuscript.

Place	Date	Hour	Summary of Events and Information	Remarks and references to Appendices
	JULY 24-29		In Reserve. On the 24th and 25th the Battalion had baths in RANSART. On the afternoon of the 25th all Details who had been left out during the last tour rejoined the Battalion, and were replaced by others. On the 24th Lieutenant T. A. COMBE, Lieutenant M. H. PONSONBY, 2/Lieutenant A. M. P. de LISLE and 2/Lieutenant D. L. KING joined the Battalion. Companies carried on training under Company arrangements whilst in Reserve, one Company route marching daily, but all training was severely handicapped by rain, which turned the trenches into a morass and involved continuous work to render them habitable. During this part of the tour an increasing stream of Americans have joined the Brigade for instruction. The following Special Message of the Day, issued by G. O. C. 1st Guards Brigade, is indicative of the feeling of spirited comradeship now existing between ourselves and our gallant allies. "From Guards Division 'Q'. To Transport Officer, 1st Guards Brigade. ---------- Draw 6 Bottles Whisky from Div: Soldiers' Club and deliver to Brigade H. Q. for American Officers attached. JMMU 'Q' ----- ----- ----- ----- ----- ----- ----- -----	

WAR DIARY
or
INTELLIGENCE SUMMARY.

(Erase heading not required.)

Army Form C. 2118.

Place	Date	Hour	Summary of Events and Information	Remarks and references to Appendices
			From G.O.C., 1st (Guards Brigade. To Guards Division 'G'. ------ On behalf of all Officers of the American Army attached to the Brigade under my Command, I wish to express my deepest thanks for the courteous present of Whiskey foreshadowed in your message. I am requested to add that these Officers accept this gift as a proof of the solidarity of the union existing between the American and British nations, which will endure until the whiskey runs out. (signed) C. R. C. de CRESPIGNY, Brigadier General, Commanding 1st Guards Brigade". -:- -:- -:- -:- -:- -:-	
	JULY 29/31.		In Support. On the 29th the Battalion moved up from the Reserve to the Support line at HENDECOURT. Weather fine and all the trenches have dried up.	

(signed)

Lieut: Colonel.
Commanding 2nd Battalion Grenadier Guards.

Army Form C. 2118.

WAR DIARY
or
INTELLIGENCE SUMMARY.

(Erase heading not required.)

Instructions regarding War Diaries and Intelligence Summaries are contained in F.S. Regs., Part II. and the Staff Manual respectively. Title pages will be prepared in manuscript.

AUGUST. 1918.
Summary of Events and Information

Hour, Date, Place		Remarks and references to Appendices
Aug. 1/4	The Battalion remained in support at HENDECOURT, the days being occupied with a competition in silent raiding until the rain made this unadvisable. The nights were spent in digging a trench for buried cable and filling it in. On August 2nd Captain A. H. Penn, M.C. relinquished the post of Adjutant to the Battalion and went to the 2nd Guards Brigade Staff under instruction. Lieutenant R. G. Briscoe, M.C. took over the work of Adjutant. Captain Penn's departure was a very severe loss to the Battalion : his organizing skill, faultless memory, unequalled tact and unfailing humour made him perhaps? one of the best adjutants in France.	
Aug. 4/10	The Battalion relieved the 1st Battalion Irish Guards in the front line. The tour was somewhat complicated by the presence of six platoons of Americans attached to the Battalion, but all officers and men were unanimous in welcoming our Allies and praising their activity and resource in what were for them novel circumstances.	
	On August 7th No. 1 Company relieved No. 4 Company and No. 2 relieved No. 3 Company in the front line. The weather remained fine and very hot throughout this tour and the trenches became perfectly dry. Enemy activity was very slight and the Battalion had only 3 casualties (including 1 killed).	
	On August 9th the Americans left the line and a slight company rearrangement of Platoons was effected.	
Aug. 10/16	In Reserve at RANSART. The weather was very fine throughout and much invaluable training was done which included, musketry, dribbling, the platoon in advance, and silent patrolling. A shooting competition also was held, each platoon entering a section to compete in rapid and snap-shooting. A prize was offered for Company teams of Sergeants and one for Corporals, and a team of Officers was defeated by a very narrow margin by a team of picked sergeants. On August 12th the duties of Intelligence Officer were taken over by Lieutenant O. F. Lawrence, as 2/Lieut. S.C.K. George had previously retired to Hospital with dysentery. Lieut. R. McCliver had filled the gap for two or three days. Captain F.H.J Drummond, M.C. also went to Hospital on August 13th and Lieut. H.B.G. Morgan	

Army Form C. 2118.

WAR DIARY
or
INTELLIGENCE SUMMARY.
(Erase heading not required.)

Instructions regarding War Diaries and Intelligence Summaries are contained in F. S. Regs., Part II. and the Staff Manual respectively. Title pages will be prepared in manuscript.

Place	Date	Hour	Summary of Events and Information	Remarks and references to Appendices
	Aug 16/18		took over No. 4 Company temporarily.	
			On the night of the 16th the Battalion relieved 1st Battalion Coldstream Guards in the support line of the Right Brigade Sector as the 2nd Guards Brigade was being withdrawn for training. The Companies were somewhat widely separated but trenches were clean and comfortable. Only two days were spent in this line, the time being occupied in becoming acquainted with the new front and in certain fatigues.	
	Aug 18/20		On the night August 18/19th the Battalion relieved the 2nd Battalion of the 320th American Regiment in the front line of the Right Brigade sector. Battalion H.Q. were in BOIRY ST. MARTIN, No. 4 Company in the sugar factory, Nos. 2 & 3 Companies in the sunken road by the Crucifix and No. 1 Company held the front line system on a wide frontage. The trenches were very poor, even cover from view being a rarity, but enemy activity was slight and very few casualties were sustained. The days were fine and hot and both the nights were occupied with patrolling activity. On the night August 19/20th we established two advanced posts some 400 to 500 yards from our line to prevent the enemy coming down by night into a wide area of dead ground in front of MOYENVILLE as this area was to be	

WAR DIARY
or
INTELLIGENCE SUMMARY.

(Erase heading not required.)

Army Form C. 2118.

Place	Date	Hour	Summary of Events and Information	Remarks and references to Appendices
	AUG: 20/25		the forming up ground for the 1st Battalion Coldstream Guards on the night August 20/21st. These two posts were held by us throughout the 20th and were relieved by the Coldstream Guards a few hours previous to their attack. On the night August 20/21st the Battalion withdrew to the Reserve line, Centre Brigade, at RANSART. The two support companies, the reserve company and Battalion H.Q. left at dusk while No. 1 Company remained until relieved by the Coldstream Guards. Enemy shelling was not above normal and there was no reason to suppose that he had discovered the British plans. The attack began at 4.55 a.m. August 21st. On the 23rd the Battalion moved up into trenches and dugouts in BOIRY, this position being now unshelled owing to the advance, and remained here until the 25th.	
	AUG: 25		On the 25th the Battalion marched off moved up to take over the front line. The Battalion marched off at 5.0 p.m. - halted until dark in a field W. of MAISON ROUGE - then moved up to relieve the 2nd Battalion Scots Guards.	

Army Form C. 2118.

WAR DIARY
or
INTELLIGENCE SUMMARY.
(Erase heading not required.)

Instructions regarding War Diaries and Intelligence Summaries are contained in F. S. Regs., Part II. and the Staff Manual respectively. Title pages will be prepared in manuscript.

Place	Date	Hour	Summary of Events and Information	Remarks and references to Appendices
	AUG.26		The enemy appeared to be apprehensive, firing heavily at dawn and early morning on all positions which might be used as forming-up areas. On the night of the 26th. 2/Lieut. H. A. FINCH and 8 O.R. went out on patrol to get in touch with the enemy. The patrol did not return. 2/Lieut. FINCH was found killed 1,000 yards in front of our line when the Battalion advanced on the 27th. (For the account of operations on the 27th and 28th see attached narrative.)	
	AUG.30		The Battalion moved to accomodation in trenches around WINDMILL Cross Roads, arriving at 5.0 p.m.	
	AUG.31		The day was spent in reorganizing and cleaning equipment etc. All the officers and O.R. rejoined the Battalion from Details.	

Lieut. Colonel,
Commanding 2nd Bn. Grenadier Gds.

2nd BATTALION GRENADIER GUARDS.

Narrative of Operations by Lieut: Colonel G.E.C.RASCH, D.S.O. Commanding 2nd Battalion Grenadier Guards.

Period - August 26th - 28th. 1918.

On the evening of August 26th a warning order was received that the advance would be continued the next day.

The following officers were with the Battalion :-

Headquarters.

Commanding .... Lieut: Colonel G.E.C.RASCH, D.S.O.
Adjutant .... Lieut. R. G. BRISCOE, M.C.
Intelligence Officer .... Lieut. G. F. LAWRENCE.
Medical Officer .... 1st Lieut. E. L. MAJOR. (U.S.M.O.R.C)

No. 1 Company.

Lieut. M. H. PONSONBY.
Lieut. N. M. JESPER.
Lieut. C. C. T. GILES.

No. 2 Company.

Captain O. MARTIN-SMITH.
Lieut. C. GWYER.
2/Lieut. A. M. P. de LISLE.

No. 3 Company.

Captain J. C. CORNFORTH, M.C.
Lieut. H. WHITE.
Lieut. R. M. OLIVER.
2/Lieut. F. J. LANGLEY.

No. 4 Company.

Lieut. H. B. G. MORGAN.
2/Lieut. J. A. PATON.

At midnight a conference was held at Battalion H.Q. attended by all Company Commanders, when the situation and objectives of the advance were explained as far as they were known. Definite orders were not received until 1.30 a.m. The rôle of the Battalion was to push forward at zero with the 2nd Battalion Coldstream Guards in its left and 62nd Division on its right and penetrate and occupy the enemy defences in and south of ECOUST and LONGATRE.

The situation was complicated by the fact that there was only a short time before dawn and all Companies had to be moved into their forming up positions before it was light. Fortunately strong patrols had been pushed out earlier in the evening to occupy the sunken road running through B.10.b & d. which was to be the forming up ground for No. 3 Company, who were to lead in the advance in extended order. No. 2 Company was to form up in HAILY COPSE as left support company in diamond formation, - No. 4 Company in MORY SWITCH with two platoons south of sunken road form in B.10.b & d. in diamond formation, - No. 1 Company as reserve company in MORY SWITCH in B.9.b.& d. in diamond formation. Battalion H.Q. formed up in centre of No. 1 Company. The forming up was carried out successfully before it was light unobserved by the enemy. The night was fine and there was little shelling. Unfortunately while No. 1 Company were moving across the open to their forming up position a shell fell in the centre of No. 1 Platoon, fatally wounding Lieut. M.H. PONSONBY, who was commanding the Company, and causing casualties to the whole platoon except 4 O.R. Lieut. JESPER took over command of the remaining three platoons of the company.

Zero was at 7.0 a.m. on August 27th. when a field-gun barrage was put down on a line 500 yards in front of the leading company, creeping forward at the rate of 100 yards in two minutes. At zero the Battalion advanced from its forming up position and within a few minutes of advancing came under intense M.G. fire from the German M.G. nests in BANKS TRENCH and BANKS RESERVE, and from this moment any movement resulted in casualties.

The frontage allotted to the Battalion was 1500 yards which made flank connection of the utmost difficulty.

Captain J. C. CORNFORTH, M.C. led his Company forward from the sunken road and found that owing to the intensity of the M.G. fire and the proximity of the enemy a prolonged advance on his left was impossible - all the more because the Battalion on his left had been already held up. At this point Lieut. R. M. OLIVER was killed. Captain CORNFORTH therefore led forward his right half Company hoping thereby to relieve the pressure on his left and compel the enemy to retire by this outflanking move. During this advance the machine gun fire grew more and more intense and the farther forward he advanced the more casualties were suffered from withering and accurate enfilade fire from his left. The advance of this half of No. 3 Company was held up temporarily by a very strongly entrenched machine gun nest in BANKS TRENCH which swept the whole the forward slope of the ground leading up to it. Enfilade fire from the left flank was still equally severe and in the capture of this position very heavy casualties were suffered, 2/Lieut. F.J.LANGLEY being killed.

At this point No. 1 Company, who throughout their advance had suffered heavily, was sent up to reinforce No. 3 Company and assist in capturing the position. Lieuts. JESPER and GILES had already been wounded and, having no officers, the remainder of this Company from this time came under the command of Captain CORNFORTH. With these reinforcements BANKS TRENCH was rushed and occupied just North of L'HOMME MORT, but the M.G. fire from the left flank had not abated and now fire was opened on them from BANKS RESERVE.

Not having enough troops to extend to the flanks and drive the enemy from the northern position of BANKS TRENCH, it was decided to remain in the position already gained. Consolidation and reorganization were impossible during daylight owing to the intensity of the fire; so also was communication to the flanks and the rear.

No. 2 Company at Zero moved out in diamond formation from RALLY COPSE and immediately came under the most intense M.G. fire from the N.E. and East. Captain Martin-Smith at once ordered his Company to extend. During the extension he himself and 2/Lieut. de LISLE were wounded, Lieut. GWYER shortly afterwards being killed. The 50 O.R. which remained in the Company then came under the command of L/S. S. FROST. Further advance was impossible, and this Company consolidated as far as enemy fire would permit along the sunken road in B.30.b.

No. 4 Company advanced on the right boundary of the Battalion along MORY SWITCH and the southern end of BANKS TRENCH, eventually establishing a position in VRAUCOURT TRENCH in C.13.d., keeping up to the barrage the whole time, but suffering heavy casualties from both flanks and the front. This Company captured a German Battalion Commander and 180 O.R. during the advance.

Lieut. MORGAN, having penetrated the enemy's position to a depth of 2000 yards beyond any other British troops, being fired on from all sides, decided to withdraw his Company after dark in order to get into touch with troops on his flanks.

On the night of August 27th the Battalion consolidated a line running parallel to and 200 yards west of BANKS TRENCH, with one company of the Irish Guards brought up on the left to fill the gap between the Battalion and the 2nd Battalion Coldstream Guards.

During the evening the M.G. fire grew less intense and there were signs of the enemy having been forced to retire. This was found to be the case, for on August 28th the Battalion was able to push strong patrols and advanced the line to BANKS RESERVE, gaining ground to the extent of some 1700 yards. This line was handed over to 1st Battalion Gordon Highlanders on the night of August 28th.

On relief the Battalion moved back to the trenches east of HAMELINCOURT. Lieut: Colonel G.N.C.RASCH, D.S.O. Captain CORNFORTH, Lieut. ERISSON and Lieut. MORGAN were the only officers who came out with the Battalion, and companies came out at the following strength :-

```
No. 1 Company      32 O.R.
No. 2    "         51  "
No. 3    "         76  "
No. 4    "         48  "
```

The following letter has been received by the 1st Guards Brigade from Major General G. P. T. Feilding, C.B., C.M.G., D.S.O.

I wish to thank all ranks of the 1st Guards Brigade for their gallantry and staunchness in action from August 26th to August 28th.

When the 1st Guards Brigade relieved the 3rd Guards Brigade in the line, the enemy was fighting hard with fresh troops to maintain his positions on the high ground between MORY AND CROISILLES while countering the thrust delivered to the north by the XVIIth and Canadian Corps. The Guards Division had been ordered to press him continually and to gain all ground possible towards ECOUST so as to prevent him from disengaging troops and guns while the attack of XVIIth and Canadian Corps was being pressed on our left flank.

All Battalions of the 1st Guards Brigade discharged this duty splendidly. The attack delivered by the 2nd Battalion Grenadier Gds. and 2nd Battalion Coldstream Gds. on August 27th not only inflicted heavy losses on the enemy and brought in large numbers of prisoners but also compelled him next day to relax his hold upon the high ground south of CROISILLES. The 1st Battalion Irish Guards did most valuable work under trying conditions in taking over part of the line after the attack on the 27th, and distinguished themselves by their vigorous patrolling forward on the following day. The full result of the hard fighting done by the Brigade was gathered only after its relief on the night of August 28/29th; for, on the morning of the 29th, the patrol of the relieving Division were able to push right forward into the outskirts of ECOUST.

Nos. 1 & 3 Companies, 4th Bn. Guards Machine Gun Regiment, deserve all full share of credit for their work while attached to the 1st Guards Brigade.

The 1st Guards Brigade has never fought more gallantly and I wish to thank all ranks most warmly for the endurance and devotion which they displayed.

(Signed) G. Feilding,
Major General,
Commanding Guards Division.

August 31st 1918.

The total casualties during this operation were as follows :-

KILLED.

Lieut. G. F. Lawrence.
Lieut. R. M. Oliver.
Lieut. U. Gwyer.
Lieut. H. White.
2/Lieut. F. J. Langley.
2/Lieut. H. A. Finch.   and   59 Other Ranks.

DIED OF WOUNDS.

Lieut. M. H. Ponsonby   and   1 Other Rank.

WOUNDED.

Captain O. Martin-Smith.
Lieut. N. H. Jesper.
Lieut. C. C. T. Giles.
2/Lieut. J. A. Paton.
2/Lieut. A.H.P. de Lisle.   and   194 Other Ranks.

MISSING.

24 Other Ranks.

Total Casualties : 12 Officers and 278 Other Ranks.

Lieut: Colonel.
Commanding 2nd Battalion Grenadier Guards.

Army Form C. 2118.

2nd Bn. Grenadier Gds.

WAR DIARY
or
INTELLIGENCE SUMMARY.
(Erase heading not required.)

Place	Date	Hour	Summary of Events and Information	Remarks and references to Appendices
			SEPTEMBER, 1918.	
	SEPT.1		The Battalion remained near ADINFER, the Division being out of the line.	
	SEPT.2		During the morning Companies practised field training – in the early afternoon orders to move were received at 3.30 p.m. The Details under Lieut. H.B.G.Morgan returned to BERLES AU BOIS. At 5.30 p.m, the Battalion under the Command of Major G.G.T.Harcourt-Vernon, D.S.O. moved up to HAMELINCOURT and took over bivouacs evacuated by the 3rd Battalion Grenadier Guards. They were situated just in front of our old front line astride the POISIEUX-HAMELINCOURT Road. Lieut. Colonel G.E.C.Rasch, D.S.O., who was indisposed owing to a chill, remained near ADINFER; the first BRIGADE were now in reserve.	
	SEPT.3		At 9:30 a.m, the Battalion, less the 1st Line Transport, moved in fighting order to the vicinity of ST. LEGER. Soon after their departure the 1st Line Transport and Q.M.Stores moved to ERVILLERS. In the afternoon further orders to move were received. At 5.0 p.M. the Battalion moved off and marched via VAUX and VAUX-VAUCOURT to LAGNICOURT. On arrival no accomodation was found but Companies were not long in making	

Army Form C. 2118.

WAR DIARY
or
INTELLIGENCE SUMMARY.
(Erase heading not required.)

Place	Date	Hour	Summary of Events and Information	Remarks and references to Appendices
	Sept 7 -11.		use of the scrap material which was lying about. Battalion H.Q. was in a German shed at C.22.a.9.1. (Sht,57c,N.W.) Companies were in DUNELM AVENUE in bivouacs.	
			The Battalion was at one hour's notice from 9.0 a.m. daily. Field Training and Drill were carried out during the mornings. The weather remained fair and very warm.	
			On September 4th the 1st Line Transport moved to NOREUIL and on September 5th it moved back slightly and found good accomodation in C.15.c. and C.21.a.(Sht,57c.N.W.) Watering was a difficult problem during this period.	
			On September 6th Lieut. R.P.le P.Trench was sent to the 4th Field Ambulance Sick and was evacuated to the C.C.S. His place was taken by Lieut R.H.R. Palmer in command of No. 3 Company.	
			The Battalion relieved the 3rd Battalion Grenadier Guards in the Front Line.	
			The following Officers accompanied the Battalion :-	
			Headquarters. Commanding Major G.C.F.Harcourt-Vernon, D.S.O.	
			Adjutant Lieut, S.T.S.Clarke, M.C.	
			Medical Officer 1st Lieutenant E.L.Major.	

Army Form C. 2118.

WAR DIARY
or
INTELLIGENCE SUMMARY.
(Erase heading not required.)

Instructions regarding War Diaries and Intelligence Summaries are contained in F. S. Regs., Part II. and the Staff Manual respectively. Title pages will be prepared in manuscript.

Place	Date	Hour	Summary of Events and Information	Remarks and references to Appendices
	Sept:8		at D.30.c.5.0. Left Support. No. 1 Company - three platoons in slits about about D.30.c and J.6.b with Company H. Q. at D.30.c.50. Aid Post at K.29.c.98. The enemy showed no real signs of activity, barring his artillery which was constantly active. The Front and Support lines were shelled pretty regularly in the morning; at 'stand to' with both gas and high explosive. In addition there were various set points which were shelled at intervals including BOURSIES and the BAPAUME-CAMBRIAI Road. The enemy showed most activity at night and threw a great deal of gas shells about. The HINDENBURG Front Line was held by the enemy in strength and every night endeavours were made with some success to get in touch with him by means of patrolling. No. 2 Company, whose line was more indefinite than that of No. 4 Company, showed more activity in this respect. Captain F.A.M.Browning, D.S.O. left to go as A.D.C. to the G.O.C. the 4th Army. His place was taken by Lieut. H.B.G.Morgan who came up from Details.	
	Sept:11		At 6.30 p.m. the troops on our immediate left and right carried out an offensive	

Army Form C. 2118.

WAR DIARY
or
INTELLIGENCE SUMMARY.
(Erase heading not required.)

Summary of Events and Information

No. 1 Company.   Captain F.A.M.Browning, D.S.O.
                 2/Lieut. R.C.M.Bevan.
                 2/Lieut. A.F.Alington.

No. 2 Company.   Lieut. W.H.S.Dent.
                 2/Lieut. Hon. S.E.Marsham.
                 2/Lieut. D.L.King.

No. 3 Company.   Lieut. T.A.Combe.
                 Lieut. R.H.R.Palmer.
                 Lieut. R.T.Sharpe.

No. 4 Company.   Captain F.H.J.Drummond, M.C.
                 Lieut. C.C.Cubitt.
                 2/Lieut. P.V.Pelly.

The Battalion experienced a quiet relief, though the relief was not complete until 3.0 a.m. on the 8th. Battalion H.Q. was at D.29..40.75 Edition 7b,(Local). Right Front Company line - No. 2 Company - K.1.b.8.6.. - K.2.a.2.2. - K.2.c.5.2. - K.2.d.2.0. with a reserve platoon and Company H.Q. in WALSH TRENCH at K.7.b.95.30.

Left Front Line. No. 4 Company.had 4 platoons in the front line from E.26.a.0pl. to K.1.b.8.6. Company H.Q. with a platoon from No. 1 Company was near Cross Roads K.1.a.85.35.

Right Support, No. 3 Company. - J,6,c.5.9. - K.7.a.6.6. with Company H.Q.

Army Form C. 2118.

WAR DIARY
or
INTELLIGENCE SUMMARY.
(Erase heading not required.)

Instructions regarding War Diaries and Intelligence Summaries are contained in F. S. Regs., Part II. and the Staff Manual respectively. Title pages will be prepared in manuscript.

Place	Date	Hour	Summary of Events and Information	Remarks and references to Appendices
	Sept. 12/13		operations. MOEUVRES and the Canal bank on both sides of the BAPAUME—CAMBRAI Road being their respective objectives. The troops on our left were successful in retaking MOEUVRES, but only penetrated as far as the Canal on part of their front. Those on the right achieved their objectives entirely. Nos. 2 & 4 Companies carried out successful minor operations in conjunction with the main operations, No. 4 Company's left platoon under 2/Lieut. P.V.Pelly inflicted casualties on the enemy by bombing and No, 4 Company established two posts in advance of its original line. The Battalion was relieved this night by the 2nd Battalion Scots Guards and 1 platoon of the 1st Battalion Grenadier Guards on the right. It was a lengthy relief, relief not being complete until nearly 4.0 a,m, on the 12th. On relief the Battalion proceeded to bivouacs in the area D.26.(Edition 1/20000 7b local). The Battalion remained at D.26. The accomodation, which on our arrival was poor, was greatly improved.	
	Sept. 14.		On the night of the 14th the Battalion went back to the immediate	

WAR DIARY
or
INTELLIGENCE SUMMARY.
(Erase heading not required.)

Army Form C. 2118.

Instructions regarding War Diaries and Intelligence Summaries are contained in F. S. Regs., Part II. and the Staff Manual respectively. Title pages will be prepared in manuscript.

Place	Date	Hour	Summary of Events and Information	Remarks and references to Appendices
	25		neighbourhood of LAGNICOURT. Battalion H.Q. was at C.22.a.8.1. and the Companies in DUNELM AVENUE (57c N.W.). Training was carried out during the mornings under Company arrangements. 2/Lieuts. K.B.Bibby and E.M.Neill joined the Battalion. At 4.0 p.m. the Battalion moved up to LLAMA POST and relieved the 1st Batt. Grenadier Guards. The Battalion remained at LLAMA POST. The weather was indifferent. The Battalion carried out Training under Company arrangements. The Battalion remained here until the night of the 26/27th. On the 25th the G.O.C. Guards Division saw all Officers and Platoon Sergeants of the Battalion and explained the general plan of the attack which was shortly to take place.	
	26			
	29		Narrative of Operations for the 27th and 28th attached. The day was spent in reorganising and cleaning equipment.	
	30		Arm Drill and Company Training. One blanket was issued per man.	

Major.
Commanding 2nd Battalion Grenadier Guards.

2nd Battalion Grenadier Guards.

NARRATIVE OF OPERATIONS SEPTEMBER 27th 1918.

The Battalion marched off from the trenches East of LAGNICOURT at 1.20 a.m. on the morning of the 27th.

Major G. C. F. Harcourt-Vernon, D.S.O. was in Command of the Battalion. The following Officers went in with the Battalion.

Headquarters. Commanding, Major G. C. F. Harcourt-Vernon, D.S.O.
Adjutant, Captain R. G. Briscoe, M.C.
Intelligence Officer, 2/Lieut. Hon. S. E. Marsham.
Medical Officer, 1st Lieut. E. L. Major.

No. 1 Company.
Captain L. St. L. Hermon-Hodge.
2/Lieut. R. C. M. Bevan.
2/Lieut. E. M. Neill.

No. 2 Company.
Lieut. W. H. S. Dent.
2/Lieut. D. L. King.
2/Lieut. B. K. Bibby.

No. 3 Company.
Lieut. R. H. R. Palmer.
Lieut. T. A. Combe.
Lieut. R. T. Sharpe.

No. 4 Company.
Captain F. H. J. Drummond, M.C.
Lieut. C. C. Cubitt.
2/Lieut. P. V. Pelly.

Companies led off in the following order :- No. 1, 2, 3, 4 and Battalion H.Q.

It had started raining earlier in the night which made the tracks very slippery. This, added to the fact that some of the bridges, which had been put across the trenches on the day previous, had been broken, caused some delay, and prevented the pack animals which were following Companies with hot food containers from keeping up with the Battalion. They were sent off round by road, but failed to arrive before the Battalion left the assembly position.

The Battalion arrived at its assembly position in WALSH TRENCH and WALSH SUPPORT at 4.30 a.m. Enemy artillery had been exceptionally quiet during the march up - only a few shells falling in BOURSIES as the Battalion passed through.

Zero was at 5.20 a.m.

At Zero the 2nd Guards Brigade attacked from our front line to take the RED LINE. The role of this Battalion was to follow up behind the 1st Battalion Irish Guards and pass through them on the BROWN LINE. The Battalion moved off from its assembly position in the normal approach march formation of platoon blobs, Nos. 1 & 2 Companies in front line, Nos. 3 & 4 Companies in Support line with Battalion H.Q. in rear of the centre of the Battalion.

The Ridge just West of the CANAL DU NORD was being heavily shelled, but the Battalion passed over it suffering few casualties and the Canal itself was crossed without any difficulty there being numerous ladders on each bank.

According to plan the Battalion was to advance to the HINDENBURG SUPPORT LINE (RED LINE) in SOAP TRENCH and SHIP TRENCH, and advance from there to the forming up area at 8.20 a.m. The Battalion, however, did not leave the RED LINE until 8.50 a.m. This delay was caused first by No. 4 Company slightly losing direction and becoming engaged by heavy M.G. fire from the left but chiefly because SUMMER LANE had not been completely cleared of the enemy in consequence of which one platoon was sent out to wipe up this M.G. nest before the Battalion could advance. 2/Lieut. P. V. PELLY and his platoon succeeded in dealing with this enemy position capturing 8 prisoners. Meanwhile the Battalion was reorganised in SHIP TRENCH and continued the advance at 8.50 a.m.

On crossing the ridge in K.17.a. the Battalion came under heavy M.G. fire from the direction of GRAINCOURT and KNAVE TRENCH which caused some casualties, 2/Lieut. P. V. PELLY being wounded.

(2)

From K.18.Central to the BEETROOT FACTORY the Battalion came under fire from field guns firing over open sights in L.7.a. and close range machine gun fire from K.12.d. - ORIVAL WOOD and L.13.b.

On reaching their forming up positions in SILVER STREET from K.18.a. to the BEETROOT FACTORY, Companies at once sent out patrols to endeavour to make ground towards ORIVAL WOOD and silence the batteries and machine guns which were causing considerable casualties, but owing to the volume and accuracy of the enemy fire, little headway could be made.

Lieut. T. A. COMBE was wounded whilst taking his patrol out down the light railway in K.12.c. and later 2/Lieut. R. C. M. BEVAN was wounded whilst leading his patrol from the BEETROOT FACTORY.

At this time GRAINCOURT had not been taken and the enemy could be seen reinforcing KNAVE TRENCH and DEGAL TRENCH in L.1 & 2.

At 12.15 p.m. patrols were again sent out forward but were unable to make ground as the enemy were firing with great accuracy from both flanks and from our immediate front.

About 4.30 p.m. troops of the 2nd Division began to arrive. In conjunction with the Kings Regiment who advanced Eastwards towards the FLESQUIERES - CANTAING Road, the Battalion advanced towards ORIVAL WOOD.

The left Company, (No. 2) reached L.7.c.1.7. where they were hung up by enfilade fire from their left flank. The centre, (No. 3) pushed through ORIVAL WOOD but were unable to debouch from its North edge. The right, (No. 1) reached L.8.c.1.8. where they were in touch with the Kings on their right.

The South Staffords advanced over the ridge in L.13.b. but were unable at that time to get more than 300 - 400 yards to the East of the FLESQUIERES - CANTAING Road.

About 6.15 p.m. the 172nd Brigade attacked KNAVE TRENCH from about K.12.b. This attack made but little progress penetrating to KNAVE TRENCH about L.1.a.3.8. but unable to get further East.

During this attack the Battalion advanced and reached a line L.7.a.5.4. - L.7.b.0.6. - L.8.a.0.4. - L.8.a.6.2. being in touch with troops of the 2nd and 57th Divisions respectively on right and left.

About 7.30 p.m. another attack was made by the 57th Division on KNAVE TRENCH without success.

During the night the Battalion reorganised and held approximately the line given above. At 2.0 a.m. orders were received to withdraw.

During the attack on ORIVAL WOOD, 7 field guns and 8 howitzers were captured - 8 more guns could be seen within 400 yards of our line but could not be reached. They were however out of action. About 40 prisoners were taken.

Total Casualties:- 6 O.R. Killed, 3 O.R. Died of Wounds, Lieut. R.T.SHARPE, Lieut. T.A.COMBE, 2/Lieut.R.C.M.BEVAN, 2/Lieut. P.V.PELLY and 86 O.R. Wounded, and 2 O.R. Missing.

The Battalion started to withdraw at 3.0 a.m. and marched back to the British old front line East of the Canal, arriving about 5.30 a.m. The Cookers arrived shortly afterwards and the men had breakfast and started making shelters and accomodation in the trenches.

1.10.18.

Major.
Commanding 2nd Battalion Grenadier Guards.

1st Gds. Bde. Gds. Divn.

War Diary.

2nd Bn. Grenadier Guards.

October 1918.

WAR DIARY
INTELLIGENCE SUMMARY
(Erase heading not required.)

Army Form C. 2118

Instructions regarding War Diaries and Intelligence Summaries are contained in F. S. Regs., Part II. and the Staff Manual respectively. Title Pages will be prepared in manuscript.

Place	Date	Hour	Summary of Events and Information	Remarks and references to Appendices
	1918		**OCTOBER 1918.**	
	Oct 1.		The Battalion took over accommodation East of DEMICOURT, this consisted of trench shelters which were improved where possible. The weather was changeable. Training, including route marching was carried out.	
	Oct 2.		Major C. F. A. WALKER, M.C. arrived to take over command of the Battalion - Lieut. Colonel G. E. C. RASCH, D.S.O. returned to ENGLAND to take over command of the 1st Provisional Battalion.	
	Oct 3/6		The Battalion remained near DEMICOURT and training was carried out. An unfortunate accident occurred to No. 4 Company. A trench subsided, burying and killing two men.	
	Oct 7/21 Oct 22.		Narrative of Operations from 7th to 21st attached. Enemy was shelling spasmodically in reply to heavy shelling by our guns, but the luck of the Battalion held and few casualties were suffered. The Battalion was relieved in the evening by the 24th Battalion Royal Fusiliers. The relief was complete by 19.30. The Battalion marched to the ST.PYTHON-ST. VAAST Road, where after a wait of about ½ hour, it embussed, the destination, CARNIERES was reached about 23.00. Hot water was ready for the men to wash their feet, also a good meal. Everyone very pleased with the prospect of a good night's sleep - good accomodation was found for all. The men had suffered severely from the cold and wet, for they had no shelter but the slits they dug.	
	Oct 23.		Reveille and Breakfast under Company arrangements. Rifles and feet were inspected and the men set to to clean themselves up.	
	Oct 24.		The Battalion bathed, rifles were inspected by the Brigade Armourer Sergeant, Gas masks by the Brigade Gas N.C.O. Inspection of rifles, Lewis guns, clothing etc. by Companies, completed.	
	Oct 25.		A training programme was made out ready to be started upon the next day. Training was carried out as follows :- No. 1 Company. No. 2 Company. No. 3 Company. No. 4 Company. Route March. Platoon Training. Platoon Training. Route March.	
	Oct 26.		Training was carried out as follows :- No. 1 Company. No. 2 Company. No. 3 Company. No. 4 Company. Platoon Training. Route March. Route March. Platoon Training.	

WAR DIARY

INTELLIGENCE SUMMARY

Army Form C. 2118

Place	Date	Hour	Summary of Events and Information	Remarks and references to Appendices
	Oct.27		No training was carried out.	
	Oct.28		The G.O.C. Guards Division inspected the Battalion at 12.00.	
	Oct.29/30		Training as usual.	
	Oct.31		The Battalion moved to billets in ST. HILAIRE, leaving CARNIERES at 12.0S., arriving at ST.HILAIRE at 14.00.	

P.M.... Capt. M.

Lieut. Colonel.
Commanding 2nd Battalion Grenadier Guards.

NARRATIVE OF OPERATIONS,
by
Major C. F. A. Walker, M.C.
Commanding 2nd Battalion Grenadier Guards.

Period, October 8th - 21st.

Reference, Map 57b N.W. 1/20000.

The following Officers were with the Battalion :-

Headquarters.
Commanding, Major C.F.A.Walker, M.C.
Adjutant, Captain R.G.Briscoe, M.C. relieved on October 19th by
Lieut. G.T.S.Clarke, M.C.
Intelligence Lieut. W.H.S.Dent, relieved on October 14th by
Officer. 2/Lieut. A.F.Alington.
Medical Officer. Lieutenant E. L. Coffin.

No. 1 Company.
Lieut. L.Holbech, M.C.
Lieut. C.L.F.Boughey.
2/Lieut. E.K.Neill.

No. 2 Company.
Captain G.E.Wilson.
2/Lieut. D.L.King.
2/Lieut. C.J.N.Adams.

No. 3 Company.
Captain J.C.Cornforth, M.C. relieved
by Captain L.St.L.Hermon-Hodge on
October 15th.
2/Lieut. K.B.Bibby.
2/Lieut. E.G.E.Harcourt-Vernon.

No. 4 Company.
Lieut. R.E.R.Palmer, relieved by
Lieut. H.B.G.Morgan, M.C. On
October 13th.
Lieut. C. C. Cubitt.
2/Lieut. B.R.Osborne.

During the night of 7/8th October the Battalion moved into trenches about MARCOING. On the morning of the 8th, the Battalion crossed the ST. QUENTIN CANAL at MASNIERES. The crossing was being shelled at the time but happily the Battalion avoided casualties. Accomodation was found in trenches between MASNIERES and CREVECOEUR.

At a conference held at 1st Guards Brigade Headquarters that evening it was decided that the 1st Guards Brigade should form up for the attack on a line of old German trenches S.W. of SERANVILLERS (H.3.Central - H.9.b. - H.20.c.) 2nd Battalion GRENADIER Guards on the left and 2nd Battalion COLDSTREAM Guards on the right - 1st Battalion IRISH Guards in reserve. The 2nd Guards Brigade was to operate on the left and the New Zealand Division on the right. 1st objective - the FORENVILLE - la TARGETTE Road, 2nd objective - the railway running North and East of WAMBAIX. Up to the 2nd objective the Battalion was to be preceded by a barrage, after that it was to advance in the direction of CATTENIERES and gain touch with the enemy should they retire. The boundary between the 2nd Battalion Grenadier Guards and the 2nd Battalion Coldstream Guards lay along the main street through SERANVILLERS through WAMBAIX in H.16.a, it then turned right-handed along railway to H.11.d.2.2. and through the middle of CATTENIERES. Zero was to be at 4.30 a.m.

As the barrage was to descend on the LA TARGETTE-ESNES Road and rest there for 10 minutes, all covering troops were withdrawn 200 yards S.W. of this road before Zero - the New Zealand Division held part of this road to the south of the Battalion's frontage.

Formation of the Battalion : No. 3 Company, right front Company, No. 4, left front company- No. 2, Support company; No. 1, reserve company.

The two leading Companies were able to move forward to the road through H.14.c. at Zero - 15 minutes.

At Zero the two leading Companies went forward deployed in two waves and were followed at 200 yards by the support Company. Three hundred yards in rear the Reserve Company followed.

The leading Companies were ordered to catch up to the barrage while it rested on the LA TARGETTE Road and then to follow it, pushing straight through all villages and trenches in their path. The Support Company was made responsible for mopping up.

The Support and Reserve Companies advanced in artillery formation preceded by strong patrols with orders to maintain that formation until forced to deploy by machine gun or rifle fire.

The barrage was good and the Battalion reached the 2nd objective without difficulty. A few prisoners, 2 howitzers, 1 field gun and several machine guns and trench mortars were captured.

About 09.00 strong patrols were sent out by the leading Companies and the advance continued through CATTENIERES and the line of the sunken road running through H.6.d, consolidated. As soon, however, as the troops emerged from CATTENIERES or came over the ridge on the left of CATTENIERES, they came under severe machine gun fire from the factory at BOISTRANCOURT and casualties were suffered. Seeing that a natural glacis lay between the Battalion and BOISTRANCOURT the O.C. Battalion considered it best not to undertake any further advance till night-fall.

At 01.00 on the morning of October 10th the Support and Reserve Companies (Nos. 1 & 2) lined up on each side of the road leading through H.6.d. to BOISTRANCOURT and rushed the factory, encountering hardly any opposition (only 6 shots were fired at them). They then dug-in from C.25.c.05.80. North of the Factory, the right flank dropping back to the CAMBRIA Road in I.1.b.4.7.

Casualties to Battalion, - 1 O.R. killed and 12 wounded.

At 05.00 on October 10th the 1st Battalion Irish Guards passed through the Battalion and continued the pursuit. Later in the day the Battalion was ordered to move forward to FRESNOY FARM where it spent the night of 10/11th October. The Battalion was now in Brigade Reserve.

On October 11th the Battalion moved into BEVILLERS and on October 13th to QUIEVY, on October 17th to BOUSSIERES and on the evening of October 18th to ST. HILAIRE.

October 19th was spent in receiving and preparing orders for the forthcoming attack. The following were with the Battalion & took part in the attack :-

Headquarters.
Commanding, Major, C.F.A.Walker, M.C.
Adjutant, Lieutenant S.T.S.Clarke, M.C.
Intelligence Officer, 2/Lieut. A.F.Alington.
Medical Officer, Lieutenant N. L. Coffin.

No. 1 Company.
Lieutenant L. Holbech, M.C.
Lieutenant C. L. F. Boughey.
2/Lieutenant B. M. Neill.

No. 2 Company.
Captain G. E. Wilson.
2/Lieut. B. L. King.
2/Lieut. C. J. M. Adams.

No. 3 Company.
Captain L. St. L. Hermon-Hodge
2/Lieutenant K. E. Bibby.
2/Lieut. E.G.F.Harcourt-Vernon.

No. 4 Company.
Lieutenant H. B. G. Morgan, M.C.
Lieutenant C. C. Cubitt.
2/Lieutenant B. R. Osborne.

The Battalion had orders to attack at 02.00 on the morning of the 20th, under cover of a heavy Field Artillery barrage and cross the River SELLE over the bridges already laid by the R.E. & 4th Battalion Coldstream Guards. Tapes from the assembly position on the railway in V.29.b.15.25. - V.23.d.4.5. had been laid to the bridges. During the crossing the five brigades of Field Artillery supporting the 1st Guards Brigade were to play on the road from V.30.a.5.6. to V.24.c.2.5. At Zero plus 23, the crossing of the river being ef the Battalion was to advance under the barrage which moved forward 100 yards every four minutes and capture the 1st objective (GREEN LINE). On reaching the 1st objective (VALENCIENNES-SOLESMES Road, W.25.b.2.6. - W.19.d.05.90.) the barrage played on a line 300 yards east of the above till Zero plus 126. At Zero plus 126 the barrage was to lift 100 yards every four minutes over and past the last objective (RED LINE, W.20.Central - W.20.a.35.65) which was then to be captured. It was to remain playing 300 yards east of the 2nd objective for four minutes and then to cease.

At 21.45 the Battalion moved off behind the 1st Battalion Irish Guards to take up its assembly position. Drizzling rain was incessant and though the moon was full the night was dark. After one or two minor delays, but without any hostile interference, the railway was reached at 00.10 and the Battalion proceeded to take up its assembly position. No. 1 Company, right front; No. 2 Company, left front; No. 3 Company, support ; No. 4 Company, reserve ;

As soon as the assembly position was taken up the tapes leading thence to Bridges over the river were reconnoitred by guides from each platoon. All arrangements and reconnaisances for the attack were complete by 01.15.

The barrage dropped possibly one minute before the correct Zero hour and though it was heavy it was inclined to be a trifle patchy. However, the river was crossed without any difficulty and at Zero plus 23 the advance was continued towards the 1st objective. Prisoners now began to come in in small parties. The 1st objective was reached and taken up to sheduled time and no serious resistance had been offered. Some 50 prisoners had been taken and only the slightest casualties suffered.

At Zero plus 126 the advance to the 2nd objective was commenced and hostile resistance increased a little necessitating some bayonet work on the part of No. 1 Company. The resistance was all machine gun fire mostly from the right as the troops on our right were not yet through SOLESMES.

By the time the 2nd objective was reached some 200 prisoners had been captured, with 2 field guns and several machine guns and trench mortars. As soon as the 2nd objective was reached the front Companies dug in on the RED LINE as shown on the map; No. 3 Company dug in in echelon on the right flank and No. 4 Company in rear of No. 3 Company, in position to protect the right rear of the Battalion in case of a counter-attack. These precautions were rendered necessary owing to the fact the troops on our right were not due to arrive in position for several hours after our last objective had been achieved. Battalion H.Q. dug in behind the VALENCIENNES - SOLESMES Road in W.19.c. V.V.

About 07.30 hostile artillery which up to now had taken no part in the proceedings began to assert itself and constant shelling was kept up with 77mm., 4.2 cm. & 5.9cm. guns and howitzers till dusk the support positions and Battalion Headquarters receiving the majority of attention.

During the night, except for sporadic gas shelling, hostile artillery was fairly quiet.

Casualties during these operations suffered by the Battalion were 1 Officer wounded and 52 O.R. killed or wounded.

23.10.18.

Commanding 2nd Battalion Grenadier Guards.

WAR DIARY
or
INTELLIGENCE SUMMARY.

(Erase heading not required.)

Army Form C. 2118.

November, 1918.

1/4th Leinster Regt.

Place	Date	Hour	Summary of Events and Information	Remarks and references to Appendices
CAMBIANO	1ST		Still at CAMBIANO. The Battalion had Baths in the morning.	
	2ND		Morning was spent in cleaning Billets and preparing for the move in the afternoon. At 14.00 the Battalion marched off with CAPELLE as destination. The road was packed with traffic which made the going very slow. It rained heavily during the afternoon, but cleared up in the evening. The Battalion arrived at CAPELLE at 19.15. Accommodation consisted of Bivouac sheets which the advance party had started to put up. A few hostile shells fell near the Bivouacs during the night but only one casualty was suffered.	
	3RD		The morning was spent in handing in Haversacks and Spare kit, and drawing S.A.A. Bombs, etc., preparatory to the attack which was to take place the next day. In the evening the Commanding Officer held a Company Commanders Conference and explained the plan of attack. As in attached narrative.	
	4TH	4pm	The Battalion went forward into Billets in WARGNIES LE PETIT arriving about 11.00. The afternoon was spent in Foot inspection and cleaning out Billets which were in a very foul state, owing to the recent German occupation.	2
				3
	5TH	6pm	The morning was spent in cleaning clothing and equipment. During the day the village was intermittently shelled, but fortunately no casualties were inflicted.	6
	6TH	7pm	In the morning two Companies were detailed to work on the roads near AMBROITANT leaving Billets at 07.00. At mid-day the order was received the Battalion was to march to BAVAY that afternoon. At 14.00 the Battalion marched off, picking up the two Companies on fatigue on the way. BAVAY was reached at 18.30. Billets were excellent. Owing to craters in the road, transport was unable to accompany the Battalion. It did not arrive until 21.00, and even then was unable to reach the billeting area as the bridges of the railway were blown up.	7
	8TH	9pm	The morning was spent in drawing S.A.A. Bombs, etc., for the further advance which was to take place the next day. The Battalion left BAVAY at 2.00 in the following order, No. 1, 2, 3, 4, and Bn. Hd. Qrs. The route followed was the main BAVAY - MAUBERGE road.	9

WAR DIARY
or
INTELLIGENCE SUMMARY.
(Erase heading not required.)

Army Form C. 2118.

Instructions regarding War Diaries and Intelligence Summaries are contained in F. S. Regs., Part II. and the Staff Manual respectively. Title pages will be prepared in manuscript.

Place	Date	Hour	Summary of Events and Information	Remarks and references to Appendices
			The Battalion was in Brigade reserve closely supporting the 2nd. Battalion Coldstream Guards, who were on the left, and the 1st. Battalion Irish Guards, who were on the right. The plan of action was for No.2 Coy. to support the 2nd. Btn.Coldstream Guards, and for No.1 Company to support the 1st.Btn.Irish Guards, taking the main BAVAY-MAUBERGE road as the centre of the Brigade frontage. No.3 Coy. was in support with orders to be prepared to form a defensive flank in either direction (The Battalion was still organised in three companies, as no reinforcements had arrived). The march was uneventful until LAS MOTTES was reahhed where the Brigade halted for about three-quarters of an hour. It had been given out that this was to be the forming up area for the 1st.Guards Brigade preparatry to passing through the 2nd.Guards Brigade, but the 2nd. Guards Brigade had been able to advance during the night, andpush forward into MAUBERGE. At 05.30 The Battalion entered DOUZIES and advanced the high ground east of MAUBERGE marching on the main road 4men until the MONS GATE was reachdd, then wheeling to the left and forming a defensive flank roundthe suburb of PONT ALLONT without any opposition being met. No.1 Coy. formed the defensive flank of the Brigade. Nos.2 & 3 Companies went into Billets in PONT ALLONT This was completed by 01.30. During the evening No.1 Coy. was withdrawn into Billets after the 2dd. Btn.Coldstream Guards had consolidated the outpost line.	
	10th		The Battalion rested in PONT ALLONT.	
	11th		At 07.00 the following wire was received:- "Hostilities will cease at 11.00 hours to-day". At 15.00 the Battalion was ordered to take over the outpost line from the 2nd.Btn.Coldstream Guards. and the 1st.Btn.Irish Guards at ELESMES and AASSEVENT, which consisted of picqueting the main roads into the town.	
	12th		The inlying Picquet was found by the Coy. in waiting, the outlying Picquet by the Coy. coming out of waiting. The morning was spent in steady drill and cleaning billets.	

Army Form C. 2118.

WAR DIARY
or
INTELLIGENCE SUMMARY.

(Erase heading not required.)

Instructions regarding War Diaries and Intelligence Summaries are contained in F. S. Regs., Part II. and the Staff Manual respectively. Title pages will be prepared in manuscript.

Place	Date	Hour	Summary of Events and Information	Remarks and references to Appendices
	13th		Steady drill. Clothing inspection was carried out. Details rejoine the Battalion, and the Battalion was re-organised into four Company with three Platoons per Company.	
	14th		The Battalion was alloted the Baths at MAUBERGE. A Solemn Mass of thanksgiving for the cessation of hostilities was celebrated in the Collegiate Church at MAUBERGE at 10.00. All Roman Catholics in the Battalion attended.	
	15th		Two Companies carried out Route march, steady drill was carried out by the remainder of the Battalion.	
	16th		A Thanksgiving service was held in the Square, MAUBERGE for all denominations except Roman Catholics, 25 O.Rs. per Company attended. The remainder of the Battalion carried out Platoon training.	
	17th		Voluntary service at 11.00.	
	18th		The Battalion marched off at 0730. and arrived at Billets in ESTINNE-La-MONT at 13.00. The Billets were excellant and inhabitants received the Battalion with open arms.	
	19th		The Battalion marched off at 08.00 and arrived in ANDERLUES at 12.30. The Battalion was billeted in small houses averaging 4 men per house, the majority of the men had beds to sleep in.	
	20th		The Battalion marched off at 0.750 and arrived in MONTIGNE-SUR-SAMBRE at 13.30. The Army Commander marched at the head of the Brigade during this march, and inspected all Battalions on the march.	
	21st		Arm drill and physical training was carried out.	
	22nd		Training as yesterday.	
	23rd		Battalion had Baths.	
	24th		The Battalion marched off at 07.30 arriving in BAMBOIS at 13.00. The FAVES road was covered with ice during the first two hours of the march, which made the going slippery and slow.	
	25th		The Battalion marched off at 08.30, there was a heavy mist dring the morning which eventually turned into rain. The Battalion arrived at WEPION at 12.30.	
	26th		A wet day. Billets were cleaned.	
	27th			

WAR DIARY
or
INTELLIGENCE SUMMARY.

(Erase heading not required.)

Army Form C. 2118.

Instructions regarding War Diaries and Intelligence Summaries are contained in F. S. Regs., Part II. and the Staff Manual respectively. Title pages will be prepared in manuscript.

Place	Date	Hour	Summary of Events and Information	Remarks and references to Appendices
	28th			
	29th 30th		The Battalion marched off at 07.50. The First line Transport (less Cookers and Mess Cart) were-x was brigaded, owing to the steepness of the hills. The Battalion arrived in billets in the ASSESSE area about 12.30. Billets were very scattered, No.1 Coy. in MIERS, Nos.4 & 3 Coys. in LA HAMEAU, Bn.Hd.Qrs. and No.2 Coy. in LA VAGNE. It rained hard during the last two hours of the march. Steady drill and physical training under company arrangements. Adjutant's parade followed by kit inspection and physical training under company arrangements.	

Major,
Commanding 2nd. Battalion Grenadier Guards.

30-11-18.

NARRATIVE OF OPERATIONS
By
Lieut: Colonel C. F. A. Walker, M.C.,
Commanding 2nd Battalion Grenadier Guards

DATE 4th November 1918.

Reference, Map France Sheet 51a 1/40,000.
Sheet 51. d6

The Battalion marched off from the Camp at CAPELLE at 4:50 a.m. The Lewis Gun Limbers marched with Companies.

The following officers were with the Battalion:-

Battalion H. Q.
Commanding.............. Lieut: Colonel C. F. A. Walker, M.C.
Adjutant................. Captain R. G. Briscoe, M.C.
Intelligence Officer..... Lieutenant L. Holbech, M.C.

No: 1 Company.	No: 2 Company.
Captain L. St: L. Hermon-Hodge.	Lieutenant W. H. S. Dent.
2/Lieutenant D. L. King.	2/Lieutenant C. J. N. Adams.

No: 3 Company.	No: 4 Company.
Lieutenant R. H. R. Palmer.	Lieutenant C. C. Cubitt.
2/Lieutenant K. B. Bibby.	2/Lieutenant B. R. Osborne.
2/Lieutenant E. C. H. Harcourt-Vernon.	

The Battalion marched off to the forming up area by the following route:- Cross Roads Q.30.a - Railway Bridge Q.8.a - Cross Roads LAGNISSETTE - VILLERS-POL.

There was slight enemy shelling at the PONT DU BUAT, where No: 1 Coy: suffered several casualties. There was no other hostile shelling until the Batt: reached VILLERS POL, where the crossings of the stream and the village itself were being heavily shelled, but fortunately few casualties were suffered. From LAGNISSETTE, Batt: H. Q. did not follow the route of the Batt: but advanced along the main road to WARGNIES LE PETIT (which was the mainline of communication during the advance) keeping level with Reserve Coy: The Batt: formed up on the BLUE LINE at 7:20 a.m. - No: 4 Coy: (Left Front Coy:) and No: 3 Coy: (Right Front Coy:) 100 yards east of the JENLAIN-LE QUESNOY ROAD. No: 2 Coy: Support Coy: and No: 1 Coy: Reserve Coy: just west of the Road.

The role of the Batt: was to follow up the 2nd Batt: Coldstream Guards who were to capture the GREEN LINE. The Batt: was then to pass through and capture the RED LINE and push the advance forward by bounds to high ground North East of AMFROIPRET.

The rain stopped in the early morning, but a heavy thick mist hung over the ground, and when the Batt: advanced from the BLUE LINE at 7:30 a.m. it was only possible to see about 200 yards ahead. After the leading Coys: had moved forward about 800 yards they saw troops in front of them moving along behind our barrage. These they believed to be the 2nd Batt: Coldstream Guards advancing to the GREEN LINE. It was not discovered till later that they were in reality the enemy retiring.

As No: 4 Coy: passed over the high ground in G.32.b, the mist lifted and they came under heavy machine gun fire from the Sunken Road in G.27.c. Lieut: C. C. Cubitt was wounded and the Coy: suffered a considerable number of casualties. 2/Lieut: B. R. Osborne led two platoons forward by short rushes to a line running from G.27.c.1.1 to G.33.a.48. From this position further advance was impossible owing to intensity and accuracy of the machine gun fire. Field guns also fired from north east of the village over open sights at any movement of our troops. 2/Lieut: B. R. Osborne went forward to make a personal reconnaissance of the enemy positions and was killed by a machine gun bullet while returning to report the situation. No: 4 Coy: was now without an officer, and No: 18523, Sergeant E. Carter took charge of the Coy:

No: 3 Coy: advanced through the southern part of the wood in G.33.c and on debouching from the eastern edge came under severe machine gun and rifle fire from the enemy who were entrenched in slits 200 yards east of the wood. Lieut: R. H. R. Palmer ordered his Coy: to advance by short rushes covered by mutual supporting fire. By this method the enemy position was captured and the entire garrison was killed or taken prisoner. Three machine guns were captured and one minenwerfer.

This Coy: was unable to advance farther as the forward slope was swept by enemy machine gun fire from the southern edge of the village.

2.

and they dug in slits on a line running from G.32.b.0.1. - G.33.c.7.2.

No 2 Coy: followed up in Support of the two leading Coys: - one platoon dug in 150 yards west of No: 4 Coy: - the other two platoons assisted No: 3 Coy: in clearing up the situation just east of the wood.

No: 1 Coy: in Reserve dug in from about G.32.b.7.7. to G.33.c.4.2.

Batt: H. Q. was at G.32. c.8.9.

This was the position of the Batt: at 10:0 a.m. Every effort was made to push forward by the leading Coys: However on the left and centre of the Batt: no movement was possible. On the right 2/Lieutenant B.G.F. Harcourt-Vernon succeeded in pushing forward with his Platoon to within 50 yards of the road in G.33.d.

During the afternoon artillery fire was brought to bear on the enemy positions in and south of the village of WARGNIES LE PETIT, which enabled Nos: 2 & 3 Coys: to occupy a line from G.34.a.1.1. to G.4.a.6.7 where touch was gained with the 3rd Batt: Grenadier Guards on the right and the 42nd Division on the left. No: 4 Company remained in the same position No: 1 Coy: dug in on a line 20 yards in front of the eastern edge of the wood.

At 6:30 p.m. 1st Batt: Irish Guards went through the Batt: and the Batt: concentrated in the wood G.33.a.& c and reorganised. Nos: 3 & 4 Coys were amalgamated into a Composite Company under Lieut: R. H. R. Palmer.

Total casualties during the day were:-

2/Lieutenant E. R. Osborne.	Killed.
Lieutenant C. C. Cubitt.	Wounded.
2/Lieutenant C. J. N. Adams.	Wounded.

Other ranks.

10	Killed.
89.	Wounded.
9.	Missing.

Captures:-

120.	Prisoners.
7.	Field Guns.
8	Machine Guns.
1.	Trench Mortars.

Lieut: Colonel.
Commanding 2nd Battalion Grenadier Guards.

Army Form C. 2118.

WAR DIARY or INTELLIGENCE SUMMARY.

December, 1918. 2nd Bn. Grenadier Guards

Place	Date	Hour	Summary of Events and Information	Remarks and references to Appendices
	1st.		At LA FAGNE. To-day is being celebrated as "Grenadier Day" by the 18th. (Bengal) Lancers in commemoration of having fought with this Battalion at the Battle of GOUZEAUCOURT. Divine Service was held at 11.00. In the afternoon, the Officers of the Battalion played the Officers of Divisional Headquarters at Football, the result being decidedly in our favour, 2 goals to 1. The weather was very cold.	
	2nd.		Training and Drill was carried out under Company arrangements.	
	3rd.		The day was very wet. Companies carried out Physical training. The Major General held a Conference of Commanding Officers at Brigade Headquarters.	
	4th.		Remained at LA FAGNE.	
	5th. 6th.		The Battalion marched from LA FAGNE to VERLEE & BUZIN.	
	7th.		The March was continued to AISNE & ROCHE-A-FRENE, where good accomodation was found.	
	8. 9.10		The M/62M Battalion arrived at ABREFONTAINE; here the Accomodation was not good owing to overcrowding, the Canadian Light Horse taking over too many Billets.	
			The Battalion remained at ABREFONTAINE. On the Sunday a Voluntary service was held On Monday and Tuesday Billets were cleaned up, and steady drill and Physical training carried out.	
	11.		The Battalion marched from ABREFONTAINE to BORN. It was a rainy day. The German Frontier was crossed at POTEAU where the Major General took the salute. On arriving at BORN excellent accomodation was found; the Civilian inhabitants seemed submissive.	
	12.		The Battalion paraded at 10.45 and marched to MURRENGEN & HUNNINGEN. Bn.Hd.Qrs, 3, 1, and 4 Companies were billeted in the former place, No.2 Coy in the latter. It rained all the day, accomodation good.	

WAR DIARY
or
INTELLIGENCE SUMMARY.

(Erase heading not required.)

Army Form C. 2118.

Instructions regarding War Diaries and Intelligence Summaries are contained in F. S. Regs., Part II. and the Staff Manual respectively. Title pages will be prepared in manuscript.

Place	Date	Hour	Summary of Events and Information	Remarks and references to Appendices
	13.		The Battalion paraded at 07.50, and arrived at OBERHAUSEN at 15.00. The march was over hilly country in which Pine forests abounded. The weather was wet. Bn.Hd.Qrs. Nos.2,3,& 4 found accomodation at OBERHAUSEN, No.1 Company at WEISGEN. Billets were comfortable.	
	14		Paraded at 08.00, and arrived at CALL at 12.30, and found good Billets.	
	15		The starting point was passed at 08.00 and SINZENICH reached at 12.00. For a change the weather was fine. 2/Lieut: G.R. de Beer joined the Battalion.	
	16		The starting point was passed at 08.20, the Battalion arrived at LECHENICH, at 12.40 in fair weather. Excellent accomodation was found. Since leaving OBERHAUSEN the inhabitants have been amicable and hospitable.	
	17		Passed the Starting point at 08.20. EFFEREN was reached at 11.45. The march took place in fair weather.	
	18		The Battalion marched to WIDDERSDORF, ~~STARTING~~ passing the Starting point at 08.10 and arrived at 11.00. The weather was stormy and some rain fell.	
	19		The Battalion remained at WIDDERSDORF. Reveille at 08.00. Companies did half an hour's Arm Drill and cleared equipment.	
EHRENFELD	20		EHRENFELD, our final destination was reached at 15.00, the Battalion was billeted in two Schools, Nos. 1 & 4 Coys. were in LEYENDECKER STRASSE, Nos. 2 & 3 were in PLATEN STRASSE. The accomodation has the makings of comfort and in time everyone should be comfortable. The Officers' Messes were in SIEMENS STRASSE, all quite good. 2/Lieut: F.G. Salmon joined the Battalion.	

Army Form C. 2118.

WAR DIARY
or
INTELLIGENCE SUMMARY.
(Erase heading not required.)

Place	Date	Hour	Summary of Events and Information	Remarks and references to Appendices
	21.		The day was spent in settling down and cleaning up. The following Officers joined the Battalion. Lieutenant C.T. Chowne 2/Lieutenant G.K. Mitchell 2/Lieutenant D.M. Horsford 2/Lieutenant G.H. Peters 2/Lieutenant J.B. Grinling 2/Lieutenant A.F. Bowes-Lyon.	
	22.		Divine Service attended by 75 other ranks per company was held in the Theatre which is doing duty as the Mens' Canteen.	
	23. 24.		Three quarters of an hour's Arm drill was carried out in the morning, and preparation made for Christmas Day. There was some anxiety as to the arrival in time of the provisions for Christmas dinners, though luckily they turned up at the last moment.	
	25.		Christmas Day. Parade Service held at 11.15 in the SCHILLER MUSEUM, PIUS STRASSE. The Battalion had their Christmas Dinner at 12.30 by double Companies, Nos.1 & 4 and Nos. 2 & 3 being together, and Concert afterwards. The arrangements were excellent, and everyone was very pleased. The Officers dined together at 20.00 hours, and had a most successful evening.	
	26. 27.		Companies did three quarters of an hour's arm drill and physical training. The weather was very poor and uncertain.	
	28.		Route marched through COLOGNE. The route followed was up the VENLOER STRASSE to the SCHIFFEROSKE ½ AND THEN ACROSS the RHINE to the HOHENZOLLERN BRIDGE, and back to COLOGNE; passed the Cathedral and back to Billets by the JUDDENR.THER STRASSE. It was a fine day, the march was much enjoyed and everyone was most interested at seeing the RHINE for the first time.	

Army Form C. 2118.

WAR DIARY
or
INTELLIGENCE SUMMARY.
(Erase heading not required.)

Place	Date	Hour	Summary of Events and Information	Remarks and references to Appendices
	29		Divine Service was attended by 75 O.Rs. per Company held in the Church in ROTHEUROS. The weather has been poor.	
	30		The Battalion did three quarters of an hour's Arm drill and Physical training, and has been finding Guards at various places.	
	1		Battalion Parade under the Adjutant in BLUCHER PARK a good place for Battalion drill. The Young Officers were taken by a C.S.M. in special drill and saluting.	

Lieut:Colonel.
Commanding 2nd. Battalion Grenadier Guards.

WAR DIARY
INTELLIGENCE SUMMARY.

2nd Bn. Grenadier Gds. January 1919.

Place	Date	Hour	Summary of Events and Information
EHRENFELD COLOGNE	January 1919 1st to 31		Since the Battalion has settled down comfortably in EHRENFELD and has led a semi-peacetime existence, it is difficult to make a daily tabulation of events.

Probably the most important event of the month was the demobilisation of "Pivotal Men" and "Old Soldiers", and since the 28th of December 1918 some 200 N.C.Os. and Guardsmen have left us, including amongst them many of the most redoubtable members of the Battalion whose loss after years of valuable service is greatly felt. Amongst the Officers, Captain F.H.J. Drummond, M.C., and Lieut. H.G. MORGAN A.C. and 2/Lieutenant Hon: S.E. Marsham, both of No. 4 Company have returned to England on leave pending demobilisation.

Important in the history of the Battalion is the arrival of the Colours from England. A Colour Party consisting of Lieutenant W.H.S. Dent, M.C., Lieutenant L. Holbech, D.S.O., M.C., Sergeant Wilson, Sergeant Blackburn, D.C.M., M.M., and Sergeant Carter, D.C.M., left COLOGNE on the 23rd. December 1918, and returned on the 7th, January. On arrival they were met at the Station by the Drums and an escort under the command of Major G.C.F. Harcourt-Vernon, D.S.O., M.C., and marched back to Barracks.

Training for the most part of Drill and Physical Training or Route Marching, has been carried out daily, and has not been hampered much by bad weather. CLASSES HAVE ALSO BEEN HELD FOR THE INSTRUCTION OF YOUNG N.C.Os. & YOUNG GUARDSMEN.

The Battalion has had to find various Guards and has now one Company away in COLOGNE permanently, which is employed in guarding the railway.

Education under able arrangements made by Captain Revd: and Hon: C.F. Lyttleton, C.F., has been started, and there can be no doubt about its success. Classes in a variety of subjects are now being held under the tuition of both Officers and N.C.Os., and a number of |

Army Form C. 2

WAR DIARY
or
INTELLIGENCE SUMMARY
(Erase heading not required.)

Interesting Lectures have been given.

A fair amount of recreation consisting of Football, Boxing, and other games has been going on, and the Pioneers have been most indefatigable in erecting apparatus for this purpose. The Battalion Association XI, who through demobilisation have lost several of their best players, has played several matches. The results have been two matches won, two matches drawn, and one lost.
The Officers have suffered a somewhat heavy defeat at the hands of the 2nd. Battalion Coldstream Guards by 4 goals to D.

On the 14th. January the Battalion marched over to the STATWALD Park by companies and watched the presentation of Colours to the 4th. Battalion Grenadier Guards by H.R.H. The Prince of Wales.

There are plenty of facilities for amusement for xthexwhxlexfxrxthe Battalion in the town for the whole of the Battalion has had a pleasant time since its arrival.

C Nether Lieut:Colonel,
Commanding 2nd. Battalion Grenadier Guards.